My eLab | Efficient teaching, effective learning

D0128904

My eLab is the interactive environment that gives you access to self-graded exercises and additional study resources related to your textbook. Be sure to register for **My eLab** to ensure your success!

TO REGISTER

❶ Go to **http://mybookshelf.pearsonerpi.com**

❷ Click on "**NOT REGISTERED YET?**" and follow the instructions. When asked for your access code, please type the code provided underneath the blue sticker.

❸ To access **My eLab** at any time, go to http://mybookshelf.pearsonerpi.com. **Bookmark this page for quicker access.**

Access to My eLab is valid for 6 months from the date of registration.

WARNING! This book CANNOT BE RETURNED if the access code has been uncovered.

5710

Note: Once you have registered, you will need to join your online class. Ask your teacher to provide you with the class ID.

TEACHER Access Code

To obtain an access code for My eLab, please contact your Pearson ELT consultant.

 | 800 263-3678
help@pearsonerpi.com

@HelpPearsonERPI

W135562 (A55820)

leap intermediate

DR. KEN BEATTY

READING AND WRITING

Learning English for Academic Purposes

PEARSON

Montréal Toronto Boston Columbus Indianapolis New York San Francisco Upper Saddle River
Amsterdam Le Cap Dubaï Londres Madrid Milan Munich Paris
Delhi México São Paulo Sydney Hong-Kong Séoul Singapour Taipei Tōkyō

Managing Editor
Sharnee Chait

Project Editor
Linda Barton

Proofreader
Mairi MacKinnon

Coordinator, Rights and Permissions
Pierre Richard Bernier

Text Rights and Permissions
Rachel Irwin

Art Director
Hélène Cousineau

Graphic Design Coordinator
Lyse LeBlanc

Book and Cover Design
Frédérique Bouvier

Book Layout
Interscript

The publisher thanks the following people for their helpful comments and suggestions:

Jerry Block, Fraser International College

Celina Costa, George Brown College

Michelle Duhaney, Seneca College

Linda Feuer, University of Manitoba

Carleen Gruntman, Laval University

Brianna Hilman, University of Calgary

Kristibeth Kelly Delgado, Fanshawe College

Marcia Kim, University of Calgary

Izabella Kojic-Sabo, University of Windsor

Jennifer MacDonald, Dalhousie University

Tiffany MacDonald, East Coast School of Languages

Karen Rauser, University of British Columbia

Cyndy Reimer, Douglas College

Darren Wilson, Bow Valley College

Dedication

To my three sisters, Irene, Diane and Elaine, who first helped me read and scribble.

Text Credits

Chapter 1, pp. 7–9 Excerpts from *Essentials of Entrepreneurship and Small Business Management*, 7th Edition by N.M. Scarborough © 2014 Pearson. Reprinted with permission by Pearson Canada Inc. pp. 14–15 Excerpts from "Youth Entrepreneurs: Why Launching a Business from Your Childhood Bedroom is More Possible than Ever (and Here's Proof)" by A. Hasham © 2012 *The Star*.

Chapter 2, pp. 31–32 "Man vs. Robot" by P. Nowak © 2013 *Macleans*. pp. 35–36 Excerpts from "Half of All Jobs Today Will Disappear by 2030 and Other Scary Predictions" by E. Sherman © 2014 Erik Sherman. Originally appeared on AOL.com.

Chapter 3, pp. 53–55 Excerpts from "Bicycling: Health Risk or Benefit?" by K. Teschke, C.G.O. Reynolds, F.J. Ries, B. Gouge, & M. Winters © 2012 *UBC Medical Journal*. pp. 58–60 Excerpts from *Campbell Biology: Concepts and Connections, Canadian Edition* by J.B. Reese, M.R. Taylor, E.J. Simon, J.L. Dickey, & K.G-E. Scott © 2015 Pearson. Reprinted with permission by Pearson Canada Inc.

Chapter 4, pp. 76–78 Excerpts from "The Walking Cure" by D. Rubinstein © 2013 *The Walrus*. pp. 82–84 Excerpts from "Benefits of Good Mental Health" by Canadian Mental Health Association © 2014 CMHA-Calgary Region.

Chapter 5, pp. 99–101 Excerpts from "3 Ways 3D Printing Could Revolutionize Health Care" by K. Doyle © 2013 Zerox Canada. pp. 105–106 Excerpts from "How Biomimicry Is Inspiring Human Innovation" by T. Vanderbilt © 2012 *Smithsonian Magazine*.

Chapter 6, pp. 122–124 Excerpts from "Guide to Augmented Reality?" by Onvert © 2014 Harmony.co.uk. pp. 129–130 Excerpts from "Tell Me a Story: Augmented Reality Technology in Museums" by Y. Ioannidis, O. Balet, & D. Pandermalis © 2014 *The Guardian*, Guardian News & Media Ltd.

Chapter 7, pp. 145–147 Excerpts from "To Adapt MOOCS, or Not? That Is No Longer the Question" by S.M. North, R. Richardson, & M.M. North © 2014 *Universal Journal of Educational Research*, Horizon Research Publishing. pp. 151–153 Excerpts from "The SOLE of a Student" by S. Mitra © 2013 NDTV.

Chapter 8, pp. 169–171 Excerpts from *Seeing Red: A History of Natives in Canadian Newspapers* by M.C. Anderson & C. L. Robertson © 2011. Courtesy of University of Manitoba Press. pp. 181–182 "Prime Minister Harper Offers Full Apology on Behalf of Canadians for the Indian Residential Schools System" by S. Harper, 2008. Office of the Prime Minister of Canada © Her Majesty the Queen in Right of Canada, 2014.

INTRODUCTION

Students learn best when they engage with materials through tasks that encourage critical thinking. In a way, writing *LEAP Intermediate: Reading and Writing* has been an extended problem-solving task. The process began with defining teacher and student needs and finding creative solutions to explaining the changing demands of academic English. Consultations with teachers, both across Canada and internationally, produced countless suggestions, but the core request was for authentic academic texts with meaningful opportunities for students to grapple with them to practise strategies that build into skills.

The bulk of the twenty-four readings in *LEAP Intermediate: Reading and Writing* are authentic and reflect a broad range of academic disciplines including business, engineering, ethics, medicine and psychology. The genres focus on different kinds of paragraphs, and also include e-mails, reports, surveys and a compare and contrast essay. Students learn how to recognize the key features of each genre and how to write them; a Models Chapter provides additional support.

Throughout, graphic organizers help students develop their note-taking, comprehension and critical thinking skills. As students develop core competencies in reading, writing and grammar, they also learn academic survival skills. Academic Survival Skill sections recognize that success in learning is based on applying exam strategies, working in groups and avoiding plagiarism through proper referencing. In terms of assessment, assignments allow students to demonstrate what they have learned in creative and individual ways. Beyond the book, extensive online resources offer additional content and explanations.

A great deal of effort has gone into making *LEAP Intermediate: Reading and Writing* an ideal resource for teachers and learners. Future editions can only improve with your input. If you have time to share what works particularly well or what could be improved, both the Pearson team and I would appreciate hearing from you.

ACKNOWLEDGEMENTS

Many thanks go to Julia Williams who started this series, wrote the first two *LEAP Reading and Writing* books and then felt confident enough to leave me cradling her baby in my arms. Editors extraordinaire Sharnee Chait and Linda Barton shaped these pages with patience and good humour; to them and to the rest of the Pearson team goes much credit. I thank my graduate students and colleagues at Anaheim University for ongoing discussions that reinforce the belief that student needs are the starting point for everything important about education. I particularly want to thank my colleague, friend, occasional co-author and Ph.D. advisor David Nunan for years of discussions on teaching and learning.

The fingerprints of teachers too numerous to name are found on these pages. For those who e-mailed me privately or spoke on issues with me at conferences, I thank you. I also appreciate the thoughtful contributions of those dedicated professionals who helped through focus groups, interviews, questionnaires and chapter reviews. I also wish to thank Erica Ferrer Ariza and staff at Universidad del Norte, Barranquilla, Colombia and Alevtina Telnova, Moscow Institute of Physics and Technology, Russia.

Dr. Ken Beatty, Bowen Island, Canada

HIGHLIGHTS

Gearing Up stimulates students' interest by tapping into their prior knowledge.

The **overview** outlines the chapter objectives and features.

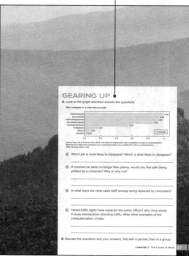

Vocabulary Build sections (three per chapter) aid comprehension and build awareness of key vocabulary on the Academic Word List.

The three **readings** in each chapter come from a variety of sources including academic journals, a transcript of a speech, essays, magazines, textbooks and websites. Difficult words are in bold in the texts and defined in the margins. Pre- and post-reading activities and questions focus on comprehension and inferences.

Focus on Writing develops the skills students need to write effective academic English.

Focus on Reading develops specific skills students need to fully understand the content and structure of academic texts. Each chapter has a **Critical Thinking** and a **Develop Your Vocabulary** sidebar that provide hints and tips to students.

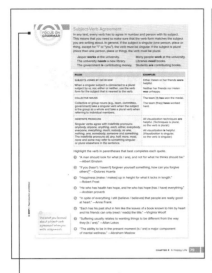

Focus on Grammar reviews important grammar features that students can apply when writing academic English.

Academic Survival Skill helps students develop essential skills for academic coursework.

The **Final Assignment** synthesizes the chapter content and theme through an in-depth writing task. Each chapter focuses on a different academic writing task.

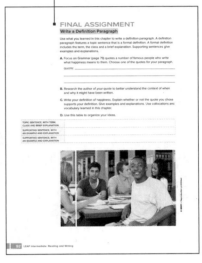

The **Warm-Up Assignment** prepares students for the Final Assignment. Each chapter focuses on a different writing task.

How confident are you? and **Vocabulary Challenge** allow students to reflect on their learning, decide what they need to review and use new vocabulary. **References to My eLab** point students toward additional content, practice and support.

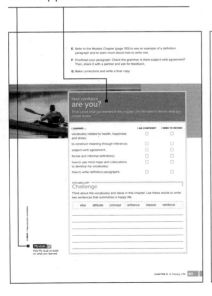

The **Models Chapter** provides students with instructions and models for the writing tasks in the textbook.

SCOPE AND SEQUENCE

CHAPTER	READING	WRITING
CHAPTER 1 **SUCCESS IN BUSINESS** SUBJECT AREAS: business, computer science	• Skimming and scanning	• Writing a paragraph
CHAPTER 2 **THE FUTURE OF WORK** SUBJECT AREAS: business, engineering, robotics	• Recognizing point of view	• Writing surveys
CHAPTER 3 **FIT FOR LIFE** SUBJECT AREAS: biology, chemistry, urban studies	• Identifying main ideas and supporting details	• Comparing and contrasting in a paragraph
CHAPTER 4 **A HAPPY LIFE** SUBJECT AREAS: genetics, psychology	• Constructing meaning by making inferences	• Using definitions
CHAPTER 5 **PRINTING THE WORLD** SUBJECT AREAS: engineering, ethics, medicine	• Evaluating research sources	• Using register and tone
CHAPTER 6 **A VIEW OF THE FUTURE** SUBJECT AREAS: artificial intelligence, engineering	• Identifying organizational patterns	• Ensuring unity and coherence
CHAPTER 7 **EDUCATION FOR ALL** SUBJECT AREAS: computer science, education	• Interpreting visual elements	• Explaining processes
CHAPTER 8 **RIGHTS AND OBLIGATIONS** SUBJECT AREAS: ethics, law, political science	• Distinguishing fact from opinion	• Writing a compare and contrast essay

GRAMMAR	ACADEMIC SURVIVAL SKILL	ASSIGNMENTS
• Simple present and simple past tenses	• Completing academic assignments	• Writing a descriptive paragraph • Writing two descriptive paragraphs
• Future tense	• Taking notes	• Conducting a survey • Writing a short report
• Punctuation	• Citing sources and references	• Describing two points of view • Writing compare and contrast paragraphs
• Subject-verb agreement	• Developing vocabulary	• Writing short definitions • Writing a definition paragraph
• Sentence types	• Applying critical thinking techniques	• Writing a formal e-mail • Writing an e-mail request for information
• Articles	• Avoiding plagiarism	• Writing a short summary • Writing a summary
• Pronoun-antecedent agreement	• Working in a group	• Writing a process paragraph • Writing a process paragraph and giving a presentation
• Active and passive voice	• Preparing for an exam	• Writing an introductory essay paragraph • Writing a compare and contrast essay

TABLE OF CONTENTS

CHAPTER 1

Success in Business

Long before graduation, many students begin to think about what they will do for a career. You might think that most students would plan one related to their studies, but a Bank of Montreal survey of Canadian university students found that only a third of students expected to find employment in their own fields. More than half expected to start their own businesses, that is, become entrepreneurs. Although many students have great ideas for new businesses, some lack the skills or the money to put those ideas into action. These challenges are being met with opportunities to raise money in new ways.

What's your ideal business?

In this chapter,
you will

- learn vocabulary related to crowdfunding and business;

- use skimming and scanning strategies when reading;

- review simple present and simple past verb tenses;

- learn how a paragraph is structured;

- learn techniques for completing academic assignments successfully;

- write descriptive paragraphs for a crowdfunding project.

GEARING UP

A. Crowdfunding uses social media to support a project by inviting people to donate money to make a new idea or business possible. This graph shows the most popular Kickstarter projects funded in 2011. Look at the graph and then answer the questions.

Kickstarter Launched Projects

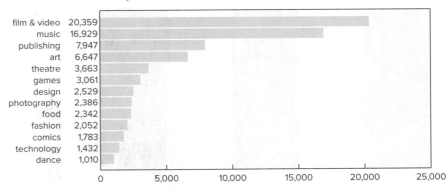

film & video	20,359
music	16,929
publishing	7,947
art	6,647
theatre	3,663
games	3,061
design	2,529
photography	2,386
food	2,342
fashion	2,052
comics	1,783
technology	1,432
dance	1,010

Source: Crisostomo, A. (2012). *Kickstarting the crowdfunding trends*. Retrieved from http://mastersofmedia.hum.uva.nl/2012/10/05/kickstarting-the-crowdfunding-trends/

1 What are the most popular and least popular types of Kickstarter projects?

_____

2 Pick a project category that interests you. What kind of project would you most likely support with a donation?

_____

3 Why do you think some project types are more popular than others?

_____

_____

4 Crowdfunding projects offer a range of rewards in exchange for support such as T-shirts or tickets to a performance. Pick a category and think of a small reward and a large reward that might be offered.

_____

_____

B. Discuss the questions and your answers, first with a partner, then in a group.

Skimming and Scanning

You read different types of text in different ways. You don't read a bus schedule or a newspaper in the same way you read a novel. You use different strategies to get the information you need. Often, this is because your time is limited or you simply want to get specific information. Skimming and scanning are two common ways to read different texts.

Skimming gives you a general impression of a text. In a piece of plain text, you may look quickly at the first and last sentences of each paragraph. If there are special features in the text, such as bullet points and quotes, then you may look at these as well. Often the title and subtitles give the main idea, as do photos, diagrams and charts. Skimming helps you decide if you want to read a text in more detail. One way to skim a document is to decide what the important ideas are.

Scanning helps you locate specific details. Use scanning when you have *who, what, when, where, why* or *how* questions. For example, you might scan an article to find the name of a person or the person's contact information. When you start with a question, look for key words that will lead you to the information you are looking for. Words such as *where* and *when* mean you are looking for a place and a time or date.

A. Consider these types of texts. Which would you skim; which would you scan? Discuss your answers with a partner.

newspapers

flight schedule

dictionary

technical drawings

B. Turn to Reading 1 on page 7. Skim the first sentence of each paragraph and fill in the table below with brief notes about things you understand and things you don't understand.

THINGS I UNDERSTAND	THINGS I DON'T UNDERSTAND

C. Scan this excerpt from Reading 1 and highlight the following information
- people who use crowdfunding sites;
- crowdfunding sites;
- how much people invest.

> Once limited to artists, musicians and filmmakers looking to finance their creative projects, crowdfunding has expanded into the world of entrepreneurship. Crowdfunding taps the power of social networking and allows entrepreneurs to post their elevator pitches and proposed investment terms on crowdfunding websites, such as Profounder, Peerbackers, Kickstarter or Indiegogo, and raise money to fund their ventures from ordinary people who invest as little as $100. Normally, the amount of capital these entrepreneurs seek is small, typically less than $10,000, and the "returns" they offer investors are mere tokens, such as discount coupons and free product samples. However, some entrepreneurs have raised significantly more money with crowdfunding and offer "real" returns.

D. Share your answers to tasks A, B and C with your partner and discuss any differences.

VOCABULARY BUILD 1

Consider other ways to organize the words. For example, draw lines to connect words associated with money.

 My eLab

Visit My eLab Documents to review the different parts of speech.

A. Below are words and phrases from the Academic Word List that you will find in Reading 1. Highlight the words you understand and then circle the words you use.

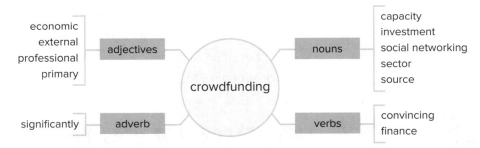

B. Fill in the blanks with the correct words or phrase to complete the sentences.

convincing	primary	significantly
external	~~professional~~	social networking

① They take their work seriously and are always _____*professional*_____.

② *Facebook* and *LinkedIn* are examples of _____.

③ Raising money is a _____ greater problem than getting a business idea.

④ Many people doubt what we can do, so our main job is _____ them.

⑤ The _____ purpose of crowdfunding is to support a new idea.

⑥ _____ funding comes from outside a company.

C. Choose the phrase that best completes each sentence. Key words are in bold.

1 To **finance** a new business involves _____.
   a) borrowing money from the owners
   b) contributing money to get it started
   c) owing money to business clients

2 To find the **source** of a problem, you should start at the _____.
   a) beginning
   b) middle
   c) end

3 When you make an **investment**, _____.
   a) it's like making a free contribution
   b) it's unlikely that it costs you anything
   c) you expect a return on your money

4 An example of a business **sector** is _____.
   a) the restaurant industry
   b) your local restaurant
   c) an idea for a restaurant

5 The **capacity** of a company is _____.
   a) how much it is likely to grow
   b) the time it takes to begin
   c) how much it can handle

6 Some benefits are **economic**, that is, _____.
   a) related to feelings of helping others
   b) based on being paid for something
   c) frequently found to be inexpensive

 **READING 1**

Looking for Money: Crowdfunding and Angels

When you start a new business, raising money is one of the greatest challenges. How can you do it? In some cases, you might have worked and saved money or you might have borrowed from friends and family. Sometimes a bank will give you a loan, but this is seldom enough to start a new business, and you have to look elsewhere. Two popular options are crowdfunding and angel investment. Crowdfunding uses social media to fund your business through the contributions of hundreds or thousands of individuals. Angel investment involves getting money from wealthy individuals or companies who exchange their support for a part of your company.

A. List two reasons people use social media.

_____

_____

B. Scan the article to find a definition of "angel investor." Why do you think *angel* is part of the term?

_____

_____

C. Google, Apple, Starbucks, Kinko's and The Body Shop are all businesses that were partially funded by angel investors. Choose one of these companies and describe what sort of angel investor might have been interested in funding it.

_____

_____

D. Read the text, and then answer the questions that follow.

Crowdfunding

entrepreneurship (n.): skill of creating and organizing new businesses

elevator pitches (n.): short proposals for new ideas

Once limited to artists, musicians and filmmakers looking to finance their creative projects, crowdfunding has expanded into the world of **entrepreneurship**. Crowdfunding taps the power of social networking and allows entrepreneurs to post their
5 **elevator pitches** and proposed investment terms on crowdfunding websites, such as Profounder, Peerbackers, Kickstarter or Indiegogo, and raise money to fund their ventures from ordinary people who invest as little as $100. Normally, the amount of capital these entrepreneurs seek is small, typically less than $10,000, and the "returns" they offer investors are mere tokens, such as discount coupons and free product
10 samples. However, some entrepreneurs have raised significantly more money with crowdfunding and offer "real" returns.

…

Congress (n.): law-making body of the USA

seed capital (n.): money to start a business

start-ups (n.): new businesses, often original and technological

equity stakes (n.): portions of the company in exchange for an investment

venture capital firms (n.): companies that raise funds to invest in new companies

primary (adj.): main or first

Crowdfunding sites typically charge a fee of about 4 percent to host a funding request, and many proposals fail to attract enough investors to reach their targets. Currently, a proposal before **Congress** would allow companies to raise up to $2 million in equity financing through crowdfunding. The proposal limits investments to $10,000 per year or 10 percent of the investor's annual income, whichever is less (Needleman & Loten, 2011).

Angels

After dipping into their own pockets and convincing friends and relatives to invest in their business ventures, many entrepreneurs still find themselves short of the **seed capital** they need. Frequently, the next stop on the road to business financing is private investors. These private investors (angels) are wealthy individuals, often entrepreneurs themselves, who invest their own money in business **start-ups** in exchange for **equity stakes** in the companies. Angel investors have provided much-needed capital to entrepreneurs for many years. In 1938, when World War I flying ace Eddie Rickenbacker needed money to launch Eastern Airlines, millionaire Laurance Rockefeller provided it. Alexander Graham Bell, inventor of the telephone, used angel capital to start Bell Telephone in 1877. More recently, companies such as Google, Apple, Starbucks, Kinko's and The Body Shop relied on angel financing in their early years to finance growth.

...

In many cases, angels invest in businesses for more than purely economic reasons—for example, because they have a personal interest or experience in a particular industry—and they are willing to put money into companies in the earliest stages, long before **venture capital firms** and institutional investors jump in. Angel financing, the fastest-growing segment of the small business capital market, is ideal for companies that have outgrown the capacity of investments from friends and family but are still too small to attract the interest of venture capital companies. Angel financing is vital to the nation's small business sector because it fills this capital gap in which small companies need investments ranging from $100,000 or less to perhaps $5 million or more. For instance, after raising the money to launch Amazon.com from family and friends, Jeff Bezos turned to angels for capital because venture capital firms were not interested in investing in a business start-up. Bezos attracted $1.2 million from a dozen angels before landing $8 million from venture capital firms a year later (Sherrid, 1997).

Angels are a **primary** source of start-up capital for companies in the start-up stage through the growth stage, and their role in financing small businesses is significant. Research at the University of New Hampshire shows that more than 318,000 angels and angel groups invest $22.5 billion a year in 66,000 small companies, most of them in the start-up phase (Sohl, 2012). In short, angels are one of the largest and most important sources of external equity capital for small businesses. Their investments in young companies nearly match those of professional venture capitalists, providing vital capital to eighteen times as many small companies. (602 words)

Angel Financing

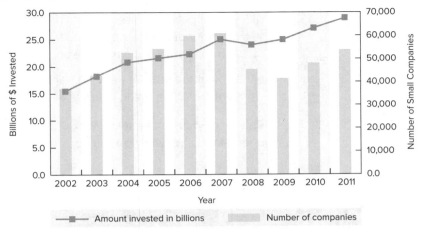

Source: Center for Venture Financing, Whittemore School of Business and Economics, University of New Hampshire, http://www.wsbe.unh.edu/crv-news

References

Needleman, S. & Loten, A. (2011, November 1). When friending becomes a source of start-up funds. *Wall Street Journal,* p. B5.

Sherrid, P. (1997, October 13). Angels of capitalism. *U.S. News & World Report*, 43–45.

Sohl, J. (2012, April 3). The angel investor market in 2013: The recovery continues. Center for Venture Research, University of New Hampshire.

Scarborough, N.M. (2014). *Essentials of entrepreneurship and small business management* (7th ed., pp. 474–476). New York, NY: Pearson.

E. Choose the correct phrase to complete each sentence. Try not to look back at the reading. When you have finished, check your answers.

SENTENCES		PHRASES
1 Crowdfunding was once limited to ...	_d_	a) angel investors.
2 Profounder, Peerbackers, Kickstarter and Indiegogo are examples of ...	_____	b) small businesses.
3 Not finding enough support from crowdfunding makes entrepreneurs seek ...	_____	c) to start his new business.
4 Crowdfunding websites make a profit by ...	_____	d) creative projects.
5 Alexander Graham Bell probably didn't have enough money ...	_____	e) venture capital companies.
6 In terms of growth, The Body Shop probably needed money to ...	_____	f) crowdfunding websites.
7 Angel investors provide more funding than crowdfunding sites but less than ...	_____	g) open new stores.
8 Angel investors are extremely important to developing ...	_____	h) charging a fee.

F. Discuss the answers to these inference questions with a partner.

1. Why might Congress want to limit the amount that can be raised by crowdfunding for a new company? Why might small business owners and crowdfunding companies not like this decision?

2. Look at the table in Reading 1 and the details for 2007 to 2011. What do you think was happening in terms of angel investment during this time?

G. Return to Focus on Reading, task B, on page 4. Review what you now understand and what you still don't understand. Discuss with your partner.

FOCUS ON GRAMMAR

Simple Present and Simple Past Tenses

When you read the text on pages 7–9, you may have noticed examples of the simple present and simple past tenses. Use the simple present tense for

• actions that are happening now: I **write** about crowdfunding;

• repeated actions: I **write** every day;

• facts, opinions and general truths: I **don't write** for corporations.

SIMPLE PRESENT TENSE	
For the affirmative, add -s to the base form of the verb for the third-person singular.	I **write**. He/She/It **writes**. We/You/They **write.**
Add -es to verbs ending in -sh, -ch, -s, -x, -o.	She **watches** the financial news on television.
For the negative, add *do not* (*don't*) or *does not* (*doesn't*) before the verb.	I **do not** (**don't**) **read** the financial news. He **does not** (**doesn't**) **read** the financial news.
To ask a question, put *do* or *does* before the subject.	**Do** you know about crowdfunding? **Does** she know about social networking?

EXCEPTIONS	
VERB *to have*	**VERB *to be***
I **have** (**I've**)	I **am** (**I'm**)
you **have** (**you've**)	you **are** (**you're**)
he/she/it **has** (**he's/she's/it's**)	he/she/it **is** (**he's/she's/it's**)
we/you/they **have** (**we've/you've/they've**)	we/you/they **are** (**we're/you're/they're**)

A. Highlight the word in parentheses that is the correct verb form.

1. The company (support / supports) crowdfunding.

2. I (pass / passes) investment ideas to my friends.

3. The start-up (push / pushes) investors to get involved.

4. She (catch / catches) a bus to work each day.

5. We (hit / hits) our funding goal in three weeks.

6. I (toss / tosses) the reports on my desk each afternoon.

Use the simple past tense of regular verbs for actions that began and ended in the past.

SIMPLE PAST TENSE	
For the affirmative form, add -ed to the end of the verb.	She start**ed** TalentEgg four years ago.
For the negative (contracted) form, add did not (didn't) before the verb.	She **did not** (didn't) start TalentEgg four years ago.
To ask a question, put did before the subject.	**Did** she start TalentEgg four years ago?
SPELLING	
For verbs that end in y, change the y to i and add -ed.	(try) He **tried** to find a job after college.
For short verbs that end in a vowel + consonant, double the consonant before adding -ed.	(clap) Everyone **clapped** when her presentation ended.

Many past-tense verbs have *irregular* forms. You have to memorize them.

SIMPLE PAST TENSE OF IRREGULAR VERBS		
AFFIRMATIVE FORM	**NEGATIVE (CONTRACTED) FORM**	**QUESTION FORM**
(pay) He **paid** for their services.	(pay) He **did not** (didn't) **pay** for their services.	(pay) **Did** he **pay** for their services?
(give) She **gave** a lot of her time to the project.	(give) She **did not** (didn't) **give** a lot of her time to the project.	(give) **Did** she **give** a lot of her time to the project?
VERB *to be*		
AFFIRMATIVE FORM	**NEGATIVE (CONTRACTED) FORM**	**QUESTION FORM**
I/He/She/It **was** late. You/We/They **were** late.	I/He/She/It **was not** (wasn't) late. You/We/They **were not** (weren't) late.	**Was** I/he/she/it late? **Were** you/we/they late?

My eLab 📁

Visit My eLab Documents to see the Irregular Verbs List.

❗
Use what you learned about the simple present and simple past tenses when you write assignments.

B. Write the verb in parentheses in the simple past tense.

1 The climate for youth entrepreneurs (seem) _____*seemed*_____ better than ever.

2 Of the 1,000 entrepreneurs (survey) _____, 88 percent believed mentoring programs would boost that support further in the next three years.

3 The online portal (connect) _____ students with jobs and employers (recruit) _____ off campuses across the country.

4 At each special place he visited, he (collect) _____ a small souvenir.

5 My team are all Gen Y-ers and we (understand) _____ the market better than anyone else.

Develop Your Vocabulary:
Mind maps reflect the
way your mind organizes
information by linking
ideas. Use mind maps to
develop your vocabulary,
adding new words and
concepts to those you
already know.

A. Below are words from the Academic Word List that you will find in Reading 2.
Highlight the words you understand and then circle the words you use.

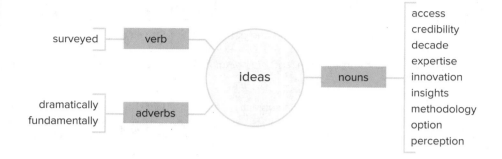

surveyed — **verb**

dramatically
fundamentally — **adverbs**

ideas

nouns

access
credibility
decade
expertise
innovation
insights
methodology
option
perception

B. Fill in the blanks with the correct words to complete the sentences.

| access | credibility | dramatically | methodology | perception |

1 Everyone agreed it was a fact; it wasn't his _____.

2 No one believed him; he had no _____.

3 The fireworks slowly stopped; they didn't end _____ at all.

4 They started the project without any plan; because of that, there was no
_____ to the work.

5 We didn't have passes to get in; there was no public _____.

C. Fill in the blanks with the correct words to complete the paragraph.

| decade | fundamentally | insights | surveyed |
| expertise | innovation | option | |

After a _____ of _____,
the company is staring to introduce new products.
The company has dramatically increased its
_____ in computing and attracted money
from venture capitalists. One of the company's
_____ was that it needed to better
understand its customers. It _____
many young people who use their phones for banking
and found they are _____ different
than the older generation. The younger generation prefer
the _____ of never going to a bank.

D. Work with a partner and practise using the words in task A in sentences.

Youth Entrepreneurs

An entrepreneur is someone who starts a business. Often the business is new and risky. The Internet has made it possible for many new entrepreneurs to become successful. In some cases, Internet entrepreneurs create new services that don't require factories or stores. This lowers their costs. The Internet also increases the number of people a new business can reach. But to reach people successfully, entrepreneurs need strong communication skills to sell their ideas. That is, they need to use words to help communicate their ideas and convince people to support them.

A. Skim the five numbered points in Reading 2 to get a general idea of what each is about. Then, match these sentences to each point.

_____ People familiar with technology can make money.

_____ More money is available.

_____ It's less expensive to start a business.

_____ It's easier to learn about starting a business.

_____1___ New leaders inspire young people.

B. Scan the article to find the sentence on musicians and entrepreneurs. Why does the writer compare these two occupations?

_____

_____

C. The article mentions Gen Y, which stands for *Generation Y* and refers to children born between the 1980s and the early 2000s. They are also called *millennials*. Based on what you know about this generation, do you agree or disagree with these statements?

GEN Y GRADUATES ...	AGREE	UNCERTAIN	DISAGREE
❶ delay getting married or starting a career.	☐	☐	☐
❷ want flexibility on the job.	☐	☐	☐
❸ are less concerned about helping the community.	☐	☐	☐
❹ are more open to new ideas.	☐	☐	☐
❺ want frequent feedback from managers.	☐	☐	☐

D. Discuss your answers with a partner. When you finish, read the text and then answer the questions that follow.

Youth Entrepreneurs

factors (n.): things that influence outcomes

digital natives (n.): those who have grown up using new technologies

venture capitalists (n.): investors in risky businesses

mentorship (n.): advising a less-experienced colleague

pros and cons (n.): advantages and disadvantages

The climate for youth entrepreneurs seems better than ever, particularly in the knowledge sectors where young people have the advantage of low start-up costs and technology know-how. Ajay Agrawal, a professor at University of Toronto's Rotman 5 School of Management, puts this down to five **factors**.

1. *Culture:* From Facebook's Mark Zuckerberg to Dropbox's Drew Houston to Tumblr's David Karp, there's a growing parade of leadership examples for young people. Becoming a CEO has become more imaginable.

2. *Technology:* The **digital natives** have the insights and expertise to find profit- 10 able niches in the rapidly growing world of mobile, Internet and social media innovation.

3. *Lean methodology:* Cost barriers to starting up your own business have fallen dramatically. With careful planning it can be done with $10,000 or less rather than $100,000.

15 4. *Access to capital:* Not only are investors more willing to fund twenty-two-year-olds than they were a decade ago, there has been an increase in funds available from **venture capitalists** to the federal and provincial governments.

5. *Infrastructure:* The opportunities for **mentorship**, training and funding have grown through organizations like the Canadian Youth Business Foundation, Nspire and 20 The Next 36. Universities are also actively promoting youth entrepreneurship through the University of Waterloo's Conrad Business Entrepreneurship and Technology Centre and Ryerson's Digital Media Zone, as examples.

According to an Ernst & Young survey released late last year, there has been a marked improvement in training, funding and support for young entrepreneurs in the last five 25 years. Of the 1,000 entrepreneurs surveyed, 88 percent believed mentoring programs would boost that support further in the next three years.

Rod McNaughton, director of the University of Waterloo's Conrad Centre, says he has noticed a shift in perception towards entrepreneurs as well.

Traditionally, even if parents were small busi- 30 ness people, they'd encourage their kids to become professionals, he says. "Going home and saying you want to be an entrepreneur was like going home and saying you want to become a musician." But now entrepreneurs 35 are becoming almost a professional class.

The question is whether this entrepreneurial wave is different, he says. He thinks there could be changes in technology and society that are fundamentally shifting in favour of 40 smaller, new businesses.

So what are the **pros and cons** of being a young CEO?

...

Lauren Friese, Founder of TalentEgg. Age: Twenty-eight

45 • *Her story:* She started TalentEgg four years ago after seeing how challenging it could be for students to find work after graduation. The online portal connects students with jobs and helps employers recruit off campuses across the country and market themselves towards Gen Y.

• *Advantages:* Start-ups are a good Gen Y option. "It's become more accepted for
50 young people to start their careers in entrepreneurial companies, whether they started them or are working in them." The appeal is being able to [have] more than just a narrow job, to have a say in what goes on and access to leadership.

• Challenges:

Building credibility: "When I founded TalentEgg I was twenty-four, but I looked fifteen
55 then and I look fifteen now. Right away I knew that I wasn't going to go into a meeting and look like the other people selling stuff in my market, so I decided I wasn't going to pretend. I'm a recent graduate, my team are all Gen Y-ers and we understand the market better than anyone else."

Lack of experience in business: "I worked to turn that to my advantage too ... by
60 saying I can approach problems with an open mind."

• *Advice:* "I don't think you could find an entrepreneur out there who could honestly tell you they've never wanted to quit. I think feeling that kind of intense emotion about your business is part of the game." Being an entrepreneur takes hard work, **perseverance** (something that got her through the **recession**) and the ability to
65 step back and reassess what you're doing.

• *Role models:* Her parents, who are both entrepreneurs, and case studies about the many successful entrepreneurs out there.

(668 words)

———
Hasham, A. (2012, March 2). Youth entrepreneurs: Why launching a business from your childhood bedroom is more possible than ever (and here's proof). *The Star*. Retrieved from www.thestar.com/business/2012/03/02/youth_entrepreneurs_why_launching_a_business_from_your_childhood_bedroom_is_more_possible_than_ever_and_heres_proof.html

E. *Who, what, when, where, why* and *how* questions are often the basis of a news article. Fill in the information about the reading by answering these questions. Write your answers in complete sentences.

QUESTIONS	ANSWERS
❶ WHO is Lauren Friese?	*She is a young entrepreneur who started TalentEgg.*
❷ WHAT does her company do?	
❸ WHEN did she found (start) her company (at what age)?	
❹ WHERE does the company operate?	
❺ WHY did she start TalentEgg?	
❻ HOW does she deal with her lack of experience?	

F. Indicate whether these statements are true or false, according to the text.

STATEMENTS	TRUE	FALSE
1 More than 80 percent of businesses believed mentoring would increase.	☑	☐
2 Parents now encourage their children to become entrepreneurs.	☐	☐
3 Society is now more in favour of larger and older businesses.	☐	☐
4 TalentEgg was founded to help students find work while they study.	☐	☐
5 Working for a start-up can provide access to leadership.	☐	☐
6 Lauren Friese first thought her age would be a disadvantage.	☐	☐
7 It's almost impossible to find an entrepreneur who has wanted to quit.	☐	☐
8 Friese's parents and case studies were her role models.	☐	☐
9 Friese believes that being an entrepreneur is easy; all it takes is a little bit of luck.	☐	☐

FOCUS ON WRITING

Writing a Paragraph

The paragraph is the basis of many kinds of writing, including essays. A paragraph is a group of connected sentences on the same topic. Paragraphs are structured with a topic sentence, supporting sentences and a concluding sentence.

A. Read this excerpt from Reading 3 and the explanatory notes to learn how a paragraph is structured.

The **topic sentence** is the first sentence of a paragraph. It lets readers know the main idea, but doesn't give detailed information. It usually includes a topic and controlling idea (underlined). The controlling idea suggests what will follow.

The **concluding sentence** brings the ideas together. It restates the topic sentence in a different way or summarizes supporting sentences or is a transition to a new topic.

> Crowdfunding is often used to raise money for products, experiences, public causes and services. Products include the manufacture of a new design or invention such as a new type of skateboard. Crowdfunding also helps to host an experience such as a dance performance. A public cause is to support an individual or group in need, such as raising adequate funds for a child's expensive operation. Services might include funding a meals program for the poor. In the case of the film *Be Brave*, crowdfunding was a way for a sister to help make her dying brother's dream come true.

Supporting sentences support and expand on the idea or ideas of the topic sentence. They may include facts, examples and explanations. There might be three or more supporting sentences in a paragraph. A few sentences may help explain a single detail.

B. Read these sentences and then number them in the correct order to form a paragraph with a topic sentence, four supporting sentences and a concluding sentence.

_____ A title for the film was chosen, *Be Brave,* and a film crew accompanied Erin to Mexico to return the bone to the cave.

_____ After Daniel's death, Erin found the bone among Daniel's possessions.

___*1*___ By the time he died, Daniel Northcott had succeeded in making a forty-minute video, but he had hoped for more.

_____ He asked his sister, Erin, to find a way to finish the film and also to return the bone.

_____ It gave an overview of what he wanted done with the footage, but it was incomplete.

_____ Three years passed before Erin found someone willing and able to take on the film project: Mikki Willis of Elevate Studios.

C. Use these phrases to write topic sentences.

1 business professionals / three important skills

Most business professionals share three important skills.

_____

2 recipe / success / energy, time, focus

_____

_____

3 many people / not understand / investment

_____

_____

4 new challenges / graduates / become entrepreneurs

_____

_____

_____

5 any business / improved / listening / customers

_____

_____

_____

D. Reread your topic sentences and highlight the controlling idea that suggests what will follow in the paragraph. Hint: it's often the second part of the sentence. In the example, it's "three important skills."

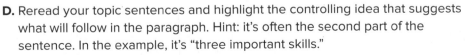

WARM-UP ASSIGNMENT
Write a Descriptive Paragraph

Write a paragraph to describe a project you might finance using crowdfunding. Choose from one of the categories in Gearing Up on page 3.

A. Write a topic sentence to introduce the project and include a controlling idea. Then, write three supporting sentences and a concluding sentence. Use this table to outline your ideas.

TOPIC SENTENCE	
SUPPORTING SENTENCE	
SUPPORTING SENTENCE	
SUPPORTING SENTENCE	
CONCLUDING SENTENCE	

> *Use feedback from your teacher and classmates on this Warm-Up Assignment to improve your writing.*

B. Write your paragraph. Refer to the Models Chapter (page 187) to see an example of a descriptive paragraph and to learn more about how to write one.

C. Proofread your paragraph. This means looking carefully to correct any errors and considering ways you can make your message clearer. Use this checklist.

☐ Do you have a topic sentence with a topic and a controlling idea?

☐ Do your supporting sentences flow smoothly from point to point?

☐ Does your concluding sentence bring your ideas together?

☐ Check your verb tenses. Do your subjects and verbs agree?

☐ Check your punctuation.

☐ Have you used the present and past verb tenses correctly?

☐ Read your paragraph out loud. This will allow you to hear errors you might not see.

☐ Put your writing aside for a period of time. When you come back to it, you may spot errors or awkward sentences you missed earlier.

☐ Reread your assignment and compare your paragraph to what you were asked to do. Have you met all the criteria? What could you improve?

D. Make corrections and write a final copy.

My eLab 🗁
Visit My eLab Documents for a writing checklist including tips on proofreading and editing.

A. Below are words from the Academic Word List that you will find in Reading 3. Highlight the words you understand and then circle the words you use.

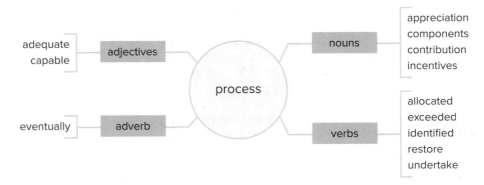

adjectives: adequate, capable

adverb: eventually

process

nouns: appreciation, components, contribution, incentives

verbs: allocated, exceeded, identified, restore, undertake

B. Match each word to its definition. For words you are not sure of, check the context of the word in the reading for clues. Use a dictionary to check your answers.

WORDS		DEFINITIONS
❶ appreciation	_____	a) set aside or distributed
❷ allocated	_____	b) in greater number or amount
❸ eventually	_____	c) in time
❹ exceeded	_____	d) plan to do something and begin
❺ incentives	_____	e) recognition of someone's or something's good qualities
❻ undertake	_____	f) things that motivate or encourage

C. Synonyms are words that have similar meanings. Highlight the word that has the closest meaning to each word in bold.

❶ Every **contribution** to a project is important and deserves thanks.
  a) theft   b) practice   c) donation

❷ Just do a/an **adequate** job; there's no need to spend too much time on it.
  a) lacking   b) abnormal   c) satisfactory

❸ Anyone who is not **capable** should not be asked to do the job.
  a) dressed   b) skilled   c) untrained

❹ Each of the **components** of a business plan must work together.
  a) parts   b) spares   c) investments

❺ We **identified** three problems that had to be fixed.
  a) changed   b) recognized   c) grown

❻ The crowdfunding campaign hoped to **restore** the old library.
  a) destroy   b) rebuild   c) change

D. VOCABULARY EXTENSION: *Undertake* is an example of a compound word. A *compound word* is made up of two or more smaller words. Considering the meaning of the individual words makes the compound word easier to understand. Rewrite these compound words dividing them into the two or three smaller words from which each is made.

1. forthcoming   *forth coming*
2. guideline   _____
3. nevertheless   _____
4. nonetheless   _____
5. ongoing   _____
6. overlap   _____
7. overseas   _____
8. straightforward   _____
9. undertake   _____
10. widespread   _____

Visit My eLab to complete Vocabulary Review exercises for this chapter.

E. Discuss the meaning of each word in task D with a partner.

READING ③

Crowdfunding: *Be Brave*

Crowdfunding projects come in many sizes; some have goals of raising less than a thousand dollars while others aim for much more. An example is films, which are expensive to make and are not guaranteed to be popular once they are completed. A good crowdfunding campaign can help raise the money and generate interest in the film as well.

A. Imagine you had a thousand dollars to spend on crowdfunding. What are some reasons you might be willing to help crowdfund a film?

_____

_____

B. Scan the reading to find the names of people mentioned in the article. Which name is mentioned most? Which name is mentioned least?

_____

_____

C. Read the text, and then answer the questions that follow.

Crowdfunding: *Be Brave*

manufacture (n.): making of something using a mechanical process

sacred (adj.): holy

Crowdfunding is often used to raise money for products, experiences, public causes and services. Products include the **manufacture** of a new design or invention such as a new type of skateboard. Crowdfunding also helps to host an experience such as

5 a dance performance. A public cause is to support an individual or group in need, such as raising adequate funds for a child's expensive operation. Services might include funding a meals program for the poor. In the case of the film *Be Brave*, crowdfunding was a way for a sister to help make her dying brother's dream come true.

When he was twenty years old, Daniel Northcott began ten years of travelling the

10 world with his video camera. Eventually, he would undertake trips across forty-two countries on four continents, visiting different cities, war zones and **sacred** sites. He

sacrificed (v.): given up, or offered, for the sake of something more important

cursed (adj.): given pain and suffering

overview (n.): general summary

perks (n.): benefits

pledges (n.): promises to do something

credit (n.): recognition for something

ended up with more than one thousand hours of film. At each special place he visited, he collected a small souvenir, often in the form of a circular or ball-shaped object. On one of his last trips, he visited a sacred cave in Mexico. The floor was covered with
15 the ancient bones of people who had been **sacrificed** there. Daniel took one bone, despite the warning of his guide who said that he would be **cursed**.

Later, the curse seemed to come true. Tragedy struck Daniel in the form of leukemia, a cancer of the blood. Despite being sick, he allocated time to continue to film and focused on two objectives. The first objective was to make a full-length film from the
20 one thousand hours he had shot, and the second was to return the bone to the sacred cave. But he was unable to remember where he'd put the bone.

When Daniel died, at age twenty-nine, he had succeeded in making a forty-minute video that gave an **overview** of what he wanted done with the footage, but it was incomplete. He asked his sister, Erin Northcott, to find a way to finish
25 the film and to return the bone. After Daniel's death, Erin found the bone among her brother's possessions. Three years passed before Erin found someone capable of taking on the film project: Mikki Willis of Elevate Studios. A title for the film was chosen, *Be Brave,* and a film crew accompanied Erin to Mexico to restore the bone to the cave.

30 Both the film and the trip were funded through an Indiegogo campaign called *Be Brave—The True Story of Daniel Northcott*. The campaign website included many essential components. A video explained the purpose of the project in a personal way. Text and photos gave more information about the film, how crowdfunding works, the people involved in the project, what the funds would
35 be spent on and answers to frequently asked questions. There was also contact information and a section on incentives called *perks*, which were rewards for **pledges**.

The campaign identified the need to raise $183,000 and quickly exceeded that amount. People interested in helping fund the film had twelve levels of perks
40 they could receive in return for their pledges. These started with a thank-you on the website for a $10 contribution, to an executive producer **credit** on the final film for a $10,000 contribution. Between these amounts were perks in the form of posters, T-shirts, DVDs, hand-made art and other shows of appreciation.

In the end, the use of crowdfunding did more than simply raise enough money to
45 make the film *Be Brave*. The website and the perks served to draw attention to the issues raised in the film and attract more people to see it.

(600 words)

References

Northcott, E. (2013). *Be brave—The true story of Daniel Northcott*. Retrieved from http://www.indiegogo.com/projects/be-brave-the-true-story-of-daniel-northcott

Steinberg, D. (2012). *The Kickstarter handbook: Real-life success stories of artists, inventors and entrepreneurs*. Philadelphia, PA: Quirke Books.

Williams Marks, P. (2013). *Hacking Kickstarter, Indiegogo: How to raise big bucks in 30 days (Secrets to running a successful crowdfunding campaign on a budget)*. Los Gatos, CA: Smashwords.

D. Match the words or phrases to the part each played in the Crowdfunding: *Be Brave* story.

WORDS/PHRASES		PART PLAYED
❶ $10	_____	a) film Daniel Northcott made before dying
❷ $10,000	_____	b) crowdfunding organization
❸ $183,000	_____	c) company that made the final film
❹ forty-minute video	_____	d) location of the sacred cave
❺ sacred bone	_____	e) donation for an acknowledgement on the website
❻ Daniel Northcott	_____	f) Daniel's sister
❼ Elevate Studios	_____	g) film director
❽ Erin Northcott	_____	h) amount it was necessary to raise
❾ Indiegogo	_____	i) cursed souvenir that Daniel brought home
❿ leukemia	_____	j) a cancer of the blood
⓫ Mexico	_____	k) maximum donation for an executive producer credit
⓬ Mikki Willis	_____	l) traveller who shot one thousand hours of video

E. Connect the phrases to create a summary.

PHRASES		
❶ Erin Northcott was asked ...	_____	a) one thousand hours of video to work with.
❷ Daniel had collected ...	_____	b) agreed to help.
❸ He tried ...	_____	c) for a stolen bone to be returned to a cave in Mexico.
❹ Before he died, he asked ...	_____	d) to raise money to make the project happen.
❺ A film director ...	_____	e) by her dying brother, Daniel, to make a film.
❻ Crowdfunding was used ...	_____	f) to make a film from his videos but died of cancer.

F. Write a topic sentence and a concluding sentence to turn the sentences in task E into a complete paragraph.

TOPIC SENTENCE: _____

_____

CONCLUDING SENTENCE: _____

_____

Completing Academic Assignments

You go to college or university to learn. Assignments and exams are ways to demonstrate both what you have learned and how you think. It's important to be effective and efficient when you work on assignments. You can be effective by asking questions about the assignment and by getting the help you need. You can be efficient by planning your time for research and writing, particularly if you are working with others.

KEY QUESTIONS	WHAT TO DO
What is the assignment?	Read the assignment as soon as you receive it and make certain you understand each part. Ask your teacher about any missing details or anything you don't understand. Are you expected to write from your own experience or do you need references from your textbooks, the library and/or the Internet? How many references?
When is the assignment due?	Check when the assignment is due. Put a note on your calendar so you remember to hand it in.
How much time do you need to do the assignment?	Consider how much time you need to do the assignment. Where will you find the information to complete it? Do you need to spend time online or in a library looking for resources?
When will you do the assignment?	Plan time on your calendar to get the work done. It's usually best to block out more hours than you think you will need. Also, block out a second session to review and revise the assignment. If you have to work with other students, plan your sessions at the start.
What information and/or tools do you need to do the assignment?	Check to make sure you have everything you need for the assignment before you start. You might need books, tools or software programs.
Where else can you get help?	Get help from other students. It's a good way to learn how others solve the same assignment problems. Librarians can help you find resources and writing guides.
When you have finished the assignment, how will you check it?	Some teachers provide a checklist with criteria. Make sure your assignment meets the highest standards: check spelling, grammar, citations and references.

A. The following assignment is not clear. Write three questions you might have for your teacher.

> Write about a successful business. Due next Friday.

1 _____

2 _____

3 _____

B. Discuss your questions with a partner and rewrite the assignment to make it clear.

_____

_____

FINAL ASSIGNMENT

Write Two Descriptive Paragraphs

Use what you learned in this chapter to write two descriptive paragraphs on your crowdfunding project.

A. Start with the paragraph you wrote for the Warm-Up Assignment. Review the supporting sentences and reconsider your choice of descriptive words (adjectives and adverbs) to make the writing more interesting. Revise and expand it, making improvements based on feedback you received.

B. Write a second paragraph about why you are suitable for undertaking the project. Think about what you have to offer in terms of acquired skills, sports and club participation, part-time jobs or subjects studied.

C. Use this table to outline your ideas.

TOPIC SENTENCE	
SUPPORTING SENTENCE	
SUPPORTING SENTENCE	
SUPPORTING SENTENCE	
CONCLUDING SENTENCE	

D. Write a draft of your paragraphs. Review the Vocabulary Build sections to see which vocabulary you can include. Review Focus on Grammar (page 10) to make sure you are using the correct verb tenses to describe what you did in the past and what you do now. Refer to the Models Chapter (page 187) to see an example of a descriptive paragraph and to learn more about how to write one.

E. Proofread your draft paragraphs. Use the checklist in the Warm-Up Assignment on page 18.

F. Make corrections and write a final copy.

How confident are you?

Think about what you learned in this chapter. Use the table to decide what you should review.

I LEARNED ...	I AM CONFIDENT	I NEED TO REVIEW
vocabulary related to crowdfunding and business;	☐	☐
skimming and scanning strategies;	☐	☐
simple present and simple past verb tenses;	☐	☐
the structure of a paragraph;	☐	☐
techniques for completing academic assignments;	☐	☐
how to write a descriptive paragraph.	☐	☐

VOCABULARY
Challenge

Think about the vocabulary and ideas in this chapter. Use these words to write two sentences that summarize success in business.

capable	eventually	investment
contribution	insights	professional

_____

_____

_____

_____

_____

My eLab 🖉

Visit My eLab to build on what you learned.

CHAPTER 2
The Future of Work

Many jobs are changing or disappearing while new ones are being created every day. Certain jobs are being taken over by computers and robots that work more consistently and at a lower cost than humans. You may not be able to compete in some ways, but developing strong critical thinking and effective communication skills will ensure that you are always prepared for new challenges and opportunities.

Which skills are you learning for a career in the twenty-first century?

In this chapter, you will

- learn vocabulary related to skills and jobs;
- recognize points of view;
- use the future tense with *will* and *be going to*;
- learn how to take notes;
- prepare and conduct a survey;
- write a short report.

GEARING UP

A. Look at the graph and then answer the questions.

Will a computer or a robot take your job?

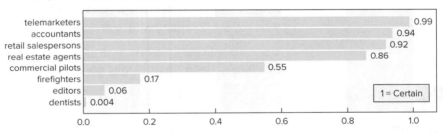

Source: Frey. C.B. & Osborne, M.A. (2013). *The future of employment: How susceptible are jobs to computerisation?* Retrieved from http://www.futuretech.ox.ac.uk/sites/futuretech.ox.ac.uk/files/The_Future_of_Employment_ OMS_Working_Paper_1.pdf

1 Which job is most likely to disappear? Which is least likely to disappear?

_____

2 If commercial pilots no longer flew planes, would you feel safe being piloted by a computer? Why or why not?

_____

_____

3 In what ways are retail sales staff already being replaced by computers?

_____

_____

4 Timed traffic lights have replaced the police officers who once stood in busy intersections directing traffic. Write other examples of the computerization of jobs.

_____

_____

B. Discuss the questions and your answers, first with a partner, then in a group.

Recognizing Point of View

When you read, try to understand the writer's point of view, which may favour one idea, person or group over another. For example, an article about robots might be quite different depending on whether it is written by an engineer who designs robots or by a worker who has lost a job to a robot. You cannot always know a writer's background, but thinking critically about what is written can help you understand the writer's point of view.

Ask these questions:

- Does the writer provide supporting evidence: facts, statistics or references?
- Does the writer ignore evidence that would support a different point of view?
- Does the writer back general statements with evidence in the form of examples and explanations?

A. Read this excerpt from Reading 1. Think about the underlined numbered sections. What questions might you have about the writer or about what has been written? Discuss with a partner.

> <u>Man vs. Robot</u> [1]
>
> It's easy to tell when a new technology has reached critical mass—discussions over its long-term effects start kicking into overdrive. <u>That's happening now with robots</u> [2] and how they are going to affect the human job market.
>
> <u>Conventional thinking has always held</u> [3] that automation and robots have historically been good things, because when a machine takes over a task, the <u>human who used to do it is forced</u> [4] to do something smarter and better.

B. Review the four points from the excerpt and decide which are neutral and which indicate the writer's point of view (POV).

POINTS	NEUTRAL	WRITER'S POV
❶ *Versus* (vs.) in the title suggests the idea of a contrast. Does the idea of a fight between robots/technology and people indicate the writer's POV?		✓
❷ Serious articles present references to back up claims. Does a lack of evidence indicate the writer's POV?		
❸ Does a general statement suggesting that everyone has always thought the same thing indicate the writer's POV?		
❹ The phrase *is forced* has a negative meaning and could be replaced by a word like *chooses*. Does the writer's use of *is forced* indicate the writer's POV?		

C. Identify writer point of view in each sentence. Write your answers and then discuss them with a partner.

SENTENCES	KIND OF POINT OF VIEW
1 Robots will eventually make people look like outdated technology, such as typewriters.	*The writer gives a general statement without any evidence.*
2 Overall, technology is eliminating far more jobs than it is creating.	
3 Machines are taking over human tasks faster than humans can come up with new and better things to do.	
4 We can't even imagine the jobs we'll create because of this increasing automation.	

**VOCABULARY
BUILD 1**

> **!**
>
> *Develop Your Vocabulary:
> Keep a notebook or
> a file on your computer
> tablet or phone to store
> new vocabulary. Write
> definitions and check
> them regularly. Add
> related words that you
> encounter.*

A. Below are words and phrases from the Academic Word List that you will find in Reading 1. Highlight the words you understand and then circle the words you use.

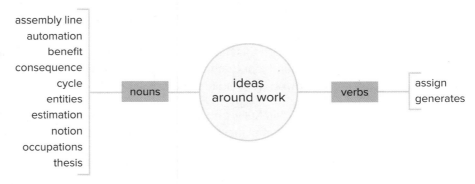

assembly line
automation
benefit
consequence
cycle
entities
estimation
notion
occupations
thesis

nouns — **ideas around work** — **verbs**

assign
generates

B. Highlight the best definition for each word.

1 consequence a) beginning of an action   b) result of an action

2 cycle   a) series of events   b) type of wheel

3 entities   a) things with a distinct identity   b) entry points to ideas

4 notion   a) small comforting thing   b) belief about something

5 occupations   a) jobs or professions   b) hobbies or challenges

6 thesis   a) final conclusion   b) statement or theory

C. Fill in the blanks with the correct words to complete the paragraph.

assembly line	automation	estimation
assign	benefit	generates

One _____ of organizing work around a/an _____ was that it was easy to _____ one worker to do another's job. But today, _____ is replacing workers. An industrial robot _____ greater profits and can work twenty-four hours a day, seven days a week. By one _____, if an industrial robot costs $50,000 to $80,000, it can pay for itself within a few months.

READING ❶ **Man vs. Robot**

New technologies seldom completely replace a job worldwide. Instead, they tend to take over parts of jobs. In 2012, 159,346 robots were shipped for use in factories worldwide, with 70 percent going to China, Germany, Japan, Korea and the USA.[1] Although this has created jobs for engineers and computer scientists, there is a general fear that technology will take away far more jobs than it will create. Is the job you want likely to be replaced?

A. Kevin Kelly, one of the writers mentioned in Reading 1, talks about the types of jobs that machines will eventually do. Think of at least one job for each category.

	HUMAN	MACHINE
EXISTING JOBS	❶ Jobs today that humans do—but machines will eventually do better.	❷ Current jobs that humans can't do but machines can.
NEW JOBS	❸ Jobs that only humans will be able to do—at first.	❹ Robot jobs that we can't even imagine yet.[2]

❶ _____

❷ _____

❸ _____

❹ _____

1. Industrial Robotics Statistics. (2013). Second highest number of robots sold in 2012. Retrieved from http://www.ifr.org/industrial-robots/statistics/

2. Kelly, K. (2012). *Better than human: Why robots will—and must—take our jobs.* Retrieved from http://www.wired.com/2012/12/ff-robots-will-take-our-jobs/all/

B. While you read, highlight indications of the writer's point of view. After reading, check with a partner to see if you agree.

☐ Does the writer provide supporting evidence: facts, statistics or references?

☐ Does the writer ignore evidence that would support a different point of view?

☐ Does the writer back general statements with evidence in the form of examples and explanations?

Man vs. Robot

overdrive (n.): high or excessive activity

conventional thinking (n.): usual thinking

repercussions (n.): unintended consequences

minutiae (n.): small details

exponential (adj.): growing at a fast pace

accelerating (v.): getting faster

GDP (n.): Gross Domestic Product; how much a country produces

accrue (v.): gather

It's easy to tell when a new technology has reached critical mass—discussions over its long-term effects start kicking into **overdrive**. That's happening now with robots and how they are going to affect the human job market.

5 **Conventional thinking** has always held that automation and robots have historically been good things, because when a machine takes over a task, the human who used to do it is forced to do something smarter and better. This has had traditional **repercussions** both great and small, from auto assembly line workers necessarily having to upgrade their skills or maybe even start their own businesses, to regular people simply not having

10 to remember **minutiae** like phone numbers because machines do it for them. Machines have traditionally freed our brains to worry about other, more important stuff.

However, in a recent *60 Minutes* interview, MIT professors Erik Brynjolfsson and Bruce Welty raised a worrying issue—that robotic development has now reached the **exponential** phase, which means that machines are taking over human tasks faster

15 than humans can come up with new and better things to do.

"Right now the pace is **accelerating**. It's faster we think than ever before in history," Brynjolfsson said. "So as a consequence, we are not creating jobs at the same pace that we need to."

By that estimation, robots will eventually take over all human jobs, leaving us with

20 nothing to do. This is very bad, says the *New York Times'* Paul Krugman, because that means all wealth will be controlled by the people who own the robots (assuming the machines don't turn on us and kill us all, of course):

> Smart machines may make higher **GDP** possible, but also reduce the demand for people—including smart people. So we could be looking
> 25 at a society that grows ever richer, but in which all the gains in wealth
> **accrue** to whoever owns the robots.

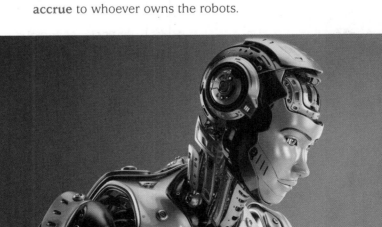

optimistic (adj.): hopeful

AIs (n.): Artificial Intelligence programs

prompting (n.): encouragement of, or inciting, some action

Wired writer Kevin Kelly, on the other hand, takes a more **optimistic** approach when he says that we can't even imagine the jobs we'll create because of this increasing automation. Humans' role in the future will thus be the same as it is now: to create

30 jobs that only people can do at first, with those tasks eventually falling to machines, whereupon the cycle will keep repeating.

… If there's one thing we can be certain of when it comes to the future, it's that it's very difficult to imagine. As Kelly puts it:

35 Before we invented automobiles, air-conditioning, flat-screen video displays and animated cartoons, no one living in ancient Rome wished they could watch cartoons while riding to Athens in climate-controlled comfort. Two hundred years ago not a single citizen of Shanghai would have told you that they would buy a tiny slab that allowed them to talk to faraway friends before they would buy indoor plumbing. Crafty **AIs**

40 embedded in first-person-shooter games have given millions of teenage boys the urge, the need, to become professional game designers—a dream that no boy in Victorian times ever had. In a very real way our inventions assign us our jobs. Each successful bit of automation gener-ates new occupations—occupations we would not have fantasized about

45 without the **prompting** of the automation.

Where Krugman's thesis falters is in the notion that it'll somehow be big entities that own the robots. With even children creating their own Lego robots, that's highly unlikely. Robots are getting better and cheaper, which means that everyone is likely to benefit from the robotic revolution.

(583 words)

Nowak, P. (2013, February 3). Man vs. robot. *Macleans.* Retrieved from http://www.macleans.ca/society/technology/man-vs-robot/

C. Choose the phrase that best completes each sentence.

1. Nowak says that traditionally, machines take over jobs _____.
   a) and cause widespread unemployment
   b) that pay untrained professionals the most
   c) and force humans to do more interesting work

2. Brynjolfsson and Welty suggest that new jobs are not being created _____.
   a) as quickly as robots and new technologies are taking old ones
   b) for robots and new technologies that will help the unemployed
   c) that are as interesting to people as jobs for robots and computers

3. Krugman assumes that the wealthiest people will _____.
   a) employ humans to do their work
   b) own as much as anyone else
   c) be those who own robots

4. Kevin Kelly thinks that humans will keep creating jobs that _____.
   a) robots will eventually take over
   b) only humans will be able to do
   c) robots and humans do together

5 The examples of Rome and Shanghai are to explain how _____.

   a) quickly our modern technologies have improved

   b) no one feels the need for things before they're invented

   c) local technologies quickly become popular internationally

6 Nowak's general point of view is that robots and other technologies _____.

   a) are likely to take over everyone's job

   b) will take over jobs that people don't want to do

   c) will only benefit the wealthy

D. Reread the article and summarize the views of the people quoted. Then, indicate whose ideas you agree or disagree with.

PEOPLE QUOTED	SUMMARY OF QUOTE	AGREE	DISAGREE
Brynjolfsson			
Krugman			
Kelly			

E. Discuss your answers to tasks C and D with your partner.

FOCUS ON WRITING

Writing Surveys

The survey in Reading 1, task D, is a simple example of a way to collect opinions. This kind of first-hand information is called *primary data* because it is collected directly. *Secondary data* is information that you read in publications or hear in presentations. Surveys collect primary data by asking questions or providing statements that people either agree or disagree with.

Many surveys use Likert scales. A Likert scale makes a statement and gives several choices, one of which is neutral. Look at the example.

❶ In twenty-five years, every home will have a robot working in it.

☐ strongly agree ☐ agree ☐ undecided ☐ disagree ☐ strongly disagree

A. In this section, you will write a survey to collect opinions on statements by the people quoted in Reading 1. Prepare your survey on a separate page. Use the Likert scale example as a model. Rewrite your summaries from task D in Reading 1 to make three statements. Keep your statements short and easy to understand.

B. Test your statements with a partner to make sure the statements are clear. Make three copies of your survey and ask three students to respond.

C. Summarize the results in a paragraph. For example: All of the students agreed ... Two or three of the students agreed ...

A. Below are words from the Academic Word List that you will find in Reading 2. Highlight the words you understand and then circle the words you use.

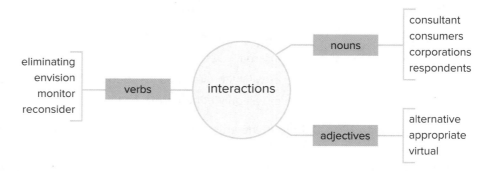

verbs: eliminating, envision, monitor, reconsider

interactions

nouns: consultant, consumers, corporations, respondents

adjectives: alternative, appropriate, virtual

B. Words with the same meaning are called *synonyms*. Words with the opposite meaning are called *antonyms*. Choose the synonym of each word.

1 consumers ☐ users ☐ producers

2 eliminating ☐ adding ☐ removing

3 monitor ☐ ignore ☐ oversee

4 reconsider ☐ review ☐ forget

5 respondents ☐ interviewers ☐ people who reply

6 virtual ☐ real ☐ simulated

C. Fill in the blanks with the correct words to complete the sentences.

alternative	appropriate	consultant	corporations	envision

1 It was _____ to thank the other members of the team.

2 As a/an _____, she helps many different companies.

3 Taking the bus or riding a bicycle is a form of _____ transportation.

4 A few small businesses grow to become large _____.

5 I _____ a future in which everyone has a personal robot.

D. Check your answers with a partner and discuss what each word means. Use a dictionary for help with words that are unfamiliar.

READING ②

Half of All Jobs Today Will Disappear by 2030

British economist John Maynard Keynes (1883–1946) predicted technology would likely cause widespread unemployment because the labour savings from technology were happening faster than we could find new jobs for workers. His focus wasn't computers, but rather steam and electric engines taking over work that previously required human involvement. Were his predictions realistic?

A. In 1900, an American railroad engineer wrote predictions for the year 2000. Have any of these predictions come true? Discuss each one with a partner and then in a group.

PREDICTION 1: Cars will disappear from large cities with all traffic either below or high above the ground, eliminating noise pollution.

PREDICTION 2: Cars will be operated by a half-kilo motor that will be cheaper than a horse and twice as powerful.

PREDICTION 3: Photographs will be telegraphed from any distance and published in newspapers an hour later.

B. Make predictions for these areas for the year 2030.

AREAS	MY PREDICTIONS
TRANSPORTATION	
JOBS	
TECHNOLOGY	
ENTERTAINMENT	

C. While you read, highlight indications of the writer's point of view as outlined in Focus on Reading, page 28.

Half of All Jobs Today Will Disappear by 2030

Building a long-lasting career means at least thinking about what might be ahead in the next ten to twenty years. So what lies ahead? A good question. We checked with the work of **futurists**, career experts and technologists to see what might happen. 5 Some of what they envision is downright scary; some of their predictions might give you hope. But any and all of them should at least get you thinking about what you should do in the near- and mid-term future.

1. Half of all jobs today will disappear by 2030.
Futurist Thomas Frey says that the world of work is going to turn upside down as two 10 billion jobs—half of all employment on the planet today—will be gone by 2030.

Why: This prediction **hinges** on massive change happening in some major industries. In the power industry alone, moving to renewable energy and **decentralized** power generation will mean many job demands in areas like coal and **ethanol** production, overhead power line maintenance, power plants and even railroad transportation 15 (to haul the fuel) will drop significantly. Self-driving cars, already a technical reality, could put a lot of taxi, bus, limousine and delivery drivers out of business. Manufacturing and retail jobs could take big hits as 3D printing eventually lets consumers make many products at home without the need to buy from a store.

*Critical Thinking:
Evaluate the credibility of what you read. Does the writer provide support in terms of proper references?*

futurists (n.): those who study current trends and innovations and make predictions about the future

hinges (v.): depends

decentralized (adj.): control moved away from central authority

ethanol (n.): fuel made from organic material

finicky (adj.): fussy

avatars (n.): figures representing people

tin can clan (n.): robots (slang)

irony (n.): discrepancy between the expected and actual state of affairs

The opportunities: There will be new areas of hiring. Corporations and communities
20 will run their own power facilities and need skilled workers. Replacing the national
grid will create jobs in construction and in recycling. Solar, wind, geothermal and
other alternative energy systems will need installation crews. People will have to
design 3D products, repair printers and sell the manufacturing "ink" they use.

…

25 2. Robots will become your co-workers and competitors.

Why: If you think of robots as something out of an old science fiction film, it is time
to reconsider your views. They already help farmers and could take over fast food
jobs. Between 2011 and 2012, employment of robots was up 40 percent worldwide.
There are already general purpose robots that cost not much more than a
30 year of minimum wage salary. The move toward robots will only increase
as technology pushes productivity by eliminating more of those **finicky** and
unreliable people who need sleep, time off and salaries. They're just going
to take a lot of different forms, giving them the advantage in many types of
work. Virtual **avatars**—faces on screens and voices on speakers—are coming
35 to a point that they can handle many customer service interactions. Medical
centres are already testing them to greet physical therapy patients in multiple
languages, ask questions about their pain and teach people appropriate
exercises, using electronics to monitor how well they follow the patterns,
according to *Technology Review*. Futurist Mike Walsh says prepare to see
40 avatars at customer service desks in retail, hotels and banking by 2030.

The opportunities: As the working world moves towards using robots, virtual
avatars and other devices, someone will have to keep the **tin can clan** doing
the right steps. There will be an increase of jobs in design, engineering and
systems management as well as a need for technicians to keep our metallic
45 co-workers up and running.

…

3. Some good-paying professions will be begging for job applicants.

Why: One **irony** of the future is that there will be plenty of good jobs that go begging
for applicants because young people often have limited views of what job opportun-
50 ities to pursue. A recent UK survey of thirteen- to sixteen-year-olds by the non-profit
Chartered Institute of Personnel and Development showed that their career aspirations
had "nothing in common" with what job markets will want in the future. They will
struggle to compete in areas and, by their choices, make getting a job ridiculously
harder for many. More than a third of the teenagers interviewed were only interested
55 in one of ten different careers: "teacher, lawyer, accountant, actor, police, IT consultant,
doctor, sportsperson, army/navy/air force/fire fighter and psychologist." The interests
of half of all respondents fell into only three of twenty-five different sectors.

The opportunity: When you consider the takeover of new technologies, remember
that someone still has to be able to open a lock, fix a leak and install a new circuit to
60 charge your new high-tech domestic help.   (719 words)

Sherman, E. (2013, September 25). Half of all jobs today will disappear by 2030 and other scary predictions.
AOL Jobs. Retrieved from http://jobs.aol.com/articles/2013/09/25/predictions-workplace/

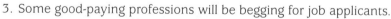

D. Connect the phrases to summarize the article.

SUMMARY		
1 When you think about a career, ...	_____e_____	a) make many products at home.
2 Futurists and technologists ...	_____	b) will be gone by 2030.
3 Frey says that two billion jobs ...	_____	c) in multiple languages.
4 Renewable energy and decentralized power generation ...	_____	d) and other alternative energy systems.
5 Self-driving cars could mean the end ...	_____	e) you should think ahead ten to twenty years.
6 3D printing will let consumers ...	_____	f) of job opportunities.
7 People will use solar, wind, geothermal ...	_____	g) take over fast food jobs.
8 Robots are more popular now and will help farmers and ...	_____	h) will mean more jobs in coal and ethanol production.
9 Virtual avatars will handle many customer service interactions ...	_____	i) humans to do them.
10 Jobs in design, engineering, systems management ...	_____	j) will help maintain robots.
11 Young people often have limited views ...	_____	k) have mixed ideas about what jobs will be like.
12 Many jobs will still require ...	_____i_____	l) of other forms of driver-based transportation.

E. Skim the article and find examples of jobs that might disappear in the future, and possible future job opportunities. Add these jobs to the columns, as well as your own job predictions. Discuss in a group.

JOBS THAT MIGHT DISAPPEAR IN THE FUTURE	POSSIBLE FUTURE JOB OPPORTUNITIES
jobs in coal and ethanol production	*jobs in recycling*

F. Review examples of the writer's point of view that you found in the reading and discuss them with a partner.

Future Tense

When you read the text on pages 35–36, you may have noticed examples of the future tense. Use the future tense to write about events that have not yet happened, but are expected to occur at a later time.

To form the future tense, use *will* + verb, or *be going to* + verb to express
- actions that will take place in the future: Miranda **will start** university classes in September;
- promises or plans: She **is going to study** robotics;
- predictions: Robots **will take** new forms in the future.

FORMS				
will	AFFIRMATIVE		NEGATIVE (CONTRACTION)	
singular	I / You / He/She/It } **will work**.		I / You / He/She/It } **will not/won't work**.	
plural	We/You/They **will work**.		We/You/They **will not/won't work**.	
	QUESTION (Move *will* before the subject.)			
	Will I / you / he/she/it } **work**?		**Will** you / we / they } **work**?	
be going to	AFFIRMATIVE		NEGATIVE (CONTRACTION)	
singular	I **am going to work**.		I **am not going to work**.	
	He/She/It **is going to work**.		He/She/It **is not/isn't going to work**.	
plural	We/You/They **are going to work**.		We/You/They **are not/aren't going to work**.	
	QUESTION (Move *be* before the subject.)			
	Am I / **Are** you / **Is** he/she/it } **going to work**?		**Are** you / we / they } **going to work**?	

Adverbs with *will* and *be going to*
Adverbs are words that describe verbs (action words). The adverb in the example sentences below is *eventually*. When you use the future tense with *will*, the adverb comes after *will*. When you use the future tense with *be going to*, the adverb comes between *be* and *going to*.

Robots **will** *eventually* take over all human jobs.
Robots **are** *eventually* **going to** be common in most homes.

A. Rearrange the words to make sentences with *will* or *be going to*.

1. of / career / the / questions / biggest / life / in / one / what / is / you / will / for / a / do

   One of the biggest questions in life is what you will do for a career.

2. of / half / 2030 / all / jobs / will / by / disappear / today

   _____

3 to / forms / are / robots / take / going / a / of / different / lot / certainly

_____

_____

4 cycle / repeating / will / the / keep

_____

5 a / your / computer / a / or / robot / job / ? / will / take

_____

_____

6 human / are / to / going / affect / robots / the / market / job

_____

_____

My eLab

Visit My eLab Documents to learn more about verb tenses.

B. Indicate whether you would use _will_, _be going to_ or either to express each action in the future tense.

ACTIONS		_will_	_be going to_	either
1	a promise to help someone find work			
2	a question about someone's plan			
3	a prediction about the future of work			
4	talking about what you want to do			

WARM-UP ASSIGNMENT
Conduct a Survey

In Reading 2, task E, you focused on jobs that might disappear and on possible job opportunities in the future. Use what you learned in Focus on Writing (page 33) to design a survey using a Likert scale questionnaire. Use the survey to find out what other students think about life twenty-five years in the future.

A. Look again at the example from page 33. Use it as a model.

> **1** In twenty-five years, every home will have a robot working in it.
>
> ☐ strongly agree   ☐ agree   ☐ undecided   ☐ disagree   ☐ strongly disagree

B. On a separate page, write five statements about life twenty-five years in the future. Use either _will_ or _be going_ to express the future event. Make sure each statement expresses a single idea. A statement such as "In twenty-five years, there will no longer be human teachers or police officers," should be written as two statements. Refer to the Models Chapter (page 188) to see an example of a survey and to learn more about how to design one.

C. Test your statements with a partner. Do the statements make sense? Does each contain a single idea? Did you avoid including a point of view?

D. Proofread your statements and then prepare your Likert scale survey. Make six copies. Note: distribute your survey by e-mail if practical.

E. Conduct your survey. Ask six students to indicate their responses.

F. Summarize the results by converting the responses into statements so that the information is easier to understand and compare. See Focus on Writing (page 33), task C for an example.

VOCABULARY BUILD 3

A. Below are words from the Academic Word List that you will find in Reading 3. Highlight the words you understand and then circle the words you use.

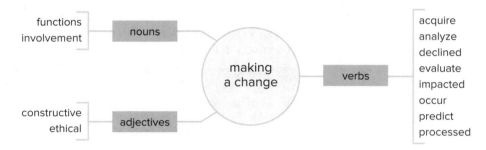

B. Highlight the word in parentheses that best completes each sentence.

❶ It's not enough to make the legal choice; you need to make the (processed / ethical) choice.

❷ They took time to (functions / evaluate) the problem, looking at each fact in turn.

❸ She decided to (acquire / involvement) more computer skills to make it easier to find a job.

❹ A/An (constructive / impacted) solution would be to help people learn on their own.

❺ It's difficult to (analyze / predict) what jobs will be available in the next thirty years.

❻ He was too busy so he (declined / occur) the offer of a second job.

C. Choose the phrase that best completes each sentence. Key words are in bold.

❶ Industrial robots' **functions** _____.
   a) are the things it can't do
   b) allow them to do different jobs
   c) are limited to one thing

❷ Our **involvement** in the project means _____.
   a) only you can do the work
   b) we will find others who help
   c) everyone will participate

3 We need to **analyze** the problem _____.

    a) to find the best solution

    b) because it doesn't matter

    c) as a way of guessing

4 All of the changes in employment have **impacted** the _____.

    a) opportunities graduates have in the workplace

    b) history of almost every job all over the world

    c) world in a way that has made no difference

5 There is a chance a change will **occur** _____.

    a) that will leave everything the same

    b) that will not affect anything

    c) in the next few hours

6 Once all the paperwork is **processed**, we will _____.

    a) have to fill out all the forms

    b) be free to start the project

    c) not be able to start the project

D. VOCABULARY EXTENSION: To analyze a problem is to look at its individual parts in detail. Analyzing is one of six ways of learning from simply remembering to the more complex task of creating. Use the key words in parentheses to write definitions for the ways we learn.

1 remember (define, recall, repeat): _____

_____

_____

2 understand (classify, describe, paraphrase): _____

_____

_____

3 apply (demonstrate, illustrate, operate): _____

_____

_____

My eLab

Visit My eLab to complete Vocabulary Review exercises for this chapter.

4 analyze (compare, contrast, criticize): _____

_____

_____

5 evaluate (argue, defend, judge): _____

_____

_____

6 create (construct, design, develop): _____

_____

_____

Academic
Survival Skill

Taking notes is a useful skill to help you remember information that you read, listen to or think about. Careful note-taking allows you to identify the sources of different ideas. This helps you to avoid plagiarism by mistakenly presenting others' ideas as your own.

When you take notes, focus on four areas

- main ideas;
- questions raised in the text;
- how the information relates to you or a task you might have;
- what you have to add in terms of questions, comments and ideas.

Note-taking is also about being efficient. Use symbols to replace words or phrases. Which words or phrases might these symbols replace? In a group, discuss other symbols you could use.

SYMBOLS	MEANING
>	*greater than*
<	
=	
≠	
+	
↑ ↓	

SYMBOLS	MEANING
/	
#	
%	
@	
* [or] !	
?	

READING ❸ — Old and New Job Skills

It is difficult to know beforehand how inventions might change the future. A painting from 1352 is the first recorded use of someone wearing eyeglasses, although they were probably invented many years earlier. The widespread use of eyeglasses is said to be responsible for the largest one-time IQ (intelligence) boost in human history by expanding the pool of potentially literate people. In the same way, the computer has probably changed the way you live and work, making knowledge more accessible. But new inventions may lead to a need for different skills and, sometimes, the loss of jobs.

A. New technology might make your perfect job disappear. Write six skills you think would be most useful to learn to prepare you for future jobs.

❶ _____

❷ _____

❸ _____

❹ _____

❺ _____

❻ _____

B. While you read, use the symbols you learned in Academic Survival Skill to take notes in the margins on the key points.

Old and New Job Skills

asbestos (n.): heat-resistant mineral that can be woven

mined (v.): dug from the earth

beaver (n.): large rodent that lives partly in the water

petroleum (n.): liquid in the earth used to make oil and gasoline

bank tellers (n.): customer service employees at a bank

Throughout history, changes in laws, technologies and demand for products and services have created the need for new job skills. Often, as new skills are required, older skills fall out of favour and are forgotten.

5 New laws are one reason some jobs appear and disappear. For example, new laws about terrorism have led to growth in the security and law enforcement sectors.[1] On the other hand, once people became aware of the dangers of a building material, such as **asbestos**, its use declined and those who **mined** and processed it lost their jobs.

Changes in demand sometimes occur when people no longer want or need a product 10 or service. This is particularly the case when new fashions make certain items of clothing more or less popular. For example, hats made from **beaver** fur were popular from the 1700s until around 1830, when silk became the preferred material. The change meant a decline in the employment of those who hunted beavers and prepared their furs. It also meant an increase 15 in employment for those involved in silk production. In modern times, the development of **petroleum**-based fabrics has similarly impacted the importance of traditional wool, 20 leather and cotton clothing.

Today, the biggest impact on job skills is new technologies, particularly computerization. Computerized bank machines have reduced the 25 need for **bank tellers**. Word processing programs have reduced the need for secretaries. Online computer-based bookstores have put many traditional bookstores out of business along with the skilled employees who once worked in them.

30 You may think that in the future you will have a job that requires computer skills. But it is difficult to predict whether more intelligent computers will require less human involvement. What is likely is that computers will take over more, reducing or eliminating the need for skilled humans. If so, then how can you prepare yourself for jobs that may not exist today?

35 The National Council of Teachers of English (NCTE) suggests that twenty-first century learners need to acquire the following six skills to be successful in the workplace.

---

1. Staples, (2009) says, "Globalization promotes military spending over social spending. Security exceptions in free trade agreements grant governments a free hand in military spending, but place limits on social spending. Thus, governments use military spending to achieve non-defence goals such as job creation, regional development, and subsidization of local corporations through defence contracts" (para. 12).

synthesize (v.): combine things into one

simultaneous (adj.): at the same time

critique (v.): analyze

1. Gain proficiency with tools of technology. If you use a computer, are you able to use all the functions of its software? Consider the most common software programs used in your field. Are you competent in using them in practical and creative ways?

40 2. Develop relationships with others and confront and solve problems collaboratively and cross-culturally. Do you have the skills to identify problems in the world around you, particularly in the workplace? Can you use teamwork skills to address these problems in constructive ways? Do you have an understanding of other cultures? Can you work with people from other cultures?

45 3. Design and share information for global communities to meet a variety of purposes. Can you create presentations for different audiences? Imagine explaining something you know to a group of friends. Now imagine explaining the same information to a group of people from another culture. Could you do it?

4. Manage, analyze and **synthesize** multiple streams of **simultaneous** information.
50 Can you take information from a variety of sources (e.g., books, social media, websites, conversations) and organize them into simpler ideas?

5. Create, **critique**, analyze and evaluate multimedia texts. Can you create websites or other multimedia presentations with sound, text, video and images? Can you look at others' multimedia work and be critical about it?

55 6. Attend to the ethical responsibilities required by complex environments. Can you make decisions about ideas of right and wrong in a variety of situations? Consider a difficult choice you might have to make in your life. On what basis would you make your choice?

These skills are the ones that are the most likely to prepare you to work with others
60 in interesting jobs. However, a report prepared for the Association of American Colleges and Universities (Bauerlein, 2010) says that the most important skills are those that would have been familiar to people in the 1700s and earlier. These skills include the ability to effectively communicate orally and in writing. These were the most important skills mentioned by 89 percent of employers. Other important skills
65 were critical thinking and analytical reasoning.

Computers and other technologies will continue to be important in the future, but the abilities to think critically and to communicate effectively might be the most important skills that future employees can learn.

(718 words)

References

Bauerlein, M. (2010, March 9). Employers want 19th century skills. *The Chronicle of Higher Education*. Retrieved from http://chronicle.com/blogs/brainstorm/employers-want-18th-century-skills/21687

Foster, J.E. & Eccles, W.J. (2013, July 23). Fur trade. *Canadian Encyclopaedia*. Retrieved from http://www.thecanadianencyclopedia.ca/en/article/fur-trade/

NCTE. (2013). The NCTE definition of 21st century literacies. *National Council of Teachers of English*. Retrieved from http://www.ncte.org/positions/statements/21stcentdefinition

Staples, S. (2009, May 3). Ten ways globalism promotes militarism. *Polaris Institute*. Retrieved from http://www.rense.com/general41/prono.htm

C. Indicate whether these statements are true or false, according to the text.

STATEMENTS	TRUE	FALSE
❶ Often, as new skills are required, older skills are forgotten.		
❷ New laws about terrorism led to a drop in security jobs.		
❸ Mining asbestos is an example of a new job opportunity.		
❹ Hats made from beaver fur replaced ones made of silk.		
❺ Computerization has reduced the need for bank tellers, secretaries and bookstore employees.		
❻ Intelligent computers will require less human involvement.		
❼ The ability to effectively communicate orally and in writing remains an important skill.		
❽ Critical thinking will no longer be an important skill in the future.		

D. Review the six skills proposed by the NCTE. Which skills do you already have? Which do you need to develop? Write the challenges you might face when learning these skills.

SKILLS	HAVE	NEED	CHALLENGES
❶ Gain proficiency with tools of technology.			
❷ Develop relationships with others and confront and solve problems collaboratively and cross-culturally.			
❸ Design and share information for global communities to meet a variety of purposes.			
❹ Manage, analyze and synthesize multiple streams of simultaneous information.			
❺ Create, critique, analyze and evaluate multimedia texts.			
❻ Attend to the ethical responsibilities required by complex environments.			

E. Discuss your answers to task D in a group.

FINAL ASSIGNMENT
Write a Short Report

Use what you learned in this chapter to write a report.

A. Base your report on the information gathered in the survey you conducted in the Warm-Up Assignment. Use this table to organize the information.

SECTIONS	NOTES	EXPLANATIONS
OVERVIEW	This report uses data collected from _____ students about their opinions on _____.	The overview lets readers know what your report is about. Use what you learned about topic sentences in Chapter 1.
BACKGROUND	Jobs are rapidly changing because of changes in technology, particularly to do with computers and robots. A survey of _____ students asked about the future of different jobs (or another topic) in the next twenty-five years.	The background explains the reason you are writing the report. What information do you have to share and why is it important?
DISCUSSION	The survey found that ... • Fifty percent of students agreed ... • Only a quarter of the students felt ... • Opinions about _____ were mixed, with _____ of _____ students saying _____ and the rest saying _____.	Include the questions from your survey and the results. Put the results together and present them with numbers and expressions that are easy to understand.
CONCLUSION	Most students seem to believe _____. However, they might not understand / be aware of _____. The data indicates that students believe that in the future, ... _____.	Reflect on the findings and add some comment or interpretation. Use *will* and *be going to* when you write about future events.

B. Write your report and review it using the checklist for writer's point of view (see Focus on Reading, page 28). Check the grammar, particularly your use of future tense. Make sure you have included the sections above. Refer to the Models Chapter (page 189) to see an example of a report and to learn more about how to write one.

C. Proofread your report. Then, share it with a partner and ask for feedback.

D. Make corrections and write a final copy.

How confident are you?

Think about what you learned in this chapter. Use the table to decide what you should review.

I LEARNED ...	I AM CONFIDENT	I NEED TO REVIEW
vocabulary related to skills and jobs;	☐	☐
how to recognize points of view;	☐	☐
the future tense with *will* and *be going to*;	☐	☐
how to take notes;	☐	☐
how to conduct a survey;	☐	☐
how to write a report.	☐	☐

VOCABULARY
Challenge

Think about the vocabulary and ideas in this chapter. Use these words to write two sentences that predict the future of work.

| alternative | analyze | appropriate | benefit | consequence | predict |

_____

_____

_____

_____

My eLab ✎
Visit My eLab to build on what you learned.

CHAPTER 3
Fit for Life

You should follow the words of motivational speaker Jim Rohn (1930–2009) to "take care of your body. It's the only place you have to live." But fitness and a good diet often seem difficult goals. It does not help that there are uncertainties surrounding the safety of certain sports and the quality of certain diets. Research can help to better inform you, but sometimes the reported results of studies are questionable because of writer bias or corporate influence.

When it comes to health and fitness, how do you make decisions about who and what to believe?

In this chapter,
you will

- learn vocabulary related to fitness and health;
- identify main ideas and supporting details;

- review capitalization and punctuation rules;
- compare and contrast text;

- learn how to cite and reference sources;
- write compare and contrast paragraphs.

GEARING UP

A. Look at the graphic and then answer the questions.

What Makes Us Healthy?

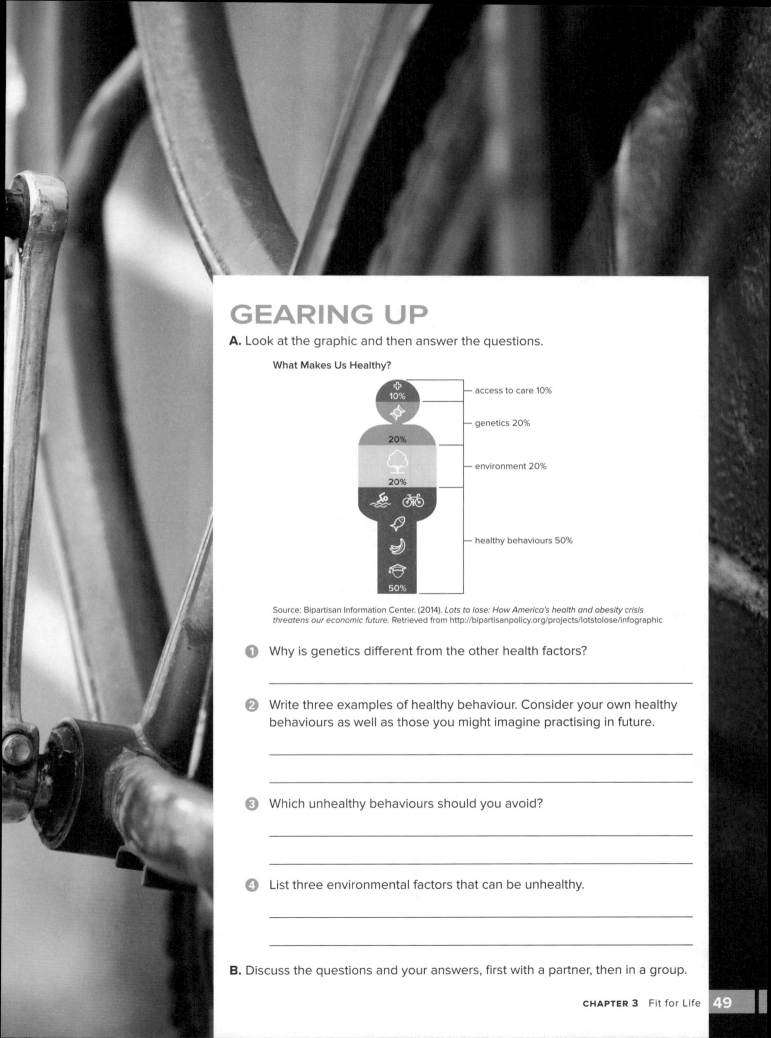

access to care 10%

genetics 20%

environment 20%

healthy behaviours 50%

Source: Bipartisan Information Center. (2014). *Lots to lose: How America's health and obesity crisis threatens our economic future.* Retrieved from http://bipartisanpolicy.org/projects/lotstolose/infographic

1 Why is genetics different from the other health factors?

_____

2 Write three examples of healthy behaviour. Consider your own healthy behaviours as well as those you might imagine practising in future.

_____

_____

3 Which unhealthy behaviours should you avoid?

_____

_____

4 List three environmental factors that can be unhealthy.

_____

_____

B. Discuss the questions and your answers, first with a partner, then in a group.

Identifying Main Ideas and Supporting Details

When you read a text, it helps to identify the main idea as well as the supporting details. The main idea is the argument that the writer puts forward. Supporting details take the form of examples, explanations and evidence. Being able to identify each element makes it easier for you to evaluate the text and decide whether the argument is convincing.

A. Read this excerpt from Reading 1 and the explanatory notes to learn how the writer states the main idea and then supports it with details.

The first sentence is the main idea; it is usually general, but may include a reference.

The text in parentheses, "less than 2 percent," is an explanation of what "very low" means.

Statistical evidence is presented and referenced.

> Canadians use active transport modes less than Europeans, so there is room for improvement. Bicycling offers the greatest opportunity for change. The percentage of trips via cycling in Canada (less than 2 percent) is very low in comparison to many northern European countries with similar climates and demographics. Cycling rates are five times higher in Finland, Germany and Sweden, and ten or more times higher in Denmark and the Netherlands (Pucher & Buehler, 2008). In addition, cycling offers an efficient transportation mode for short distance trips not easily made on foot.

The second sentence is an example of an "active transport mode" that represents an "improvement."

The last sentence is an example of a way bicycling can bring about change.

B. Read the sentences and indicate whether each is a main idea, an example, an explanation or evidence. In some cases, a sentence may have more than one function.

SENTENCES	MAIN IDEA	EXAMPLE	EXPLANATION	EVIDENCE
❶ In the last decade, there has been new interest in promoting cycling as a mode of transportation in North America (Mapes, 2009).	☑	☐	☐	☑
❷ Two of the largest cities in the United States, New York and Chicago, have set aggressive targets for increased cycling and, to meet them, have launched programs to construct connected networks of bicycle infrastructure (Pucher & Buehler, 2008).	☐	☐	☐	☐
❸ Vancouver began installing separated lanes on major streets in its downtown core in 2009 as a complement to a system of designated bike routes elsewhere in the city.	☐	☐	☐	☐
❹ In the public health realm, "active transportation" (physically active travel modes such as walking and cycling) has become a focus of attention.	☐	☐	☐	☐
❺ A recent review and other emerging evidence show that bicycle-specific facilities (e.g., cycle tracks, residential street bike routes, on-road marked bike lanes and off-road bike paths) reduce crashes and injuries to cyclists.	☐	☐	☐	☐

C. Discuss your answers with a partner.

A. Below are words from the Academic Word List that you will find in Reading 1. Highlight the words you understand and then circle the words you use.

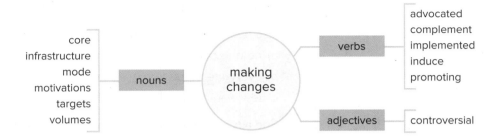

nouns		verbs	
core		advocated	
infrastructure		complement	
mode	making	implemented	
motivations	changes	induce	
targets		promoting	
volumes		adjectives	controversial

B. Fill in the blanks with the correct nouns to complete the sentences.

core	infrastructure	mode	motivations	targets	volumes

1. People have different _____ for wearing bicycle helmets.

2. Bicycles take up less room and are replacing the large _____ of cars and buses.

3. Cars are efficient over great distances but inefficient in the city's _____ .

4. Besides bicycles and cars, the subway is another _____ of transportation.

5. People often set _____ for improving their health and fitness.

6. Cars put more stress on a city's _____ , particularly roads and bridges.

C. Choose the phrase that best completes each sentence. Key words are in bold.

1. **Promoting** public transportation requires _____.

   a) making everyone aware of the dangers

   b) letting people know that it's a better choice

   c) explaining how bus schedules are unreliable

2. To **complement** the summer use of bicycles, the city _____.

   a) discourages people from walking to work

   b) offers free parking for cars in downtown areas

   c) provides free buses on snowy days in winter

③ Your company would like to **induce** you to ride a bicycle to work _____.

    a) so you can afford to drive your car on weekends

    b) to improve your fitness and cut down on parking

    c) because bicycling is the cause of many accidents

④ The decision was **controversial** because _____.

    a) no one could agree on it

    b) everyone agreed on it

    c) few wanted to discuss it

⑤ She **advocated** for the use of bicycle helmets _____.

    a) after her daughter was hurt while not wearing one

    b) because she believed that they weren't of any use

    c) when she seriously hurt her head while wearing one

⑥ The changes to the city plan were **implemented** _____.

    a) for a future date to be decided

    b) but only as an idea for discussion

    c) by the engineering department

READING ❶

Bicycling: Health Risk or Benefit?

In 1885, the Rover Safety Bicycle was invented, and bicycles replaced horses as the most popular means of individual transportation. Two years later, a rubber tire filled with air was introduced to make riding smoother, but wearing helmets was not common until the mid-1970s.

A craze for bicycles brought changes to society; for example, women's clothing became more comfortable. Other changes continue to occur as cyclists and city planners realize that the bicycle is a practical alternative to noisy and polluting cars.

A. Based on the title of this reading and on what you have read so far, can you predict what the reading will be about?

_____

_____

_____

_____

B. Read this excerpt from Reading 1. Then, with a partner, discuss how you would respond to the two concerns.

> Despite the many motivations, promotion of cycling has been controversial. Some car users have been concerned about losing road space, and bike lanes have been a prominent issue in municipal elections in both Toronto and Vancouver. In addition, there is concern about safety by both members of the public and by health professionals who have advocated helmet use.

C. Take notes while you read. Focus on the main idea and the supporting ideas.

SUPPORTING IDEA 1: North American cities are building bike lanes and _____ _____ _____ _____	**SUPPORTING IDEA 3:** _____ _____ _____ _____

MAIN IDEA:
Cycling should be
_____

SUPPORTING IDEA 2: _____ _____ _____ _____ _____	**SUPPORTING IDEA 4:** _____ _____ _____ _____ _____

Bicycling: Health Risk or Benefit?

BIXI (n.): bicycle sharing system

In the last decade, there has been new interest in promoting cycling as a mode of transportation in North America (Mapes, 2009). Two of the largest cities in the United States, New York and Chicago, have set aggressive targets for increased cycling
5   and, to meet them, have launched programs to construct connected networks of bicycle infrastructure (Pucher & Buehler, 2008). Canadian cities are also seeing changes, as illustrated in our three largest cities. Montreal has a system of separated bike lanes throughout its downtown core and implemented its pioneering **BIXI** bike share system in 2009. Toronto adopted the BIXI system in the summer of 2011, and

designated (adj.): chosen or appointed

multifaceted (adj.): having many sides

congestion (n.): crowded area

connectivity (n.): several parts fitting together

demographics (n.): statistical data about a population

prominent (adj.): important or standing out

accrue (v.): accumulate over time

mitigate (v.): make less serious

pedestrian (adj.): related to people walking

10 is considering building separated lanes. Vancouver began installing separated lanes on major streets in its downtown core in 2009 as a complement to a system of **designated** bike routes elsewhere in the city.

The motivations for these changes are **multifaceted**. At the municipal level, they include the impossibility of managing traffic **congestion** via increased roadways, 15 green city strategies aimed at reducing air pollution and greenhouse gases, and a recognition that the vitality of cities is better promoted by people who are not enclosed in vehicles, but walking, cycling and interacting with each other (Frank, Engelke, & Schmid, 2003). In the public health realm, "active transportation" (physically active travel modes such as walking and cycling) has become a focus of attention following 20 research showing that the design of cities and the **connectivity** of streets affect both our likelihood of walking and our health (Frank, Engelke, & Schmid, 2003).

Canadians use active transport modes less than Europeans, so there is room for improvement. Bicycling offers the greatest opportunity for change. The percentage of trips via cycling in Canada (less than 2 percent) is very low in comparison to many 25 northern European countries with similar climates and **demographics**. Cycling rates are five times higher in Finland, Germany and Sweden, and ten or more times higher in Denmark and the Netherlands (Pucher & Buehler, 2008). In addition, cycling offers an efficient transportation mode for short distance trips not easily made on foot.

Despite the many motivations, promotion of cycling has been controversial. Some 30 car users have been concerned about losing road space, and bike lanes have been a **prominent** issue in municipal elections in both Toronto and Vancouver. In addition, there is concern about safety by both members of the public and by health professionals who have advocated helmet use (Winters, Davidson, Kao, & Teschke, 2011; D. Thompson, Rivara, & R. Thompson, 2000).

35 …

Given the substantial health benefits that **accrue** from bicycling as a mode of transportation, the new public health focus on promoting its use is well-founded. It is also reasonable to promote means to **mitigate** any risks. A number of evidence-based strategies for managing risks exist. Cyclists can be encouraged to wear helmets, which 40 reduce the chance of head and face injuries in the event of a crash (D. Thompson, Rivara, & R. Thompson, 2000; Elvik, 2011). However, helmets do not prevent crashes from happening in the first place. The methods used to protect cyclists in the Netherlands, where helmet use is rare and injury rates are low, appear to have been successful in this regard (Pucher & Buehler, 2008). Their approach has been to construct bicycle-45 specific facilities, the design of which varies depending on motor vehicle traffic volumes and speeds. Typically, on major streets, "cycle tracks" are used to physically separate cyclists from faster (motor vehicle) and slower (**pedestrian**) traffic. On residential streets, motor vehicle traffic is restricted and kept slow, with speed limits of 30 km/h.

A recent review and other emerging evidence show that bicycle-specific facilities 50 (e.g., cycle tracks, residential street bike routes, on-road marked bike lanes and off-road bike paths) reduce crashes and injuries to cyclists (Lusk et al., 2011; Reynolds, Harris, Teschke, Cripton, & Winters, 2009; Teschke et al., 2011). Most of these route types are favoured by all types of people, from young men to older adults with children, from regular cyclists to those who are just considering cycling (Winters & Teschke, 2010). They 55 should help motivate cycling and thus help induce safety in numbers. In addition, route types separated from traffic are likely to have lower air pollution and noise exposures.

reap (v.): gather

The good news is that developments in North American cities are much more focused on creating favourable environments for cycling, similar to the Dutch model. Whether we **reap** the benefits depends on all of us. *(739 words)*

> This article features many citations to support its ideas. Citations can be distracting when you read but are necessary in academic writing.

References

Elvik, R. (2011). Publication bias and time-trend bias in meta-analysis of bicycle helmet efficacy: A re-analysis of Attewell, Glase and McFadden, 2001. *Accident Analysis and Prevention, 43*, 1245–51.

Frank, L., Engelke, P., & Schmid, T. (2003). *Health and community design: The impact of the built environment on physical activity.* Washington, DC: Island Press.

Lusk, A.C., Furth, P.G., Morency, P., Miranda-Moreno, L.F., Willett, W.C., & Dennerlein, J.T. (2011). Risk of injury for bicycling on cycle tracks versus in the street. *Injury Prevention, 17*, 131–5.

Mapes, J. (2009). *Pedaling revolution: How cyclists are changing American cities.* Corvallis, OR: Oregon State University Press.

Pucher, J. & Buehler, R. (2008). Making cycling irresistible: Lessons from the Netherlands, Denmark and Germany. *Transport Review, 28*, 495–528.

Reynolds, C.C.O., Harris, M.A., Teschke, K., Cripton, P.A., & Winters, M. (2009). The impact of transportation infrastructure on bicycling injuries and crashes: A review of the literature. *Environmental Health, 8*, 47.

Teschke, K., Harris, M.A., Reynolds, C.C.O., Winters, M., Babul, S., Chipman M., et al. (2011). Route infra-structure and the risk of injuries to bicyclists: A case-crossover study. *American Journal of Public Health.* Accepted pending minor revisions.

Thompson, D., Rivara, F., & Thompson R. (2000). Helmets for preventing head and facial injuries in bicyclists. *Cochrane Database System Review* CD001855.

Winters, M. & Teschke, K. (2010). Route preferences among adults in the near market for cycling: Findings of the cycling in cities study. *American Journal of Health Promotion*, 2540–47.

Winters, M., Davidson, G., Kao, D., & Teschke, K. (2011). Motivators and deterrents of bicycling: Comparing influences on decisions to ride. *Transport, 38*, 153–168.

———————

Teschke, K., Reynolds, C.C.O., Ries, F.J., Gouge, B., & Winters, M. (2012). Bicycling: Health risk or benefit? *UBC Medical Journal*, March 3(2), 6–11.

D. Match the places to the reason they were mentioned in the reading.

PLACES		WHY THEY WERE MENTIONED
1 New York and Chicago	_____	a) adopted the BIXI system in 2011
2 Montreal	_____	b) cycling is an issue in municipal elections
3 Toronto	_____	c) cycling rates are five times higher than in Canada
4 Vancouver	_____	d) helmet use is rare and injury rates are low
5 Finland, Germany and Sweden	_____	e) implemented a BIXI bike share system in 2009
6 Denmark and the Netherlands	_____	f) began installing separated lanes in downtown core in 2009
7 Toronto and Vancouver	_____	g) focused on creating favourable environments for cycling
8 the Netherlands	_____	h) cycling rates are ten times higher than in Canada
9 North America	_____	i) set aggressive targets for increased cycling

E. The title of the article questions whether bicycling is risky or beneficial to our health. Review your notes and the reading and list the health risks and benefits outlined in the article.

HEALTH RISKS	BENEFITS

F. Based on what you understand about the article, suggest a new title.

_____

FOCUS ON GRAMMAR

Punctuation

When you read the text on pages 52–54, you may have noticed examples of punctuation. Punctuation helps to clarify your meaning when you write by showing possession, pauses and emphasis. Punctuation marks go directly after the last letter of a word and are followed by a space. Note that dashes do not have spaces before or after, and apostrophes have a space after if they come at the end of a plural possessive noun.

> The **professor's** notebook [one professor's notebook]
> The **professors'** notebooks [more than one professor, more than one notebook]
> Transportation is changing—particularly in terms of bicycles.

Using colons and semicolons

A colon (:) introduces a list of things, an explanation or a formal quote longer than three lines. A colon in a title indicates that the next words are a subtitle. In book references, a colon separates the place of publication and the name of the publisher.

A semicolon (;) links two complete ideas (independent clauses).

A. Insert the missing colons and semicolons in the following examples.

1. Oscar Wilde tells the story of a man who does not age a painting of him ages instead.

2. Most of us crave foods that are fatty fries, chips, burgers, cheese and ice cream.

3. Reese, J.B., Taylor, M.R., Simon, E.J., Dickey, J.L., & Scott, K.G-E. (2015). *Campbell biology Concepts and connections* (Canadian Edition). Toronto, ON Pearson.

Common punctuation errors

It's important to memorize common punctuation rules. Look at your teacher's corrections of your work and see whether any errors are just careless mistakes or examples of not understanding something. There are many things you should not do in terms of punctuation.

• Do not use a comma before *because*.

- Do not use exclamation marks in academic writing. Instead, explain why something is important.
- Do not use the possessive apostrophe with plural years.
- Do not use the possessive apostrophe when you refer to something that belongs to *it*; the word *it's* is short for *it is*.
- Do not use contractions (replacing missing letters in a word with an apostrophe) in academic writing; it's not formal enough.

Use what you learned about punctuation when you write assignments.

My eLab
Visit My eLab Documents for additional explanations and practice on punctuation.

B. Correct this paragraph using the punctuation rules above. There is one error in each sentence.

Many university graduates can't find a job locally. A good job is something everyone needs! My mother wanted to work overseas, because she loved to travel. So, during the 1990's, she worked in Africa as a nurse. But she was lonely and the job soon lost it's appeal for her.

C. Review Reading 2 to identify examples of different punctuation marks including apostrophes, hyphens, colons and semicolons.

VOCABULARY BUILD 2

Develop Your Vocabulary: Some words, like "estimate," "rewrite" and "survey," can be both nouns and verbs. Use a dictionary to learn the correct meaning and pronunciation of both.

A. Below are words from the Academic Word List that you will find in Reading 2. Highlight the words you understand and then circle the words you use.

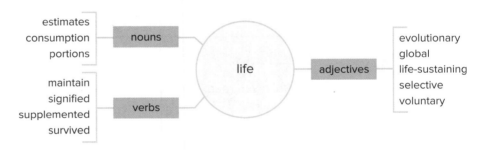

estimates
consumption
portions — **nouns**

maintain
signified
supplemented
survived — **verbs**

life — **adjectives** — evolutionary
global
life-sustaining
selective
voluntary

B. Fill in the blanks with the correct words to complete the paragraph.

consumption	life-sustaining	selective
evolutionary	maintain	voluntary

There is a debate whether the food choices we make are _____*voluntary*_____

or _____ . We all need to do _____ activities

like eat and drink. But people tend to be _____ about their

food choices as well as how they _____ their fitness. One

challenge is the _____ of junk food, as is time spent in front

of TVs and computers.

C. Draw an arrow (↓) to indicate where in each sentence the word in parentheses should be placed.

❶ (estimates) We had several ↓ for the cost of the fitness club and had to choose one.

2 (global) The club has a reach with offices in sixty-six countries.

3 (portions) The cake was divided into six and shared among the team.

4 (signified) We weren't sure what the language in the letter but it seemed serious.

5 (supplemented) When we were students, each of us our savings with part-time jobs.

6 (survived) Once when we were camping, we barely after a bear destroyed our supplies.

READING ❷

!

Calorie with a capital "C" refers to per kilogram; calorie with a lowercase "c" refers to per gram.

Body Energy: Spending It and Storing It

The calorie was first identified as a measure of energy in 1819, and ninety-nine years later author Lulu Hunt Peters wrote the first diet book that advocated counting calories in common foods as a way of reducing body weight. Counting calories remains an important part of diets and food labelling, but few people understand exactly what a calorie is and what part it plays in nutrition and fitness.

A. Read the first paragraph of the Reading 2. What is the main idea? Discuss it with a partner.

B. Scan the reading to find the word *example*. What example is provided and what does it detail?

_____

_____

C. While you read, take note of the evidence presented to support the writers' main idea.

Body Energy: Spending It and Storing It

continuous (adj.): without interruption

glucose (n.): type of sugar

Your body requires a **continuous** supply of energy just to stay alive—to keep the heart pumping, breathe and maintain body temperature. Your brain requires a huge amount of energy; its cells burn about 120 grams (g)—about half a cup of **glucose** a day,

5 accounting for about 15 percent of total oxygen consumption. Maintaining brain cells and other life-sustaining activities uses as much as 75 percent of the energy a person takes in as food during a typical day.

Above and beyond the energy you need for body maintenance, **cellular respiration** provides energy for voluntary activities. For example, consider the amount of energy
10 it takes to perform some of these activities. The energy units are kilocalories (kcal), the quantity of heat required to raise the temperature of 1 kilogram (kg) of water by 1° Celsius. (The "Calories" listed on food packages are actually kilocalories, usually signified by a capital C.) The values shown do not include the energy the body consumes for its basic life-sustaining activities. Even sleeping or lying quietly requires energy
15 for **metabolism**.

Energy consumed by various activities

ACTIVITY	KCAL CONSUMED PER HOUR BY A 67.5 KG (150 LB) PERSON*
running (13–14 km/h)	979
dancing (fast)	510
bicycling (16 km/h)	490
swimming (3.2 km/h)	408
walking (6.4 km/h)	341
walking (4.8 km/h)	245
dancing (slow)	204
driving a car	61
sitting (writing)	28

*Not including the kcal needed for body maintenance

Canada's Food Guide estimates that the average adult (ages nineteen to thirty) needs to take in food that provides about 2700 kcal of energy per day for men and about 2100 kcal per day for women. This includes the energy expended in both maintenance
20 and voluntary activity.

…

Over-nourishment, consuming more food energy than the body needs for normal metabolism, causes obesity, the excessive accumulation of fat. The World Health Organization now recognizes obesity is a major global health problem. The increased
25 availability of fattening foods and large portions, combined with more **sedentary** lifestyles, puts excess weight on bodies. A standard method of determining healthy weight is body mass index (BMI), a ratio of weight to height … A BMI of 25–30 is considered overweight, and above 30 is obese. In Canada, the percentage of obese (very overweight) people has been increasing in recent years, reaching 17.5 percent
30 in 2010. A further 3.1 percent of Canadians are overweight. Weight problems often begin at a young age: about 26 percent of Canadian children and **adolescents** are either overweight or obese.

…

hoarding (v.): storing more than you need

liability (n.): negative responsibility

ancestors (n.): those from whom you are descended

savannah (n.): grassy tropical plain

scavenging (v.): searching waste and collecting useful things

famine (n.): time when food is not easily available

gorge (v.): eat greedily

Some of our current struggles with obesity may be a consequence of our evolution-
35 ary history. Most of us crave foods that are fatty: fries, chips, burgers, cheese and
ice cream. Though fat **hoarding** can be a health **liability** today, it may actually have
been advantageous in our evolutionary past. Only in the past few centuries have
large numbers of people had access to a reliable supply of high-calorie food. Our
ancestors on the African **savannah** were hunter-gatherers who probably survived
40 mainly on seeds and other plant products, a diet only occasionally supplemented
by hunting game or **scavenging** meat from animals killed by other predators. In such
a feast and **famine** existence, natural selection may have favoured those individuals
with the physiology that induced them to **gorge** on rich, fatty foods on those rare
occasions when such treats were available. Individuals with genes promoting the
45 storage of fat during feasts may have been more likely than their thinner peers to
survive famines.

So perhaps our modern taste for fats and sugars reflect the selective advantage it con-
veyed in our evolutionary history. Although we know it is unhealthy, many of us find it
difficult to overcome the ancient survival behaviour of stockpiling for the next famine.

(619 words)

Reese, J.B., Taylor, M.R., Simon, E.J., Dickey, J.L., & Scott, K.G-E. (2015). *Campbell biology: Concepts and connections* (Canadian Edition, p. 103, pp. 564–565). Toronto, ON: Pearson.

D. Comparisons help people to better understand facts and figures. Use the figures in the table in Reading 2 to complete each comparison. For example: running uses 979 calories; bicycling uses 490. The comparison is *almost twice as many*.

ACTIVITIES			COMPARISONS
❶	Running uses _____ as bicycling.	_____	a) twenty more calories an hour
❷	Running uses _____ as sitting.	_____	b) almost thirty-five times as much energy
❸	Driving a car uses _____ as sitting.	_____	c) almost one hundred calories per hour
❹	Slow dancing uses _____ of swimming.	_____	d) almost twice as many calories
❺	Fast dancing uses _____ than bicycling.	_____	e) half the energy
❻	The difference between fast and slow walking is _____.	_____	f) more than twice as much energy

E. Number these points in the correct order to form a summary of Reading 2.

_____ 33 percent of Canadians and 26 percent of Canadian children and adolescents are overweight or obese

_____ 75 percent of energy used for normal functions

_____ access to a reliable supply of high-calorie food is recent and many find it difficult to overcome the ancient survival behaviour

BODY MASS INDEX

< 18.5	18.5-24.9	25.0-29.9	> 30.0
UNDERWEIGHT	HEALTHY	OVERWEIGHT	OBESE

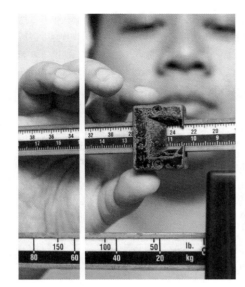

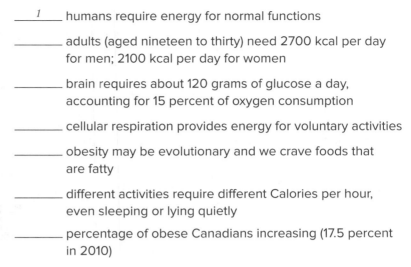

_____1_____ humans require energy for normal functions

_____ adults (aged nineteen to thirty) need 2700 kcal per day for men; 2100 kcal per day for women

_____ brain requires about 120 grams of glucose a day, accounting for 15 percent of oxygen consumption

_____ cellular respiration provides energy for voluntary activities

_____ obesity may be evolutionary and we crave foods that are fatty

_____ different activities require different Calories per hour, even sleeping or lying quietly

_____ percentage of obese Canadians increasing (17.5 percent in 2010)

FOCUS ON WRITING

Comparing and Contrasting in a Paragraph

There are many ways to structure a paragraph. For example, a paragraph can compare two or more things, listing similarities. Or, a paragraph can contrast two or more things, explaining their differences. Sometimes a paragraph can do both, compare and contrast.

A. This paragraph from Reading 2 contrasts how we ate in the past with how we eat today. Read the paragraph and then fill in the table with the points of contrast (differences). After, add anything that you think might be compared (similarities).

Critical Thinking: Using allusion, like the reference to the "African savannah," is a technique to call something to mind without mentioning it directly, in this case the first humans.

Some of our current struggles with obesity may be a consequence of our evolutionary history. Most of us crave foods that are fatty: fries, chips, burgers, cheese and ice cream. Though fat hoarding can be a health liability today, it may actually have been advantageous in our evolutionary past. Only in the past few centuries have large numbers of people had access to a reliable supply of high-calorie food. Our ancestors on the African savannah were hunter-gatherers who probably survived mainly on seeds and other plant products, a diet only occasionally supplemented by hunting game or scavenging meat from animals killed by other predators.

	IN THE PAST	TODAY
CONTRAST (DIFFERENCES)		
COMPARE (SIMILARITIES)		

B. When you write a compare and contrast paragraph, there are two ways of organizing it. How do these two paragraphs differ in organization? Discuss with a partner.

PARAGRAPH 1	**PARAGRAPH 2**
Although modern and prehistoric peoples eat seeds and other plant products, prehistoric people mostly survived on them. Some modern people hunt for food as did prehistoric peoples, but unlike modern people, prehistoric people also scavenged for meat. Fat hoarding is common to both times but today's reliable supply of high-calorie foods did not exist in prehistoric times.	Modern people eat seeds and other plant products. Some modern people hunt for food but generally do not scavenge for meat. Fat hoarding and a reliable supply of high-calorie foods are common today. However, in prehistoric times, people mainly ate seeds and other plant products, hunted extensively and scavenged for meat as well. Prehistoric people horded fat to survive because there was no reliable supply of high-calorie foods.

Paragraph 1 uses each point to talk about both modern and prehistoric people; that is called the *point-by-point method*. Paragraph 2 puts ideas about modern people together in one block then talks about prehistoric people in another block; that is called the *block method*. The words *although*, *however* and *but* highlight contrasts. Other contrast words include *yet* and *on the other hand*. Comparison words include *similarly, likewise* and *in the same way*.

C. Your topic sentence for a compare and contrast paragraph should mention both subjects being compared as well as the fact that you are comparing and contrasting some features. Write a compare and contrast topic sentence for one of the above paragraphs.

_____

_____

_____

D. The concluding sentence summarizes the similarities and differences and points out the significance of the comparison or contrast. Which concluding sentence would be the best choice for the two paragraphs?

a) Modern people have little understanding of the diets of prehistoric peoples.

b) Modern and prehistoric diets are mostly similar in terms of foods and ways of cooking.

c) Modern and prehistoric diets are different, and prehistoric diets were probably healthier.

WARM-UP ASSIGNMENT
Describe Two Points of View

Critical thinking includes the ability to consider a topic from more than one perspective. In this assignment, use what you have learned in Focus on Writing to write a paragraph comparing and contrasting two ways to keep fit. You can compare and contrast any two: diets, gym-based exercise routines or sports.

A. Use a table to sort out the similarities and differences.

WAYS TO KEEP FIT		
COMPARE (SIMILARITIES)		
CONTRAST (DIFFERENCES)		

B. Write a topic sentence that outlines the two things that you are comparing and contrasting. Add information about why the comparison and contrast is important.

C. Write a draft of your paragraph on a separate page. Use either the block method or the point-by-point method. Use compare and contrast words mentioned in Focus on Writing, task B. Refer to the Models Chapter (page 190) to see an example of a compare and contrast paragraph and to learn more about how to write one.

D. Add a concluding sentence that summarizes the similarities and differences and explain the significance. For example: For younger people ... is a better sport than ... because ...

E. Proofread your paragraph. Then, share it with a partner and ask for feedback.

F. Make corrections and write a final copy. You will use this paragraph in the Final Assignment.

Use feedback from your teacher and classmates on this Warm-Up Assignment to improve your writing.

Visit My eLab Documents for a writing checklist.

A. Below are words from the Academic Word List that you will find in Reading 3. Highlight the words you understand and then circle the words you use.

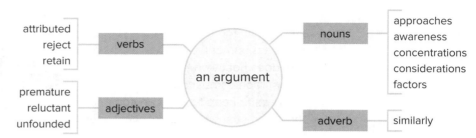

B. Fill in the blanks with the correct words to complete the sentences.

awareness	premature	reject	reluctant	retain	unfounded

1 It's easy to _____ all the diets, but you should choose one.

2 There is now a general _____ of the need to keep fit.

3 We started the project too early; it was _____ .

4 Everyone was _____ to begin so the group never started.

5 The story was completely _____ and only based on gossip.

6 Although she gave away her car, she decided to _____ her bicycle.

C. Fill in the blanks with the correct words to complete the paragraph.

approaches	concentrations	factors
attributed	considerations	similarly

Some _____ to dieting include high _____ of protein. One of the _____ that influence people's diet choices is the promise of weight loss that can be _____ solely to changes in what they eat. _____, some people focus on only changing their exercise routine, without making changes to their diets.

D. VOCABULARY EXTENSION: *Reject*, *retain* and *reluctant* are examples of words where the root cannot stand on its own without the prefix *re-*, unlike the following words. Define each word and then think about what they all have in common.

1 reactivate: _____

2 reaffirm: _____

3 reappear: _____

4 redefine: _____

5 rediscover: _____

My eLab
Visit My eLab to complete Vocabulary Review exercises for this chapter.

READING ③   Living Forever, Living Well

In *The Picture of Dorian Gray*, author Oscar Wilde (1854–1900) tells the story of a man who does not age; a painting of him ages instead. Gray is forever young, but his wicked life turns the painting into a horrible image of a man whose years have been wasted. One theme of the book is that living longer is not an advantage if one does not live well. While you cannot expect to find a magic painting to allow you to live forever, you can take steps to ensure that for the years you do live you are fit and healthy.

A. How well do you live? Contrast healthy and unhealthy factors in terms of your eating and activities.

	HEALTHY FACTORS	UNHEALTHY FACTORS
EATING		
ACTIVITIES		

B. Read this excerpt from Reading 3. Then, work with a partner and rate the importance of the factors that extend a lifespan from 1 (most important) to 7 (least important).

> There is likely a range of considerations that are extending the average lifespan. Britain's Royal Geographical Society suggests the increase can be attributed to a number of factors including "improvements in public health, nutrition and medicine. Vaccinations and antibiotics greatly reduced deaths in childhood, health and safety in manual workplaces improved and fewer people smoked."

_____ improvements in public health

_____ improvements in nutrition

_____ improvements in medicine

_____ vaccinations

_____ antibiotics

_____ health and safety in manual workplaces

_____ fewer people smoked

C. While you read, take notes on aspects of each paragraph that are compared or contrasted. For example, the first paragraph contrasts "living forever" with "being old."

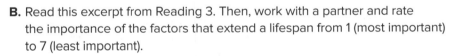

Living Forever, Living Well

An old joke observes that everyone wants to live forever, but no one wants to be old. The idea behind the observation is that if you do happen to live for a long time, you want to be fit and in good health.

immortality (n.): ability to live forever

trajectory (n.): path of an object through the air

vaccinations (n.): injections to make you immune to a disease

antibiotics (n.): medicines that fight micro-organisms

nutrient (n.): chemical or food needed to live and grow

cholesterol (n.): chemical substance found in the blood

blood pressure (n.): force with which the blood travels through the body

doses (n.): quantities of medicine

5 What is not in question is that people *are* living longer. John Martin Fischer, a University of California Riverside professor, is leading the **Immortality** Project, which is exploring what it would be like to live forever.

> On the science side, we're living at a time where we've increased our life expectancy dramatically … At the turn of the twentieth century in
> 10 developed countries the average was about forty-seven years, and at the turn of the twenty-first century it was seventy-six years, and now it's about eighty years. The **trajectory**, he says, is "radically upward." (Moxley, 2014, para. 16)

There is likely a range of considerations that are extending the average lifespan.
15 Britain's Royal Geographical Society (n.d.) suggests the increase can be attributed to a number of factors including "improvements in public health, nutrition and medicine. **Vaccinations** and **antibiotics** greatly reduced deaths in childhood, health and safety in manual workplaces improved and fewer people smoked" (para. 1).

On the individual level, those who are living longer probably have an awareness of
20 both their diets and their need for fitness. However, many people's eating habits and choice of exercise reject modern insights.

One problem area related to diet has to do with fads that are promoted by food companies and others with little or no scientific support. A recent trend has been to identify certain food items as *super foods*; among others, the list includes blueberries,
25 chocolate, oily fish, green tea and wheatgrass. The trouble is that scientific studies, if they are done at all, often focus on concentrations that might not be consumed on a daily basis by most people. For example, consuming raw garlic is encouraged because it contains a **nutrient** that is believed to help reduce **cholesterol** and **blood pressure**. However, "you'd have to eat up to twenty-eight cloves a day to match the
30 **doses** used in the lab—something no researcher has yet been brave enough to try" (NHS Choices, 2013, para. 7).

genetically modified organisms (n.): foods adapted in a lab to improve a quality

susceptible (adj.): likely to be influenced or harmed

attention span (n.): how long you can focus on something

evidence (n.): factual support

Part of the problem is that most people are reluctant to make changes to their diets and instead consider super foods like magic pills that will undo the effects of the rest of their bad eating habits. "While the miracle food remains a fantasy, it's pretty well
35 established that obesity and alcohol are the two most common causes of major long-term illness and an increased risk of premature death" (NHS Choices, 2013, para. 11).

On the other hand, superstitious criticisms of certain foods, particularly **genetically modified organisms** (GMOs), have largely proven to be unfounded. Munro (2013) writes about the retraction of a biased article published in an important French journal
40 that claimed GMOs caused cancerous tumours.

> Many scientists criticized Seralini's evidence and methods and called for the record to be set straight. One of the major flaws in the study is that Seralini used rats that are highly **susceptible** to tumours, with or without GMOs in their diets, they said. (para. 8)

45 Similarly, in terms of exercise, Palmer (2014) notes that yoga is one of the latest athletic pastimes that is being promoted for health benefits far beyond those common to most forms of exercise.

> Today, people want to believe that yoga will solve their problems. More than two hundred studies were published about the health benefits of
50 yoga last year. Yoga is supposed to cure everything from low back pain to short **attention span** to several forms of mental illness. (para. 2–3)

Yoga has some benefits, but many others are exaggerated or completely false. Most of the two hundred studies featured
55 poor methodologies and weak **evidence**.

Despite criticisms of flawed scientific studies of diet and exercise, people seem to only retain what they want to hear, particularly if it concerns promises of
60 quick fixes and easy exercise routines. People want to live forever. They do not want to be old. But they will not follow common sense and thoughtful approaches that will give them both
65 health and happiness.   (698 words)

References

Moxley, M. (2014, June 23). Living forever, the right way. *Slate*. Retrieved from http://www.slate.com/articles/news_and_politics/uc/2014/06/living_forever_the_right_way.html

Munro, M. (2013, November 28). Widely discredited study that fuelled fear of genetically modified "Frankenfoods" finally retracted. *National Post*. Retrieved from http://news.nationalpost.com/2013/11/28/widely-discredited-study-that-fuelled-fear-of-genetically-modified-frankenfoods-finally-retracted/

NHS Choices. (2013, June 12). What are super foods? Retrieved from http://www.nhs.uk/Livewell/super-foods/Pages/what-are-superfoods.aspx

Palmer, B. (2014, March 24). Researchers discredit yoga as medicine. *Herald-Tribune*. Retrieved from health.heraldtribune.com/2014/03/24/researchers-discredit-yoga-medicine/

Royal Geographical Society. (n.d.). Who wants to live forever? Long life futures. Retrieved from http://www.rgs.org/OurWork/Schools/Teaching+resources/Key+Stage+3+resources/Who+wants+to+live+forever/Why+are+people+living+longer.htm

D. Indicate whether these statements are true or false, according to the text.

STATEMENTS	TRUE	FALSE
1 Overall, life expectancies are decreasing rapidly.	☐	☐
2 A longer lifespan may be the result of improvements in public health, nutrition and medicine.	☐	☐
3 Rejecting modern insights is part of increased health awareness.	☐	☐
4 Garlic has health benefits if you eat twenty-eight cloves a day.	☐	☐
5 Most people are reluctant to make changes to their diets.	☐	☐
6 Obesity and alcohol are the two most common causes of major long-term illness.	☐	☐
7 GMOs have been proven to cause cancerous tumours in mice.	☐	☐
8 People tend to only retain what they want to hear.	☐	☐

E. Answer these questions. Then, discuss in a group.

1 Why do some people avoid vaccinations for themselves and their children?

_____

_____

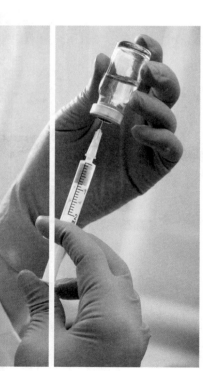

2 Why might food companies be among those promoting false or exaggerated food benefit claims?

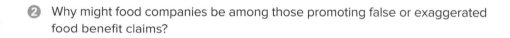
_____

_____

_____

3 If Seralini made up his evidence of GMOs causing cancer, what might have been his motivation(s)?

_____

_____

_____

4 Why would people ignore health warnings around obesity and alcohol?

_____

_____

_____

5 How would your life change if you could live for two hundred years?

_____

_____

_____

Academic
Survival Skill

Isaac Newton (1643–1727) wrote, "If I have seen farther, it is by standing on the shoulders of giants." He was acknowledging those who went before him. Citing and referencing the work and ideas of others is important in academic writing. When you write, use citations (in the text) and references (at the end of the text) to avoid plagiarism. There are a number of ways to cite and reference sources, and you may have to learn a particular one based on your area of study, but one from the American Psychological Association (APA) is widely used.

APA in-text citations

There are slightly different ways to cite text depending on whether you quote directly, with quotation marks, or you paraphrase, without quotation marks.

Author last name (date) writes "the quote" (p. 1). Note: if no page number is available, give the paragraph number, e.g., (para. x).

Munro (2013) writes, "Many scientists criticized Seralini's evidence and methods and called for the record to be set straight" (para. 8).

A. Rewrite the following information using APA in-text citation style.

1. I read a book by Jeff Mapes that was written in 2009. It's called *Pedaling Revolution: How Cyclists Are Changing American Cities*. On page 8, he says, "Motorists are learning to share the streets with a very different kind of traveller, one who often perplexes and angers them."

_____

_____

_____

2. I read on a website, posted on November 28, 2013 by Margaret Munro in the *National Post*, that she said, "But observers say the damage will be hard to undo." It was in the third paragraph of the website.

_____

_____

_____

APA references

References include details to help you find additional information in books, journals and websites. Basic information includes the writer or writers' names, the date, titles of sections and books, who published it and where it was published. Here are some examples:

BOOKS
One author
Author's last name, First Initial(s). (year). *Title of book in italics: And subtitle* [if there is one]. City, province or state or county [abbreviated]: publisher.

Gehl, J. (2010). *Cities for people*. Washington, DC: Island Press.

For two authors, use an ampersand (&), no comma, in both the references and the in-text citations [Gehl, J. & Munro, M. (2010); (Gehi & Munro, 2010)].

JOURNAL ARTICLES

Authors' last names, First Initial(s). (year). Title of the article [not in italics]. *Name of the Journal, Volume/number* [in italics], pages.

Pucher, J. & Buehler, R. (2008). Making cycling irresistible: Lessons from the Netherlands, Denmark and Germany. *Transport Review, 28*, 495–528.

WEB PAGES

Author's last name, first initial(s). [Organization responsible for the Web page if author is unknown]. (year, Month day [use n.d. if not given]). Title of the article [not in italics]. *Title of the website* [in italics]. Retrieved from [website address]

Palmer, B. (2014, March 24). Researchers discredit yoga as medicine. *Herald-Tribune*. Retrieved from health.heraldtribune.com/2014/03/24/researchers-discredit-yoga-medicine/

B. Rewrite the following information using APA referencing style.

1 A book by Oscar Wilde titled *The Picture of Dorian Gray* was published in 1891 in London by Ward Lock & Co.

_____

_____

2 A Web page article titled "What are superfoods?" has no author, but it was published on June 12, 2013, on the NHS Choices UK website. The address is http://www.nhs.uk/Livewell/superfoods/Pages/what-are-superfoods.aspx

_____

_____

_____

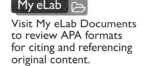

Visit My eLab Documents to review APA formats for citing and referencing original content.

FINAL ASSIGNMENT
Write Compare and Contrast Paragraphs

Use what you learned in this chapter to write two (or more) compare and contrast paragraphs with citations and references.

A. Start with your compare and contrast paragraph on two ways to keep fit from the Warm-Up Assignment. Add to what you wrote; you may include quotes to support your ideas, such as from a journal, a website or a book. Note: many journals are available online.

B. For your online search, use key words related to the diets or fitness routines or sports you wrote about, along with compare and contrast words, e.g., "similarities tennis and Ping-Pong."

C. If you quote, you need to include citations and references. Refer to Academic Survival Skill to make sure you are using the correct format.

D. Write your compare and contrast paragraph(s). Choose the point-by-point method or the block method. Refer to the Models Chapter (page 190) to see an example of a compare and contrast paragraph and to learn more about how to write one.

E. Proofread your paragraph(s). Pay special attention to punctuation. Then, share with a partner and ask for feedback.

F. Make corrections and write a final copy.

How confident are you?

Think about what you learned in this chapter. Use the table to decide what you should review.

I LEARNED ...	I AM CONFIDENT	I NEED TO REVIEW
vocabulary related to fitness and health;	☐	☐
how to identify main ideas and supporting details;	☐	☐
capitalization and punctuation rules;	☐	☐
how to compare and contrast text;	☐	☐
how to cite and reference sources;	☐	☐
how to write a compare and contrast paragraph.	☐	☐

VOCABULARY
Challenge

Think about the vocabulary and ideas in this chapter. Use these words to write two sentences that summarize eating and fitness.

approaches	controversial	maintain	motivations	portions	targets

_____

_____

_____

_____

_____

My eLab 🖉
Visit My eLab to build
on what you learned.

CHAPTER 4

A Happy Life

Although everyone wants to be happy, the concept is difficult to define and different for each person. What is common for almost everyone is the fact that what we *think* will make us happy is often not the case. Lottery winners, for example, are frequently no happier despite their new wealth. Stress can be the enemy of happiness and lead to a situation in which we might feel unable to handle daily problems. Then again, sometimes stress can have positive effects, as when an extreme challenge pushes us to an unexpected level of achievement.

What makes you happy and what causes you stress?

In this chapter,
you will

- learn vocabulary related to health, happiness and stress;

- construct meaning by making inferences;

- review the rules for subject-verb agreement;

- learn about formal and informal definitions;

- use mind maps and collocations to develop your vocabulary;

- write a definition paragraph.

GEARING UP

A. Look carefully at the pie chart and then answer the questions.

What determines happiness?

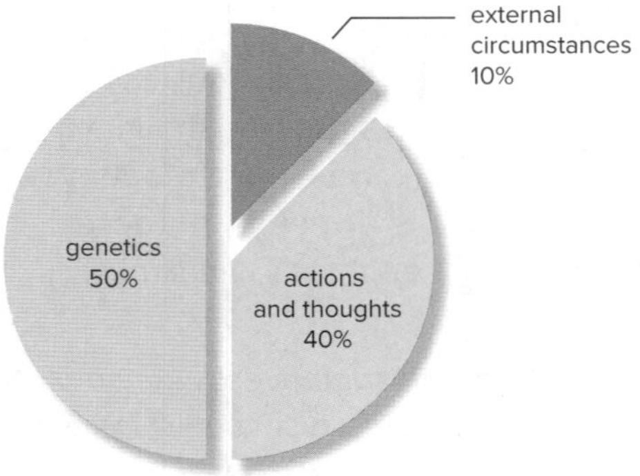

external
circumstances
10%

genetics
50%

actions
and thoughts
40%

Source: Lyubomirsky, S. (2008). *The how of happiness: A new approach to getting the life you want.*
Retrieved from http://connectinghappinessandsuccess.com/overview/happiness-concepts/2-control-your-life/

1 Genetics (inherited characteristics) and other factors can play a role
in determining happiness. Describe a family you know where everyone
seems happy, or unhappy, and suggest why this might be so.

_____

_____

2 Give three examples of external circumstances that might influence
happiness.

_____

_____

3 Give three examples of actions that make you happy.

_____

_____

4 Recalling good memories makes most people happy. Which memories
can you recall that make you happy?

_____

_____

B. Discuss the questions and your answers, first with a partner, then in a group.

Constructing Meaning by Making Inferences

When you read a word you don't understand, you can infer meaning based on the words that surround it. Constructing meaning from text involves making inferences, or drawing conclusions based on reasoning after considering evidence. When you construct meaning from text, you try to connect prior knowledge and experience with what is in the text to make good guesses.

When you read, you encounter a mix of explicit and implicit details. Explicit details are clearly explained, with no room for doubt or confusion. Implicit details are implied, or suggested, and are not clearly stated.

A. Read this excerpt from Reading 1 and the inferences in blue. Reflect on what you need to understand in order to construct meaning from the text.

You may not know the meaning of this phrase (it means medical advantages), but it is an explicit detail.

You can infer from your background knowledge that this phrase simply means walking. This is an implicit detail that you need to figure out.

> The therapeutic properties of moving around on your feet are powerful, and backed by a growing mountain of data. Walking protects you from obesity, diabetes, heart attacks and strokes.

This phrase is implicit because it is not an exact description. You infer that there is a lot of research and that research is continuing. You can also infer that the writer may not have an exact idea of how much research has been done.

This sentence is explicit; it is clear what the writer is explaining.

B. Read the sentences. What implicit or explicit meaning can you infer from the underlined sections? Discuss your answers with a partner.

1. Scientists in Scotland <u>believe</u> walking could help stave off brain shrinkage and Alzheimer's disease.

   _____

   _____

   _____

2. "The medical system is woefully out of touch," says Halifax <u>psychologist</u> Michael Vallis, a <u>professor</u> at Dalhousie University.

   _____

   _____

   _____

3. <u>But</u> when he holds clinics in Pessamit, the Innu village he comes from on the north shore of the St. Lawrence River, <u>patients often ask for pills or an operation to remedy their ailments</u>.

   _____

   _____

   _____

   _____

VOCABULARY BUILD 1

A. Below are words from the Academic Word List that you will find in Reading 1. Highlight the words you understand and then circle the words you use.

conduct
initiatives
institute
intervention
range
stress

nouns — **wellness**

adjective — depressed

verbs — alter
concluded
impose

B. Match each word to its definition. For words you are not sure of, check the context in the reading for clues. Use a dictionary to check your answers.

WORDS		DEFINITIONS
1 alter	_____	a) force something on someone or something
2 impose	_____	b) actions aimed at solving a problem
3 institute	_____	c) state of general unhappiness
4 depressed	_____	d) change
5 initiatives	_____	e) organization with a particular purpose

C. Fill in the blanks with the correct words to complete the sentences.

conduct   concluded   intervention   range   stress

1 Going to school and having two part-time jobs caused her a lot of _____.

2 The _____ involved encouraging her to quit her stressful job.

3 We said there was a/an _____ of things we did to celebrate her birthday.

4 His _____ during the emergency was extremely helpful.

5 Looking at the evidence, they _____ that walking improved happiness.

Why walk? Although walking was once the most common way for people to get around, most people today have multiple transportation options, from bicycles and motorcycles to buses and cars. Cars have shaped modern cities, creating vast suburbs of homes that are often far from shops and places of work, making walking impractical. Many people don't necessarily associate walking with happiness, but the evidence is growing.

A. What do you think are the benefits of walking? Discuss with a partner.

_____

_____

B. Read this excerpt from Reading 1. What can you infer from each of the underlined numbered phrases? Inferences might be about Vollant's degree of stress, the relationship of his pace to others on the pilgrimage, why he was stubborn or what benefit might come from his medical problems. Discuss with your partner.

> In the spring of 2008, <u>depressed over the end of his second marriage and drained by an exhausting work schedule</u> [1], Stanley Vollant, Quebec's first Aboriginal surgeon, set out to complete the Camino Francés pilgrimage into Spain <u>at a marathon runner's pace</u> [2]. After twelve forty-two-kilometre days, <u>stubbornly ignoring excruciating pain in his shin</u> [3], he developed a serious infection that almost turned into necrotizing fasciitis—but <u>his fainting spells and throbbing feet had an upside</u> [4].

C. While you read, match each phrase to the reason it is set in quotation marks or italics.

PHRASES		REASONS
❶ "fancy new machines"	_____	a) title of a video
❷ *Shinrin-yoku*	_____	b) disapproving description
❸ *23 and ½ Hours*	_____	c) non-English expression

Santiago de Compostela Cathedral, the final destination of the Camino Francés pilgrimage.

pilgrimage (n.): journey to a famous place

excruciating (adj.): intense, acute

necrotizing fasciitis (n.): flesh-eating disease

The Walking Cure

In the spring of 2008, depressed over the end of his second marriage and drained by an exhausting work schedule, Stanley Vollant, Quebec's first Aboriginal surgeon, set out to complete the Camino Francés **pilgrimage** into Spain at a marathon runner's pace.
5 After twelve forty-two-kilometre days, stubbornly ignoring **excruciating** pain in his shin, he developed a serious infection that almost turned into ***necrotizing fasciitis***—but his fainting spells and throbbing feet had an upside. One night in a mountain refuge, in a feverish dream, Vollant saw himself walking in the woods with Aboriginal youth and elders, away from alcohol and drugs, refreshing their bodies, minds and spirits. Now
10 he is in the middle of a five-year, 5,000-kilometre series of walks between every First Nations community in Quebec and Labrador and a few in Ontario and New Brunswick.

…

stave off (v.): prevent or avoid

take-away (n.): key fact

siloed (adj.): placed apart; isolated

incubator (n.): place that encourages growth

bang for your buck (n.): good value for the money

skyrocketing (adj.): increasing quickly

perfect storm (n.): bad state of affairs

precipitators (n.): causes of other events

The therapeutic properties of moving around on your feet are powerful, and backed by a growing mountain of data. Walking protects you from obesity, diabetes, heart attacks
15 and strokes. It lowers blood pressure, improves cholesterol and builds bone mass. Walking improves your balance, preventing falls. It strengthens the muscles in your arms and legs, and gives your joints better range of motion. It eases back pain, and reduces the risk of glaucoma. In Japan, researchers studying *Shinrin-yoku* (forest bathing) have concluded that walking in the woods helps the body produce anti-cancer proteins. Walk
20 for thirty minutes, five times a week, says an American educational alliance called Every Body Walk!, and the endorphin boost will ease stress, anger and confusion. Scientists in Scotland believe walking could help **stave off** brain shrinkage and Alzheimer's disease. The Canadian Centre for Occupational Health and Safety counsels that walking "with good company and in pleasant surroundings" limits depression and anxiety, and leads
25 to better sleep. The **take-away**: walking keeps you healthy and helps you live longer.

In 2011, exploring novel ways to speak directly to Canadians, Toronto physician Mike Evans made a whiteboard video called *23 and ½ Hours* that has hit nearly 3.5 million views on YouTube. It argues that in that remaining half-hour each day, the single most constructive thing you can do for your health is to be active. That is a
30 message one seldom hears in our **siloed** medical system, an **incubator** for the commercial industries that have developed around obesity, diabetes and heart disease, with the quest for cures often driven by studies financed by pharmaceutical companies. Similarly, funders who donate millions of dollars to hospitals want to buy "fancy new machines," says Evans, not support workaday initiatives to get people moving. "I would
35 do a walking intervention before anything else," he says. "Programs that get people active give you more **bang for your buck**. We need to create a Ministry of Habit."

Meanwhile, changing demographics and **skyrocketing** rates of chronic illness threaten to unleash a **perfect storm** on our cardiovascular care system, reports the Heart and Stroke Foundation of Canada. So many people will be so sick, hospitals and health care
40 workers won't be able to keep up, and provincial governments won't be able to handle the bills. "The medical system is woefully out of touch," says Halifax psychologist Michael Vallis, a professor at Dalhousie University and head of the Orwellian-sounding Behaviour Change Institute, which helps health care providers alter their patients' conduct. "It's geared toward acute problems, but lifestyle diseases are overwhelming the system."

45 Among Aboriginals, there is already an outright cardiovascular crisis, and because the population is so young and growing much faster than any other group in Canada, the social and financial costs will continue to balloon if **precipitators** are not addressed.

Critical Thinking: While you read, put yourself in the place of the writer. Ask yourself whether you would make the same choices and come to the same conclusions.

"We're such a strong demographic force," Vollant says, "that if we do something positive to change things, we'll benefit the country as a whole." But when he holds clinics 50 in Pessamit, the Innu village he comes from on the north shore of the St. Lawrence River, patients often ask for pills or an operation to remedy their ailments.

Behaviour change is hard for pretty much everybody, everywhere. Often, we are prisoners of the patterns we establish, or the patterns others impose. A re-imagined future can feel out of reach, which is why Vollant says, "You always have to concen55 trate on the next step, the next hill you're going to climb." (713 words)

Rubinstein, D. (2013). The walking cure. *The Walrus*. Retrieved from http://thewalrus.ca/the-walking-cure/

D. Connect the phrases to summarize the mental and physical benefits of walking.

SUMMARY		
1 Walking protects you and improves your health by improving ...	_____	a) stress, anger and confusion.
2 Walking in the woods helps the body produce ...	_____	b) depression and anxiety, and leads to better sleep.
3 Walking for thirty minutes, five times a week will boost endorphins and ease ...	_____	c) is to be active.
4 Walking could help stave off ...	_____	d) you live longer.
5 Walking with good company and in pleasant surroundings limits ...	_____	e) your balance and strengthening your muscles.
6 Walking keeps you healthy and helps ...	_____	f) brain shrinkage and Alzheimer's disease.
7 The single most constructive thing you can do for your health ...	_____	g) anti-cancer proteins.

E. Indicate whether these statements are true or false, according to the text.

STATEMENTS	TRUE	FALSE
1 Stanley Vollant is an Aboriginal surgeon who recommends walking as a way of improving one's physical and mental health.	☐	☐
2 Vollant dreamed of walking with elders and youth between First Nations communities.	☐	☐
3 Walking protects you from blood pressure, cholesterol and bone mass.	☐	☐
4 Japanese researchers believe walking in a forest may cause cancer.	☐	☐
5 The point of the video, *23 and ½ Hours,* is that you should be active for at least thirty minutes a day.	☐	☐
6 Vollant's patients tend to want medications and operations to deal with their illnesses.	☐	☐
7 The term *perfect storm* suggests health, in some cases, could be improved by weather.	☐	☐
8 The writer suggests that behaviour change is difficult for most people.	☐	☐

Subject-Verb Agreement

In any text, every verb has to agree in number and person with its subject. This means that you need to make sure that the verb form matches the subject you are writing about. In general, if the subject is singular (one person, place or thing, except for "I" or "you"), the verb must be singular. If the subject is plural (more than one person, place or thing), the verb must be plural.

Jasper **works** at the university.	Many people **work** at the university.
The university **needs** a new library.	Libraries **need** books.
The government **is** contributing money.	Students **are** contributing books.

RULES	EXAMPLES
SUBJECTS JOINED BY *OR* OR *NOR* When a singular subject is connected to a plural subject by *or, nor, either* or *neither*, use the verb form for the subject that is nearest to the verb.	Either Helen or her friends **were** helpful. Neither her friends nor Helen **was** unhappy.
COLLECTIVE NOUNS Collective or group nouns (e.g., team, committee, government) take a singular verb when the subject is the group as a whole and take a plural verb when referring to individual members.	The team (it) **has** won the medal. The team (they) **have** worked hard.
INDEFINITE PRONOUNS Singular verbs agree with indefinite pronouns: *anybody, anyone, anything, each, either, everybody, everyone, everything, much, nobody, no one, nothing, one, somebody, someone* and *something*. The indefinite pronouns *all, any, half, more, most, none* and *some* may refer to something singular or plural elsewhere in the sentence.	All visualization techniques **are** helpful. (*Techniques* is plural, so the verb is plural.) All visualization **is** helpful. (*Visualization* is singular, so the verb is singular.)

Highlight the verb in parentheses that best completes each quote.

1. "A man should look for what (is / are), and not for what he thinks should be." —Albert Einstein

2. "If you (hasn't / haven't) forgiven yourself something, how can you forgive others?" —Dolores Huerta

3. "Happiness (make / makes) up in height for what it lacks in length." —Robert Frost

4. "He who has health has hope, and he who has hope (has / have) everything." —Arabian proverb

5. "In spite of everything I still (believe / believes) that people are really good at heart." —Anne Frank

6. "Each has his past shut in him like the leaves of a book known to him by heart and his friends can only (read / reads) the title." —Virginia Woolf

7. "Suffering usually relates to wanting things to be different from the way they (is / are)." —Allan Lokos

8. "The ability to be in the present moment (is / are) a major component of mental wellness." —Abraham Maslow

Use what you learned about subject-verb agreement when you write assignments.

A. Below are words from the Academic Word List that you will find in Reading 2. Highlight the words you understand and then circle the words you use.

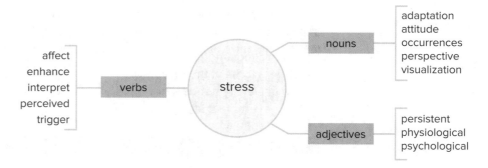

affect
enhance
interpret
perceived
trigger

verbs

stress

nouns

adaptation
attitude
occurrences
perspective
visualization

adjectives

persistent
physiological
psychological

B. Fill in the blanks with the correct words to complete the sentences.

adaptation	affect	enhance	interpret	physiological	trigger

❶ Failure to succeed on a test would _____ unhappiness.

❷ Seatbelts were a/an _____ to the design of cars to improve safety.

❸ They had lots of information, but it was difficult to _____ what it meant.

❹ Our class decided to _____ our fitness by riding bicycles to school every day.

❺ The difficulty wasn't in his mind but rather something that was

_____.

❻ She found that sunshine—or a lack of it—could _____ her happiness.

C. Choose the phrase that best completes each sentence. Key words are in bold.

❶ Looking through several **occurrences** of stressful times, she found that _____.

   a) negative stress made her happy

   b) overwork was a common factor

   c) she looked forward to them

❷ Looking for another **perspective** on his problem, he _____.

   a) decided to consult a doctor

   b) stopped reading magazines

   c) refused advice from friends

❸ The **psychological** problems they encountered were _____.

   a) nothing that they really cared about

   b) encouraged by medical professionals

   c) treated in sessions with a counsellor

④ A period of **visualization** helped the team _____.

a) imagine how they could solve the problems

b) see the images that were displayed on TV

c) forget about everything they were seeing

⑤ It wasn't obvious at first, but then they **perceived** _____.

a) almost nothing in particular

b) what they'd seen all along

c) a small light in the darkness

⑥ He had a good **attitude** which helped him _____.

a) see the worst in other people

b) see the best in other people

c) criticize other people's faults

D. VOCABULARY EXTENSION: *Physiological* and *psychological* are adjectives that relate to *physiology* (the study of biological processes) and *psychology* (the study of the mind). Write the adjective that relates to the subjects. Use a dictionary if needed.

THE STUDY OF ...	ADJECTIVES
❶ law	*legal*
❷ geography	
❸ history	

THE STUDY OF ...	ADJECTIVES
❹ economics	
❺ agriculture	
❻ art	

READING ② Take Control of Stress

When you think about stress, you might think only about its negative effects, but stress can have positive effects as well. Managing the effects of stress in a positive way makes you feel good. But for some people who experience only the negative effects of stress, there can be a loss of alertness and motivation.

A. Reading 2 suggests a number of ways to manage stress. Rate them in terms of what you think would be the most (1) and least (7) helpful. Discuss your answers with a partner.

_____ learn relaxation techniques

_____ set realistic goals

_____ exercise

_____ enjoy yourself

_____ visualization

_____ maintain a healthy lifestyle

_____ talk about it

B. While you read, highlight a definition of stress and three examples of things that cause stress.

Take Control of Stress

moderation (n.): avoidance of excess or extremes

migraines (n.): severe throbbing headaches

ulcers (n.): open sores that will not heal

irritability (n.): state of being upset at things

Stress is a fact of life. No matter how much we might long for a stress-free existence, the fact is, stress is actually necessary. It's how we respond to stress that can negatively affect our lives.

5 Stress is defined as any change that we have to adapt to. This includes difficult life events (bereavement, illness) and positive ones. Getting a new job or going on vacation are certainly perceived to be happy occurrences, but they, too, are changes, also known as stress, that require some adaptation.

Learning to effectively cope with stress can ease our bodies and our minds. Meditation 10 and other relaxation methods, exercise, visualization are all helpful techniques for reducing the negative impact of stress.

Stress can be beneficial—in **moderation**. That's because short episodes of stress trigger chemicals that improve memory, increase energy levels and enhance alertness and productivity. But chronic stress has debilitating effects on our overall health. 15 Physically, it can contribute to **migraines**, **ulcers**, muscle tension and fatigue. Canadian researchers found that chronic stress more than doubled the risk of heart attacks.

Persistent stress also affects us emotionally and intellectually, and can cause:

- Decreased concentration and memory
- Confusion
20 • Loss of sense of humour
- Anxiety
- Anger
- **Irritability**
- Fear

episode (n.): event occurring as part of a sequence

stressor (n.): something that causes unease

originates (v.): begins from

realign (v.): restore to a former position or state

feasible (adj.): possible to do

25 The link between stress and mental illness has yet to be fully understood, but it is known that stress can negatively affect an **episode** of mental illness.

Managing stress

First, it's important to recognize the source(s) of your stress. Events such as the death of a loved one, starting a new job or moving house are certainly stressful.

30 However, much of our stress comes from within us. How we interpret things—a conversation, a performance review, even a look—determines whether something becomes a **stressor**. Negative self-talk, where we focus on self-criticism and pessimistic over-analysis can turn an innocent remark into a major source of stress.

Understanding where your stress **originates** can help you decide on a course of action. 35 External stressors, like bereavement or career changes, can be managed over time and with the support of family and friends. Internal stressors, caused by our own negative interpretation, require changes in attitude and behaviour.

The goal of managing stress is to cue the "relaxation response." This is the physiological and psychological calming process our body goes through when we perceive 40 that the danger, or stressful event, has passed.

Here are some tips for triggering the relaxation response:

- Learn relaxation techniques. Practising meditation or breathing awareness every day can relieve chronic stress and **realign** your outlook in a more positive way. Good breathing habits alone can improve both your psychological and physical
45 well-being.

- Set realistic goals. Learning to say no is essential for some people. Assess your schedule and identify tasks or activities that you can or 50 should let go. Don't automatically volunteer to do something until you've considered whether it is **feasible** and healthy for you to do so.

- Exercise. You don't have to train for 55 a marathon, but regular, moderate exercise helps ease tension, improves sleep and self-esteem. Making exercise a habit is key.

- Enjoy yourself. Taking the time for 60 a favourite hobby is a great way of connecting with and nurturing your creative self.

- Visualization. Athletes achieve results by picturing themselves 65 crossing the finish line first. Use the same technique to practise "seeing" yourself succeed in whatever situation is uppermost in your mind.

- Maintain a healthy lifestyle. A good diet is often the first thing to go when we're
70 feeling stressed. Making a meal instead of buying one ready-made may seem like
a challenge, but it will be probably cheaper and certainly better for you and the
simple action of doing something good for yourself can soothe stressful feelings.

- Talk about it. Sharing your troubles with a friend may help you to put things in
perspective and to feel that you're not alone. You may also learn some other ways
75 to manage stress effectively.   (662 words)

_____

Canadian Mental Health Association. (2014). Benefits of good mental health. Retrieved from http://calgary.cmha.ca/mental_health/benefits-of-good-mental-health/#.U_JlbsVdWSo

C. Fill in the blanks with words from the reading to complete the sentences.

❶ How we respond to stress can _____ affect our lives.

❷ Meditation and other _____ methods help reduce stress.

❸ Short episodes of stress _____ chemicals that improve memory.

❹ Chronic stress has _____ effects on our overall health.

❺ Stress can negatively affect a/an _____ of mental illness.

❻ How we interpret things determines whether something becomes a/an _____.

❼ External stressors can be managed with others' _____.

❽ Internal stressors require changes in _____ and behaviour.

❾ The relaxation response happens after a/an _____ event has passed.

D. Based on your understanding of the text, what can you infer about the writer's attitude? Choose one of the answers.

☐ The writer thinks that stress is not a big problem and that people would not have it if they would just learn a few simple stress-management techniques.

☐ Although the writer thinks that there are many causes for stress, the suggestion is that the causes can be treated with one or more techniques.

☐ The writer's view of stress is that it is like a serious disease and that most people probably won't be able to take care of it themselves, even with the suggested techniques.

E. Now that you have read the article, which stress-management techniques would work for you? Which techniques would not work for you? Discuss with your partner.

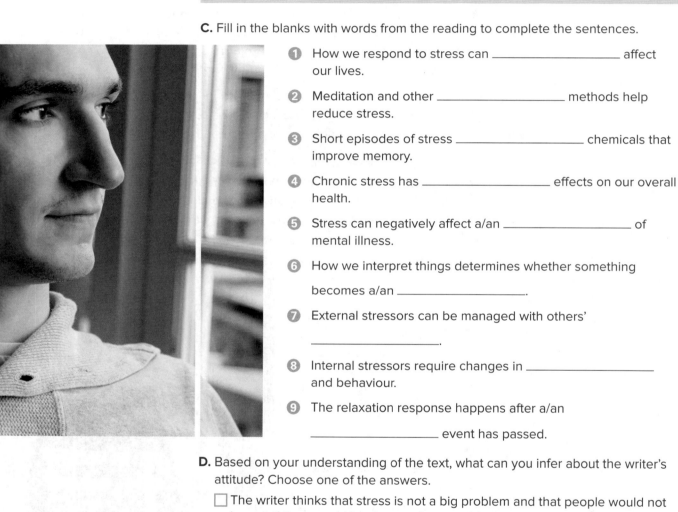

FOCUS ON WRITING

Using Definitions

Academic writing is often about introducing new ideas. Sometimes you have to explain a term or concept your readers may not be familiar with. In such cases, you can write an informal definition or a formal definition to ensure that your message is clear and that your reader will better understand the term or concept. This is particularly important when a word or phrase has more than one meaning. For example, *edge*, as a noun, can mean "an advantage, a sharp side or an outside limit." As a verb, *edge* can mean "to move gradually and carefully." If the meaning of the term or concept is not clear through context, then you should define it.

FOR INFORMAL DEFINITIONS USE ...	EXAMPLE
a synonym, e.g., for the word *danger*	This is the physiological and psychological calming process our body goes through when we perceive that the danger, **or stressful event**, has passed.
one or more examples, in commas or parentheses	This includes difficult life events **(bereavement, illness)** and positive ones.
words and phrases such as *defined as* or *relates to* or *can be explained as*	Stress is **defined as** any change that we have to adapt to.
a second sentence, e.g., when defining the term *relaxation response*	The goal of managing stress is to cue the "relaxation response." **This is the physiological and psychological calming process our body goes through when we perceive that the danger, or stressful event, has passed.**
the term with an explanation of what it is not before explaining what it is	**Stress** is **not always a problem**; it can be **the motivator** that provides a boost of energy.

FOR FORMAL DEFINITIONS USE ...	EXAMPLE
the term being defined	stress
the part of speech	noun
the class: an explanation of how it fits with similar terms	state of emotional strain
an explanation of what makes the term different from others in its class	that makes one feel overwhelmed

NOTE: Make sure your class and explanation words are in simple, easy-to-understand English. Don't repeat a form of the term in the explanation (e.g., **Relax**ed means the feeling of **relax**ing.).

A. Write informal definitions for the terms in bold. Set the definition off with commas or parentheses as needed.

1. Learning to effectively **cope** (synonym) _____ with stress can ease our bodies and our minds.

2. **Persistent stress** (example) _____ affects us emotionally and intellectually.

3. Physically, stress can contribute to migraines, ulcers, muscle tension and **fatigue** (synonym) _____.

B. Write formal definitions for these terms. Include the class and an explanation, and highlight the class in each one. Use a dictionary if necessary.

1 anxiety: _____

_____

2 performance review: _____

_____

3 healthy lifestyle: _____

_____

WARM-UP ASSIGNMENT
Write Short Definitions

Write a paragraph with three or more strategies that people can use to reduce stress.

A. For each strategy, include brief informal definitions. Use the techniques and example words or phrases in Focus on Writing if you need help. For example: Most people want to have a good quality of life, **as defined** in part by a healthy diet and enough exercise.

B. Add supporting details in the form of examples and explanations. Each detail may have its own informal definition: A healthy diet **(a balanced mix of vegetables and fruit, milk and alternatives, grains, meat and alternatives)** helps reduce cardiovascular disease, **problems with the heart and blood vessels.**

C. Write your paragraph. Refer to the Models Chapter (page 192) to see an example of a definition and to learn more about how to write one.

D. Share your paragraph with a partner. Use this checklist to assess each other's writing and then revise based on your partner's comments.

My partner

☐ spelled each word correctly

☐ avoided bland words by choosing more interesting ones

☐ included sentences that flow smoothly from point to point

☐ ensured subjects and verbs agree

☐ used present and past verb tenses correctly

☐ added correct punctuation

☐ understood the assignment and met all the criteria

Use feedback from your teacher and classmates on this Warm-Up Assignment to improve your writing.

A. Below are words from the Academic Word List that you will find in Reading 3. Highlight the words you understand and then circle the words you use.

commitment
concept
philosophy
rationalization → **nouns**

happiness

verbs → assumes
attained
constitutes
obtaining
reinforce

attitudinal → **adjective**

B. Highlight the word that has the closest meaning to each word in bold.

1 They wanted her to stay at the company, but she wouldn't make a **commitment**.

a) break   b) offer   c) promise

2 To **reinforce** the rule, he made signs and posted them throughout the school.

a) ignore   b) emphasize   c) weaken

3 They used a/an **attitudinal** survey to find out what the group preferred.

a) informal   b) opinion   c) formal

4 They found a/an **rationalization** for happiness based on five hundred people's best memories.

a) explanation   b) dismiss   c) encourage

5 He **assumes** that money can buy happiness.

a) believes   b) remembers   c) explains

C. Fill in the blanks with the correct words to complete the paragraph.

attained	concept	constitutes	obtaining	philosophy

When we do not understand something, we often look at _____ _____ as a way of exploring a/an _____ like happiness. We look at people who have _____ happiness as well as others, whose attempts at _____ happiness have failed. But we often find that what _____ happiness for one person many not be the same as for someone else.

My eLab

Visit My eLab to complete Vocabulary Review exercises for this chapter.

Defining Happiness

When physicist Stephen Hawking was twenty-one, he was diagnosed with the disease that left him paralyzed, unable to walk. However, he considers himself happy and feels he is more fortunate than many others. This is in part because he has been able to continue his work and write best-selling books. His achievements in mathematics and astronomy have been recognized internationally.

A. The approval of others is probably an important part of Stephen Hawking's happiness. Write your definition of happiness.

_____

_____

B. Read this excerpt from Reading 3, which raises and answers a question related to happiness. Based on the excerpt, what can you infer about happiness levels in your country compared to other countries? Discuss with a partner.

> Another question is whether wealthier people are happier than poorer people. Diener (2000) notes that some countries are better able to meet people's basic needs—such as for food, clean water and health—and this leads to greater happiness. But beyond satisfying basic needs, more wealth does not seem to translate to greater happiness.

C. Reading 3 gives definitions of happiness. While you read, highlight them.

Defining Happiness

limitations (n.): lack of abilities

anxious (adj.): uneasy or nervous

harmony (n.): state of being in pleasing agreement

construe (v.): interpret in a particular way

When Helen Keller (1880–1968) was nineteen months old, a brief illness made her both deaf and blind. Cut off from the world, she struggled to communicate her most basic needs (Keller, 1905). With such **limitations**, how could Keller ever be expected
5 to find happiness?

Because happiness has been considered a personal concept, it is difficult to define. Many people throughout history have tried. Greek scientist and philosopher Aristotle (384–322 BCE) wrote, "Happiness depends upon ourselves," which is not a definition but an observation that individuals are responsible for their own
10 happiness. Roman statesman and philosopher Lucius Seneca (4 BCE–AD 65) wrote of a particular quality of happiness, saying, "True happiness is to enjoy the present, without **anxious** dependence upon the future." Seneca's interpretation centres on the idea that you are happy when you are free from worry, but it, too,
15 fails to define happiness. Indian statesman Mahatma Gandhi (1869–1948) came closer with the idea that happiness has a quality of being true to yourself: "Happiness is when what you think, what you say and what you do are in **harmony**."

Is there a scientific basis for happiness? Researcher Sonja
20 Lyubomirsky (2014) suggests happiness is a matter of perspective: "… truly happy individuals **construe** life events and daily situations in ways that seem to maintain their happiness, while

self-gratification (n.): satisfaction of your own desires

fidelity (n.): faithfulness to someone or something

tactile (adj.): connected with the sense of touch

unhappy individuals construe experiences in ways that seem to reinforce unhappiness" (para. 2). Basically, this means the way you choose to remember events and
25 situations affects your happiness.

Some research concludes happiness is made up of three parts: pleasure, engagement and meaning (PBS, 2009). *Pleasure* involves things that give physical and emotional joy, such as playing a sport or seeing beautiful art. *Engagement* involves positive interactions with other people, such as studying or working with people whose company you enjoy.
30 *Meaning* relates to feeling that your work is useful and important to others.

Even with scientific rationalization, questions remain. For example, are younger people happier than older people? In fact, the opposite seems to be true. This may be because younger people tend to experience higher levels of negative emotions, such as anxiety and anger. The young also have less control over their lives because they lack both
35 independence and the ability to make many of their own decisions.

Another question is whether wealthier people are happier than poorer people. Diener (2000) notes that some countries are better able to meet people's basic needs—such as for food, clean water and health—and this leads to greater happiness. But beyond satisfying basic personal needs, more wealth does not seem to
40 translate to greater happiness.

Perhaps the most important question is whether you can change how happy you are. Studies of identical twins (De Neve, Christakis, Fowler, & Frey, 2012) suggest that genetics forms about half of your happiness level. Beyond this, your quality of life influences about 10 percent of your happiness. That means about 40 percent of your
45 happiness is determined by your choices and actions.

Helen Keller, despite the severe disabilities that left her unable to hear or see, was reportedly an extremely happy person. Why? Lyubomirsky, Sheldon and Schkade (2005) note that aspects of happiness are partly "… determined by global attitudinal or meaning-based factors. Thus, a person who 'suffers for a cause' might still feel
50 very happy because her suffering demonstrates her commitment to, and also perhaps moves her closer to obtaining, an important life-goal" (p. 25).

From this explanation we can see that one way you can make yourself happier is to set goals. Keller had a definition of happiness in keeping with this idea. She thought most people didn't understand true happiness and
55 contrasted the idea of **self-gratification** with **fidelity** to a worthwhile purpose. She felt happiness did not come from simply trying to satisfy your own desires but rather by contributing your time and skills to improve
60 the world in some way (Keller, 1905).

How was Keller's philosophy reflected in her own life? When she was seven years old, Keller was fortunate to meet a specially trained teacher, Anne Sullivan (1866–1936),
65 who introduced Keller to the idea of letters spelled out in the palm of her hand. This allowed Keller to better communicate and learn Braille, a **tactile** writing system for the blind. Despite her limitations, Keller went on to learn to speak and sing, to write twelve books and to give lectures around the world, inspiring millions of people.

70 Even if you are unable to achieve a goal that makes the world better in some small way, simply trying will likely give your life meaning and, at the same time, happiness.

(770 words)

References

De Neve, J-E., Christakis, N.A., Fowler, J.H., & Frey, B.S. (2012). Genes, economics and happiness. *CESifo Working Paper Series* No. 2946. Retrieved from SSRN: http://ssrn.com/abstract=1553633

Diener, E. (2000). Subjective well-being: The science of happiness and a proposal for a national index. *American Psychologist, 55*(1) 34–43.

Keller, H. (1905). *The story of my life.* New York, NY: Doubleday, Page & Company.

Lyubomirsky, S. (2014). Sonja Lyubomirsky [personal webpage]. Retrieved from http://sonjalyubomirsky.com/

Lyubomirsky, S., Sheldon, K.M., & Schkade, D. (2005). Pursuing happiness: The architecture of sustainable change. *Review of General Psychology, 9*(2) 111–131.

PBS. (2009). What is happiness? *This Emotional Life, PBS.* Retrieved from http://www.pbs.org/thisemotionallife/topic/happiness/what-happiness

D. Number these sentences in the correct order to form a summary of Reading 3.

_____1_____ Helen Keller's deafness and blindness cut her off from the world.

_____ About 40 percent of your happiness is determined by your choices and actions.

_____ Happiness includes elements of depending on yourself, being responsible for your own happiness and enjoying the present without worry.

_____ Happiness is based on pursuing an important life goal.

_____ Happiness is made up of pleasure, engagement and meaning.

_____ Lyubomirsky suggests happiness is a matter of perspective based on how you choose to remember events and situations.

_____ Wealthier people are not happier than poorer people who have had their basic needs met.

_____ Mahatma Gandhi thought happiness was when what you think, what you say and what you do are in harmony.

_____ Younger people are not happier than older people.

_____10_____ Happiness comes from contributing time and skills to improve the world.

E. Based on your understanding of Helen Keller's life and her perspective on happiness, what can you infer about her likely agreement with the other writers? Complete the survey and then discuss in a group.

	COMPLETELY AGREE		NEITHER AGREE NOR DISAGREE		COMPLETELY DISAGREE
❶ Happiness depends upon ourselves.	1	2	3	4	5
❷ True happiness is to enjoy the present, without anxious dependence upon the future.	1	2	3	4	5
❸ Happiness is when what you think, what you say and what you do are in harmony.	1	2	3	4	5
❹ Truly happy individuals construe life events and daily situations in ways that seem to maintain their happiness.	1	2	3	4	5

Academic
Survival Skill

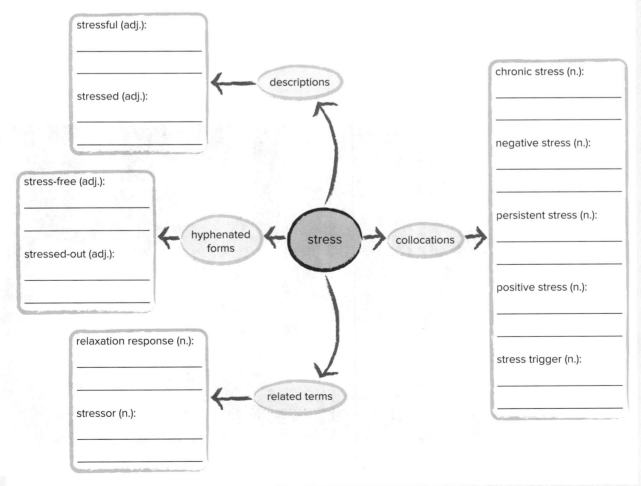

❶

Develop Your Vocabulary: While you read, learn the pronunciation of new words. This helps you recognize and reinforce the words when you hear them.

Developing Vocabulary

You will never finish learning new vocabulary. Even if you could memorize a dictionary, new words are being created every day. What you need is a system for learning words that are useful to you and your studies.

Decide which words are useful. The word *stress* is an important concept in this chapter. Not only is it repeated frequently, several forms of it are used as in collocations. *Collocations* are pairs or groups of words frequently used together. On the other hand, some words or phrases, such as *necrotizing fasciitis,* appear only once: in Reading 1. Unless you are studying medicine, it may not be a useful word to learn.

Keep a computer file or notebook and develop mind maps to show the relationships of key words, parts of speech and definitions. Add common collocations. Also include other words and phrases you know, for example *stressed out,* though not in this chapter, is an example of a phrase you can use to build your mind maps as you encounter new vocabulary.

Review your mind maps frequently and build on them. Display them around your home or desk. You can also write key vocabulary on sticky notes to carry with you as portable flash cards.

Find opportunities to use new words. Include them in your writing, in your conversations and in your communications, such as in assignments and e-mails.

Write a definition for each of these terms.

stressful (adj.):

_____

_____

stressed (adj.):

_____

_____

descriptions

chronic stress (n.):

_____

_____

negative stress (n.):

_____

_____

persistent stress (n.):

_____

_____

positive stress (n.):

_____

_____

stress trigger (n.):

_____

_____

stress-free (adj.):

_____

_____

stressed-out (adj.):

_____

_____

hyphenated forms

stress

collocations

relaxation response (n.):

_____

_____

stressor (n.):

_____

_____

related terms

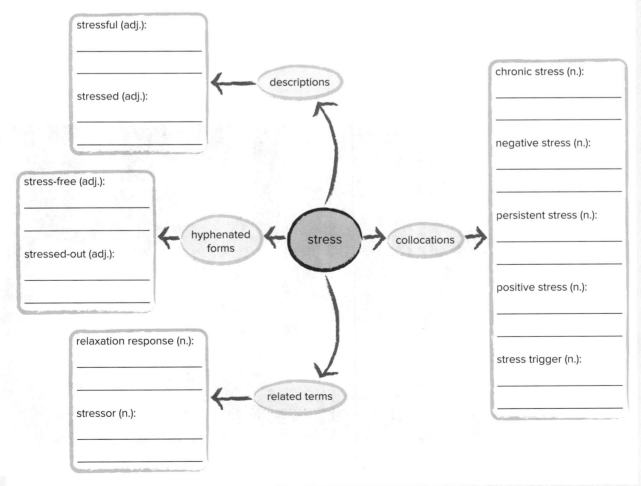

FINAL ASSIGNMENT

Write a Definition Paragraph

Use what you learned in this chapter to write a definition paragraph. A definition paragraph features a topic sentence that is a formal definition. A formal definition includes the term, the class and a brief explanation. Supporting sentences give examples and explanations.

A. Focus on Grammar (page 79) quotes a number of famous people who write what happiness means to them. Choose one of the quotes for your paragraph.

QUOTE: _____

_____

_____

B. Research the author of your quote to better understand the context of when and why it might have been written.

C. Write your definition of happiness. Explain whether or not the quote you chose supports your definition. Give examples and explanations. Use collocations and vocabulary learned in this chapter.

D. Use this table to organize your ideas.

TOPIC SENTENCE, WITH TERM, CLASS AND BRIEF EXPLANATION	
SUPPORTING SENTENCE, WITH AN EXAMPLE AND EXPLANATION	
SUPPORTING SENTENCE, WITH AN EXAMPLE AND EXPLANATION	

E. Refer to the Models Chapter (page 193) to see an example of a definition paragraph and to learn more about how to write one.

F. Proofread your paragraph. Check the grammar. Is there subject-verb agreement? Then, share it with a partner and ask for feedback.

G. Make corrections and write a final copy.

How confident are you?

Think about what you learned in this chapter. Use the table to decide what you should review.

I LEARNED ...	I AM CONFIDENT	I NEED TO REVIEW
vocabulary related to health, happiness and stress;	☐	☐
to construct meaning through inference;	☐	☐
subject-verb agreement;	☐	☐
formal and informal definitions;	☐	☐
how to use mind maps and collocations to develop my vocabulary;	☐	☐
how to write definition paragraphs.	☐	☐

VOCABULARY Challenge

Think about the vocabulary and ideas in this chapter. Use these words to write two sentences that summarize a happy life.

alter	attitude	concept	enhance	impose	reinforce

_____

_____

_____

_____

_____

_____

My eLab ✎
Visit My eLab to build on what you learned.

CHAPTER 5

Printing the World

New technologies often change the world in unexpected ways. The three-dimensional (3D) printer's first product was a plastic cup. Since then, an amazing array of objects and tools have been printed from plastics, ceramics and metals, as well as edible materials, such as chocolate, fish paste and sugar. The process works by sending a computer file to a printer that either builds up layers of material or carves a block of material. Predictions are that every home will eventually have a 3D printer for making and repairing everyday goods.

What would you use a 3D printer for?

In this chapter,
you will

- learn vocabulary related to 3D printing and biomimicry;

- evaluate research sources;

- review different sentence types;

- consider register and tone in formal and informal writing;

- apply critical thinking techniques;

- write formal e-mails.

GEARING UP

A. Look at the image and then answer the questions.

A giant 3D printer for building homes

Source: *3d printer builds a concrete house in just 24 hours.* (2014). Illustration by Yang Liu / USC Viterbi.

1 Massive 3D printers are now able to create entire homes from concrete. Who might be interested in this kind of technology?

_____

2 The Internet allows people to illegally distribute digital information, such as stolen movies and music. Which objects might be manufactured with home 3D printers using illegal plans?

_____

_____

3 3D printers can be used to customize everyday objects, for example, to create eyeglass frames that perfectly fit your face. Which personalized objects would you print in 3D?

_____

4 What uses might doctors and hospitals find for a 3D printer?

_____

_____

B. Discuss the questions and your answers, first with a partner, then in a group.

Evaluating Research Sources

Research falls into two categories: *primary research* (original investigations and experiments) and *secondary research* (reviews of primary research). Primary research may be qualitative or quantitative. Qualitative research is exploratory and aims to better understand a phenomenon, often through interviews and observations that collect information. Quantitative research begins with a hypothesis—or educated guess—about what might explain a phenomenon. Through measurable observations or an experiment, data is collected and measured statistically. The statistics can then be shown to support or reject the hypothesis.

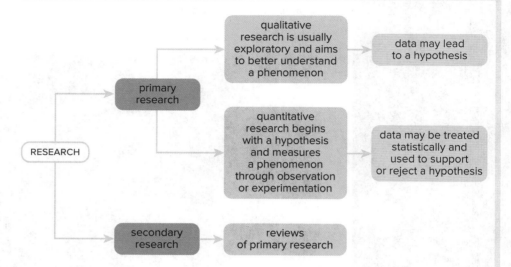

A. Fill in the blanks with the correct words or phrases to complete the sentences.

hypothesis	qualitative	secondary research
primary research	quantitative	statistics

1. The _____ research led to the creation of a hypothesis.

2. Her _____ surveys were converted to statistical data.

3. The _____ suggested that UV light could be used to harden plastic.

4. His _____ research reviewed twelve current studies.

5. The _____ research resulted in the rejection of the hypothesis.

6. Their hypothesis was supported by the _____.

B. The CRAAP Test was developed by Sarah Blakeslee, a librarian at the Meriam Library, to help evaluate research sources. Read what each letter stands for, the related questions, and then give an example of a research source you might reject.

CRAAP	QUESTIONS	EXAMPLE OF WHAT TO REJECT
CURRENCY	Is the article reasonably recent?	*Data on university student attitudes published forty years ago.*
RELEVANCY	Does the information match your research needs? Who is the intended audience: academic, professional or the general public?	
AUTHORITY	Is the information professionally written, edited and published? Is the author an expert on the topic?	
ACCURACY	Is the information based on facts that can be verified through other sources?	
PURPOSE	What is the purpose of the information? Is it biased in favour of one point of view?	

VOCABULARY BUILD 1

A. Below are words and phrases from the Academic Word List that you will find in Reading 1. Highlight the words you understand and then circle the words you use.

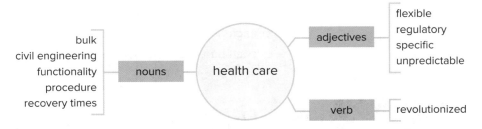

B. Highlight the words or phrases that have the closest meaning to the words or phrases in bold.

1. They looked at general problems, but we wanted the **specific** cause.

   a) typical   b) exact   c) recent

2. Results were **unpredictable** with early versions of 3D printers.

   a) well-known   b) lost   c) irregular

3. Even though their injuries were small, their **recovery times** were long.

   a) healing periods   b) payment periods   c) hospital stays

4. The **procedure** for printing a new arm bone involved more than one hundred steps.

   a) research   b) rate   c) method

5. No **regulatory** authority governs all of the many uses of 3D printers.

   a) advisory   b) governing   c) competing

C. Choose the phrase that best completes each sentence. Key words are in bold.

1 **Civil engineering** is responsible for _____.

a) designing the layout of the farm

b) construction of roads and bridges

c) all of the city's electrical problems

2 In terms of increased **functionality**, the new model _____.

a) has more buttons but fewer features

b) solves the same motivational equations

c) can do much more than previous models

3 The 3D printer has **revolutionized** parts of health care _____.

a) through the creation of individualized body parts

b) by allowing the mass production of new tools

c) in the same way all technologies save costs

4 Rather than buy all the items in **bulk**, they _____.

a) saved money by buying them one at a time

b) saved time by buying them individually

c) wasted money by buying them individually

5 Using **flexible** plastics meant that _____.

a) the parts could bend if they had to

b) each part was more likely to snap

c) each part could be much firmer

READING 1 **Three Ways 3D Printing Could Revolutionize Health Care**

From around 1760, the Industrial Revolution's steam-powered machines allowed for mass production. Individually tailored goods began to disappear. Today, it would be unusual for you to have all your clothes and daily consumer supplies made by hand. However, 3D printers may reverse the trend by offering opportunities to customize and make the things you need at home. In the medical field, 3D printers promise to provide body parts that will change the treatment you receive at hospitals and in emergency situations.

A. Artificial hips and other body parts are commonly implanted, but now other bones are being 3D printed with ceramic powder. These bones allow growth, in much the same way as a coral reef grows upon itself. Why might artificial bones be so important to medicine?

_____

_____

_____

_____

B. Read this excerpt from Reading 2. Customizable body parts are intended for a better fit. But in this age of plastic surgery, do you think people might customize body parts to further modify their appearance: for example, by creating different shaped fingernails or teeth? Discuss with a partner.

> In medicine, it [3D printing] has had most success with prosthetics, dental work and hearing aids, which can all be made from plastic or pliable materials and often need to be tailored to a specific patient. But scientists have also worked out, at least in theory, how to print blood vessels, skin, even embryonic stem cells. "The biggest advantage is that everything is customizable," Markus Fromherz, Xerox's chief innovation officer in health care, told HealthBiz Decoded.

C. In the above excerpt, "success" could be measured through primary quantitative research that assessed doctor, dentist and patient satisfaction levels. These could be compared with previous treatments to see if there was a statistically significant difference. While you read, write notes on each paragraph and decide whether the writer is reporting on research and whether that research is primary or secondary.

Three Ways 3D Printing Could Revolutionize Health Care

Originally used to cheaply and quickly make prototypes, 3D printing has lately gained momentum as a (cheap, quick) manufacturing endpoint in and of itself.

The technology redefines the phrase "broadly applicable": it's been used for archi-
5 tecture, industrial design, automotive and aerospace engineering, the military, civil engineering, fashion and food.

In medicine, it has had most success with **prosthetics**, dental work and hearing aids, which can all be made from plastic or **pliable** materials and often need to be tailored to a specific patient. But scientists have also worked out, at least in theory, how to
10 print blood vessels, skin, even **embryonic stem cells**.

"The biggest advantage is that everything is customizable," Markus Fromherz, Xerox's chief innovation officer in health care, told HealthBiz Decoded.

prosthetics (n): artificial body parts

pliable (adj.): easily bent, flexible

embryonic stem cells (n.): cells which can be used to grow other cells

optimal (adj.): best or most favourable

cartilage (n.): connective tissue in the body

mould (n.): hollow form for making copies

crowns (n.): replacement caps for teeth

trachea (n.): tube in the throat for breathing (windpipe)

viable (adj.): workable

There are three categories of health care where 3D printing could be applied, or is already, Fromherz said: for body parts or prosthetics—sometimes called "scaffolding,"
15 medical devices and human tissues.

Scaffolding

Printing technology has already revolutionized joint replacements, Fromherz said.

"Knee replacement is a very common procedure; there are six or so different types of knees that doctors use," he said, adding, "with each one you need to cut the bone
20 differently."

But with 3D printing, doctors aren't limited to those six knees. They can design one specific to each patient.

Patients with custom knees don't have to lose extra inches of bone; instead, the surgeon can cut at the **optimal** point, which could lead to faster recovery times and
25 better functionality.

Strong, flexible new knee joints mimicking bone and **cartilage** can now be printed with nylon. These surgeries are available at top-tier medical facilities like the Mayo Clinic.

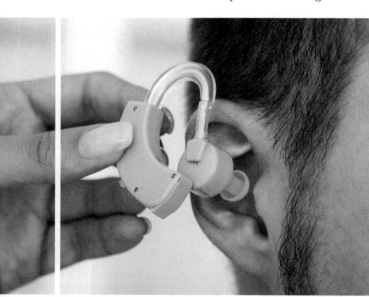

Medical devices

Most hearing aids are already 3D printed, since these
30 have always been customized to the user, and scanning, modelling and printing saves time over casting a handmade **mould** of the inner ear. What used to take a week now takes less than a day.

Similarly, making **crowns** and dental implants used
35 to take two weeks, but now can happen while the patient reads a magazine in the waiting room.

"Printing medical devices is maybe of lesser value as far as a hospital is concerned," Fromherz said.

Hospitals buy medical devices in bulk and 3D print-
40 ing their own devices, which don't often need customization, doesn't offer much advantage.

Printing may be best for when doctors need to create a new device on demand for rare, unpredictable conditions. In May 2013, doctors printed a customized splint for a newborn with a collapsing **trachea**, which saved the boy's life.

45 Human tissues

Scientists have printed artificial meat tissue suitable for eating, but making tissues and organs that maintain life has been much harder. So far, printed bits of functional liver tissue in petri dishes could be **viable** for testing drugs, and larger models have been useful for surgeons to practise technique.

50 "Printing functional human tissue will be a game changer, but it's far out," Fromherz said.

What the future holds

The next step is to build in electronics, he said. Artificial knees could include sensors to measure the pressure and health of the knee, connected wirelessly to an app or provider software.

55 If you're printing a device, body part or tissue from scratch, it won't be much more difficult to build electronics into the design, he said. Every printed device or tissue could double as a source of data.

But 3D printing isn't foolproof, and there are regulatory and use-case questions yet to be answered, he said.

60 "With a regular printer, everyone can create a document," he said. "Not everybody will be skilled or knowledgeable enough to create a knee."

Not a useful one, anyway. And it still takes at least thirty minutes to print anything. The technology may one day be most useful at military field hospitals or at the scene of an accident, where immediately creating splints, body parts or devices could save 65 lives, [but] it's not quick enough yet to be implemented.

"There will be 3D printers I'm sure in every home and hospital in the future," Fromherz said. "But right now the tech isn't fast enough." (680 words)

Doyle, K. (2013). 3 ways 3d printing could revolutionize health care. *Healthbiz Decoded*. Retrieved from http://www.healthbizdecoded.com/2013/07/how-3-d-printing-could-revolutionize-healthcare-someday/

D. Choose the phrase that best completes each sentence.

① 3D printing has become _____.
   a) used by most doctors internationally
   b) a cheap and quick means of manufacturing
   c) an expensive but efficient way to make things

② 3D printing has applications _____.
   a) that are mostly limited to medicine
   b) for a wide range of disciplines
   c) at colleges and universities

③ 3D printing has medical applications _____.
   a) for prosthetics, dental work and hearing aids
   b) for doctors with training in electronics
   c) in the area of designing new instruments

④ 3D printing allows knee replacements _____.
   a) for patients of any age and bone condition
   b) for those suffering from severe breaks
   c) with custom cuts to the connecting bones

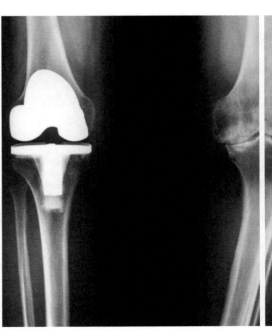

⑤ 3D printing may be most useful in hospitals when _____.

   a) doctors have lots of time to create solutions

   b) staff are properly trained in scanning

   c) doctors face unpredictable conditions

⑥ 3D printing of liver tissue is mostly useful for _____.

   a) very young children experiencing liver disease

   b) testing drugs and practising surgical techniques

   c) very old people whose livers have failed

E. Answer the questions and then discuss in a group. Look for answers beyond those in the article.

① In the section titled "Scaffolding," what would be a suitable question for future research on knee replacements?

   _____

   _____

② How might embedded electronics be useful in researching 3D printed body parts?

   _____

   _____

③ The text suggests that body tissue, such as skin, will be an important 3D printing application. How could research help support this statement?

   _____

   _____

④ It will be necessary to conduct research to see if 3D printers are useful in military field hospitals (temporary hospitals in war zones). What primary research would it be useful to conduct?

   _____

   _____

FOCUS ON GRAMMAR

Sentence Types

A mixture of simple, compound, complex and compound-complex sentences gives variety to your writing and helps keep readers' attention. To recognize and use different sentence types, it's necessary to understand independent and dependent clauses.

An *independent clause* has a subject and a verb and expresses a complete thought. A *dependent clause* can have both a subject and a verb, but it does not express a complete thought.

SENTENCE TYPES	STRUCTURE	EXAMPLE
SIMPLE	one independent clause	Biomimicry is a new discipline.
COMPOUND	two independent clauses linked by a coordinate conjunction (*for, and, nor, but, or, yet, so*)	Biomimicry is a new discipline **and** it's now used in car designs.
COMPLEX	an independent clause plus a dependent clause, linked by a subordinate conjunction (*for example, after, although, because, instead of, since, when, until*)	Biomimicry is a promising technique **because** of its many applications.
COMPOUND-COMPLEX	two (or more) independent clauses linked by a coordinate conjunction and at least one dependent clause linked by a subordinate conjunction	We should learn from nature **and** we should consider biomimetic solutions **before** dismissing biomimicry.

! Use the acronym "fanboys" to remember the coordinate conjunctions: *for, and, nor, but, or, yet, so.*

A. Add words, capital letters and punctuation to these dependent clauses to form complex sentences.

1 because biomimicry is new

_____

2 when Leonardo da Vinci was alive

_____

3 before using the 3D printer

_____

4 although based on bird wings

_____

! Use what you learned about sentence types when you write assignments.

5 since efficient designs can be found in nature

_____

_____

B. Highlight the word or phrase in parentheses that best completes each sentence.

1 George de Mestral had the idea for Velcro (after / with) observing how burrs stuck to his dog's fur.

2 Nature has found solutions to many problems, (when / for example) making faster planes.

3 We should learn from nature (and / although) use it as a source of inspiration.

4 Mark Miles looked for ways to create colour monitors, (until / during) he read an article on butterflies.

5 Trees and bones distribute strength and loads (when / so) they can be models for vehicles and buildings.

A. Below are words and phrases from the Academic Word List that you will find in Reading 2. Highlight the words you understand and then circle the words you use.

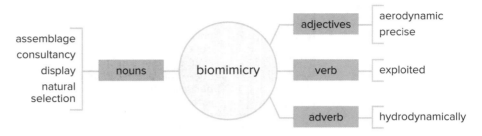

B. Fill in the blanks with the correct words to complete the sentences.

aerodynamic	display	hydrodynamically	natural selection

1 Countless plants have evolved the best traits through

_____.

2 A computer _____ makes use of new technologies to reduce its size.

3 Some squirrels have _____ flaps of skin that help them glide from tree to tree.

4 A _____ designed roof could either shed water or conserve it.

C. Highlight the best definition for each word. For words you are not sure of, check the context of the word in Reading 1 for clues. Use a dictionary to check your answers.

1 assemblage   a) collection or gathering of things   b) prepackaged box of goods

2 consultancy   a) fundraising group   b) professional practice

3 exploited   a) avoided personal interactions   b) made the full use of something

4 precise   a) accurate and exact   b) before siding with someone

D. VOCABULARY EXTENSION: The prefix *aero-* in *aerodynamic* and *hydro-* in *hydrodynamically* are commonly used in several other words. Read examples of these and other words and define what the affix means.

PREFIX	EXAMPLES	DEFINITIONS
aero-	aerosol, aerobics, aeroplane	
bio-	biology, biometrics, biomass	
cryo-	cryogenic, cryopac, cryosurgery	
hydro-	hyrdroelectric, hydroplane, hydrospa	

How Biomimicry Is Inspiring Human Innovation

Biomimicry takes its name from words for *life* and *imitate* and asks the question, "How has nature already solved this problem?" For example, the natural world has developed ways to move and filter water, to build strong structures with simple materials and to generate power. Biomimicry looks at these solutions and considers how they can be applied to problems in the human world.

A. Label the following pictures. With a partner, discuss what each might contribute in terms of supplying a biomimicry solution.

burrs	deciduous tree	kelp	nautilus shell
camel	harvester ants	Morpho butterfly	whelk

B. While you read, highlight examples of biomimicry. Which examples would be considered primary research and which secondary research?

How Biomimicry Is Inspiring Human Innovation

resilient (adj.): able to resist or withstand force

vibrant (adj.): brilliant and striking (colours)

iridescent (adj.): showing luminous colours that appear to change

pigment (n.): natural colouring

This is the idea behind the increasingly influential discipline of biomimicry: that we human beings, who have been trying to make things for only the blink of an evolutionary eye, have a lot to learn from the long processes of natural selection,
5 whether it's how to make a wing more aerodynamic or a city more **resilient** or an electronic display more **vibrant**. More than a decade ago, an MIT grad named Mark Miles was dabbling in the field of micro-electromechanical and materials processing. As he paged through a science magazine, he was stopped by an article on how butterflies generate colour in their wings. The brilliant **iridescent** blue of
10 the various Morpho species, for example, comes not from pigment, but from "structural colour." Those wings harbour a nanoscale assemblage of shingled plates, whose shape and distance from one another are arranged in a precise pattern that disrupts reflective light wavelengths to produce the brilliant blue. To create that same blue out of **pigment** would require much more energy—energy better used for flying,
15 feeding and reproducing.

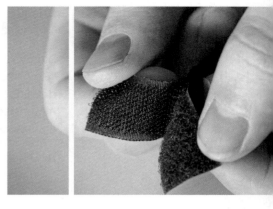

Miles wondered if this capability could be exploited in some way. Where else might you want incredibly **vivid** colour in a thin package? Of course: in an electronic device
20 display. Qualcomm, which acquired the company Miles had formed to develop the technology, used it in its Mirasol display. "We exploit the phenomena of optical interference," says Brian Gally, senior director
25 of product management at Qualcomm. Lurking beneath the glass surface is a vast array of interferometric modulators, essentially microscopic (10 to 50 microns square) mirrors that move up and down, in microseconds, to create the proper colour.

Like the butterfly's wings, "the display is taking the white **ambient** light around us,
30 white light or sunlight, and through interference is going to send us back a colour image," Gally says. Unlike conventional LCD screens, the Mirasol doesn't have to generate its own light. "The display brightness just automatically **scales** with ambient light." As a result, the Mirasol consumes a tenth of the power of an LCD reader. Qualcomm used the display in an e-reader and is offering it for licence to other companies.

35 Though biomimicry has inspired human innovations for decades—one of the most often-**cited** examples is Velcro, which the Swiss engineer Georges de Mestral patented in 1955 after studying how burrs stuck to his clothes—better technology and more nuanced research have enabled increasingly complex adaptions. Design software created by German researcher Claus Mattheck—and used in Opel and Mercedes
40 cars—reflects the ways trees and bones distribute strength and loads. A fan created by Pax Scientific borrows from the patterns of swirling kelp, nautilus and whelks to move air more efficiently. A saltwater-irrigated greenhouse in the Qatari desert will use condensation and evaporation tricks gleaned from the nose of a camel. Now, thanks in part to continuing innovations in nanoscale fabrication, manufacturers are
45 bringing an expanding array of products to market.

Biomimicry isn't itself a product but a process, drawing on natural organisms and processes in order to spark innovation. Organizations and even cities can look to ecosystems for inspiration, says Tim McGee, a biologist and member of Biomimicry 3.8, a Montana-based consultancy. In Lavasa—described as "India's first planned hill city"
50 by its developers, who hope to eventually build homes for more than 300,000 people there—the **guild** consulted with landscape architects. Thus the planting strategy included deciduous trees, forming a **canopy** to catch, and then reflect, through evaporation, nearly a third of the monsoon rain that hits it. That effect acts "like an engine that drives the monsoon inland," says McGee, which helps prevent drought there. The hydrody-
55 namically efficient shape of banyan tree leaves influenced the design of a better water-dispatching roof shingle, while water **divertment** systems were inspired by the ways harvester ants direct water away from their nests. The first Lavasa "town" has been completed, with four more projected to follow by 2020.

(655 words)

Vanderbilt, T. (2014, September). How biomimicry is inspiring human innovation. *Smithsonian Magazine.* Retrieved from http://www.smithsonianmag.com/science-nature/how-biomimicry-is-inspiring-human-innovation-17924040/#O9u2TdaUfme8uSWb.99

C. Indicate whether these statements are true or false, according to the text.

STATEMENTS	TRUE	FALSE
1 Human beings can learn from the results of natural selection.	☐	☐
2 Butterfly wings were the inspiration for a kind of airplane wing.	☐	☐
3 Butterfly colours are created by a type of electronic signals.	☐	☐
4 Velcro was developed by a Swiss engineer in 1955.	☐	☐
5 Trees and bones have structural properties that can be used in cars.	☐	☐
6 Nautilus shells are an inspiration for a greenhouse design.	☐	☐
7 The camel's nose is an example of biomimicry that is used in fans.	☐	☐
8 Lavasa is a planned city in India designed on biomimicry principles.	☐	☐

D. Explain the importance of the following terms to biomimicry.

TERMS	IMPORTANCE TO BIOMIMICRY
1 banyan trees	
2 carpenter ants	
3 deciduous trees	

FOCUS ON WRITING

Using Register and Tone

When you write, you use different language depending on who you are writing to, and why. For example, you would choose different words and different sentence structures in a casual e-mail to a friend than you would to a potential employer. These differences refer to *register* and *tone* and both describe the degree of formality in the language you use.

A. Read the information and consider some of the ways register and tone differ in formal and informal writing. Add examples of your own.

REGISTER AND TONE	IN INFORMAL WRITING	IN FORMAL WRITING
GREETING/ SALUTATION	casual greeting and first name or no name: *Hi Don,* or *Hi,*	*Dear* with title and last name: *Dear Dr. Pratt,*
VOCABULARY	more common words and slang, but avoids professional jargon: *cheap, very, lots of, kneecap, judge* _____ _____	subject-specific words and avoids slang, but may use professional jargon: *inexpensive, more, many, patella, bench* _____ _____

REGISTER AND TONE	IN INFORMAL WRITING	IN FORMAL WRITING
TRANSITION WORDS	simple words: *like, and, so, but, also*	complex words: *additionally, as a result, however, in addition, nevertheless*
PERSON	first and second person (subjective) more common: *I bought a 3D printer.*	third person (objective) more common: *One/The company will invest in a 3D printer.*
ACRONYMS, INITIALISMS AND CONTRACTED FORMS	short forms: *UN, NASA I'll, won't, don't*	full forms: *United Nations, National Aeronautical Space Administration, I will, will not, do not*
SENTENCE STRUCTURE	shortened incomplete sentences and/or simple sentences: *Coming to your office at 4.*	complete simple sentences and/or compound and complex sentences: *If you are free, my group will visit your office at 4:00 p.m.*

> Develop Your Vocabulary: Acronyms like "scuba" are pronounced like words; initialisms like "USA" are pronounced as separate letters. Learn the full forms of popular acronyms and initialisms.

B. Read this e-mail and highlight examples of formal writing that are mentioned in task A. Discuss with a partner.

> In an e-mail, "Cc" means Courtesy copy.

To:	dr.pratt@3dtech.com
Cc:	
Subject:	Advice on 3D printers

Dear Dr. Pratt,

I am writing to ask if you would be free to speak to two representatives from the Engineering Society (ES). The ES is considering the purchase of a three-dimensional (3D) printer for students to use for their projects and we would like your advice on the best 3D printer currently on the market.

Please let me know if you would be available and, if so, would a meeting at your office on Friday at 2:30 p.m. be convenient?

Yours sincerely,

Liz Jory, ES President

WARM-UP ASSIGNMENT
Write a Formal E-mail

Write a formal e-mail to your teacher asking for clarification on something in this chapter that interests you.

A. Choose a topic. For example, you might want to know how one of the organisms in Reading 2, task A (page 105) is used as a model for biomimicry, or if 3D printers used in fashion and food are the same machines used by hobbyists.

MY TOPIC: _____

B. Ask your teacher for approval of your choice of topic.

C. Follow the e-mail format you learned in Focus on Writing and use the paragraph format for the body of your message. Include a topic sentence that explains the reason you are writing. Ask two questions. Apply proper tone and register.

D. Write your e-mail. Refer to the Models Chapter (page 194) to see another example of a formal e-mail and to learn more about how to write one.

E. Share your e-mail with a partner and ask for feedback.

When you can choose your own topic, challenge yourself!

VOCABULARY BUILD 3

A. Below are words and phrases from the Academic Word List that you will find in Reading 3. Highlight the words you understand and then circle the words you use.

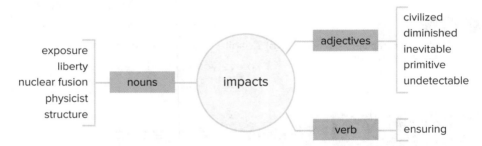

B. Fill in the blanks with the correct nouns to complete the sentences.

exposure	liberty	nuclear fusion	physicist	structure

1 A 3D printer can be used to build a small _____ such as a model of a building.

2 The _____ applied mathematical reasoning to understand the motorcycle engine.

3 Too much _____ to certain gases can hurt your lungs.

4 The discovery of _____ led to the creation of atomic bombs.

5 One important _____ we enjoy is freedom of speech.

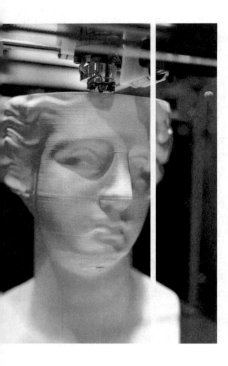

C. Choose the phrase that best completes each sentence. Key words are in bold.

① Many modern technologies seem **primitive** even though they _____.
   a) are just about to be released
   b) are the most popular ones in use
   c) were invented just a few years ago

② We would have a more **civilized** world if we had _____.
   a) fewer wars
   b) more civilians
   c) more prisons

③ **Ensuring** fairness is _____.
   a) not a university policy
   b) necessary on all exams
   c) not a university's concern

④ The need for electricity has **diminished** as _____.
   a) the overall demand has increased
   b) people use more and more appliances
   c) people use energy-efficient appliances

⑤ After 3D printers were invented, it was **inevitable** that _____.
   a) they may or may not have become popular
   b) someone would use one to create a weapon
   c) they would mostly be used in manufacturing

⑥ The poison in the food was **undetectable** _____.
   a) so everyone decided to try it
   b) despite hours spent searching for it
   c) so everyone knew it was there

My eLab ✎

Visit My eLab to complete Vocabulary Review exercises for this chapter.

READING ❸   **The Impact of Inventions**

Parents are often held responsible for the harmful actions of their children. Should inventors, in the same way, be responsible for their inventions? Most inventors do not—or cannot—always control how their inventions are used. Their aim is usually to simply discover and understand new things. This essay focuses on inventions and discoveries that unintentionally led to widespread harm.

A. Consider these three inventions. How have the computer, the skyscaper and the jet airplane each been put to both good and bad uses? Discuss with a partner.

B. Read the first paragraph of Reading 3. Based on what it says, what might you expect to read in the rest of the essay?

_____

_____

_____

C. While you read, take notes in the margins indicating the register and tone of the essay. Is it formal or informal? Is it objective or subjective? How does the tone compare with the other two readings in this chapter?

The Impact of Inventions

naive (adj.): lacking in wisdom

supersede (v.): take the place of something

wearing out (v.): outlasting

hydrogen bombs (n.): fusion weapons similar to atomic and nuclear bombs

nucleus (n.): central part of the atom

Many scientists and inventors are **naive** about the impact of their work. As a result, they assume their discoveries and inventions will only be used to improve the world. This has seldom been the case and the latest great invention, the three-dimensional (3D)
5 printer, seems to be on the same path.

Inventor Richard Gatling (1818–1903) followed this path of ignorance. During the American Civil War (1861–1865), he created the first machine gun: the Gatling gun. Most Civil War deaths did not occur on battlefields but from the wounds, illness and disease that followed. In 1877, Gatling wrote,

10   It occurred to me that if I could invent a machine—a gun—which could
        by its rapidity of fire, enable one man to do as much battle duty as a
        hundred, that it would, to a large extent **supersede** the necessity of
        large armies, and consequently exposure to battle and disease would
        be greatly diminished. (as quoted in Stephenson, 2012, p.184)

15 But the Gatling gun and other machine guns resulted in countless deaths. During the American Civil War, 646,392 died and during World War I (WWI, 1914–1919), more than thirty-seven million died, in part because of improved machine guns and other weapons (PBS, 2004). So-called civilized nations used machine guns to expand their empires; people with primitive weapons had no chance.

20 In 1903, Orville Wright (1871–1948) and his brother Wilber Wright (1867–1912) created the first successful powered plane. Like Gatling, they mistakenly believed their invention would lead to peace. Orville wrote a letter explaining his surprise at the airplane being used as a weapon, instead of just a tool to observe other armies:

        We thought governments would realize the impossibility of winning by
25   surprise attacks, and that no country would enter into war with another
        of equal size when it knew that it would have to win by simply **wearing
        out** the enemy. (letter to C.H. Hitchcock, June 21, 1917, n.p.)

In 1932, physicist Marcus Oliphant (1901–2000) helped discover the principles of nuclear fusion. During World War II (1939–1945), these principles led to the creation
30 of the atomic bomb. However, Oliphant said he was ignorant about the possibilities, "We had no idea whatever that this would one day be applied to make **hydrogen bombs**. Our curiosity was just curiosity about the structure of the **nucleus** of the atom" (IEEE Global History Network, 2013, para. 4).

Wright Brothers' Military Flyer, 1909

descendant (n.): one's child or other future relative

Orville Wright was still alive in 1945 when a **descendant** of his first airplane dropped
35 atomic bombs on Hiroshima and Nagasaki, Japan, leading to the deaths of at least
225,000 people (Asian American Studies Center, 2007). Regardless, he still held to
his belief that technology could solve more problems than it created. Orville wrote,
"I once thought the aeroplane would end wars. I now wonder whether the aeroplane
and the atomic bomb can do it" (as quoted in Tobin, 2003, p. 365).

40 The atomic bomb failed to end wars and now new technologies threaten death in
unusual ways. In 1983, inventor Chuck Hull (1939–) developed the first 3D printer.
Two years later, he commercialized the product and now dozens of different kinds of
3D printers have become available (Hickey, 2014). It was inevitable that one would
be used to create a weapon, in this case a plastic gun developed in 2013 that is largely
45 undetectable by airline security.

The gun's inventor, Cody Wilson (1988–), a University of Texas law student, claims
he invented the plastic gun as a way of ensuring personal liberty and freedom of
choice: "I'm seeing a world where technology says you can pretty much be able to
have whatever you want. It's not up to the political players any more" (as quoted in
50 Morelle, 2013, para. 17).

Essentially, anyone can now make a gun at home. How long will it be until 3D printed
weapons become a tool of mass murder? One research group suggests that 2040 is
a date that might combine the worst nightmares of Gatling, the Wright brothers and
Oliphant: "3D printers could be so advanced by 2040 they could create small
55 unmanned aircraft," (Press Association, para. 1). It takes no leap of imagination to
suggest that such craft could carry machine guns or nuclear weapons.

destined (adj.): certain to do or become something

The cycle of innocent inventions being turned into tools of death to the surprise of their inventors is an example of what philosopher George Santayana (1863–1952) observed as, "Those who don't know history are **destined** to repeat it." But another, 60 perhaps more appropriate piece of wisdom from Santayana is "Only the dead have seen the end of war."

(764 words)

References

Asian American Studies Center. (2007). Children of the atomic bomb. Retrieved from http://www.aasc.ucla.edu/cab/200708230009.html

Hickey, S. (2014, June 22). Chuck Hull: The father of 3d printing who shaped technology. *The Guardian*. Retrieved from http://www.theguardian.com/business/2014/jun/22/chuck-hull-father-3d-printing-shaped-technology

IEEE Global History Network. (2013). Mark Oliphant: Biography. Retrieved from http://www.ieeeghn.org/wiki/index.php/Mark_Oliphant

Morelle, R. (2013, May 6). Working gun made with 3d printer. *BBC News*. Retrieved from http://www.bbc.com/news/science-environment-22421185

PBS. (2004). WWI casualty and death tables. Retrieved from http://www.pbs.org/greatwar/resources/casdeath_pop.html

Press Association. (2014, July 6). 3d printer drones will take to skies by 2040, claim BAE scientists. *The Guardian*. Retrieved from http://www.theguardian.com/world/2014/jul/06/3d-printer-drones-2040-bae-futurist-aircraft

Stephenson, M. (2012). *The last full measure: How soldiers die in battle*. New York, NY: Random House.

Tobin, J. (2003). *To conquer the air: The Wright brothers and the great race for flight*. New York, NY: Simon & Schuster.

D. Use this timeline to write notes about the reading.

DATES	EVENTS	IMPACT
1861–1865	*American Civil War*	*646,392 died and many others wounded; introduction of the Gatling gun*
1903	*Wright brothers' first powered flight*	
1914–1919		
1932		
1939–1945		
1983		
2013	*Cody Wilson creates …*	
2040		

E. Evaluate each statement and decide if it supports the arguments. Choose a) or b).

STATEMENTS	STRONG OR WEAK ARGUMENTS
❶ Richard Gatling observed that most Civil War deaths did not occur on battlefields but from the wounds, illness and disease that followed.	a) Strong: convincing first-hand observation. b) Weak: it was only his observations at the time.
❷ During World War I, more than thirty-seven million died, in part because of improved machine guns and other weapons.	a) Strong: convincing statistical evidence. b) Weak: it doesn't say exactly how many more than thirty-seven million died.
❸ The Wright brothers thought governments would realize the impossibility of winning by surprise attacks.	a) Strong: the Wright brothers were well-known inventors. b) Weak: although from a primary source, this is just an opinion.
❹ Oliphant and team had no idea whatever that the principles of nuclear fusion would one day be applied to make hydrogen bombs.	a) Strong: convincing report from a primary source. b) Weak: Oliphant and team should have predicted the invention of the bomb.
❺ It was inevitable that a 3D printer would be used to create a weapon.	a) Strong: it has turned out that way. b) Weak: just opinion after the fact.
❻ Decisions to make guns using 3D printers are not up to the political players anymore.	a) Strong: sounds believable, even though it's just one person's opinion. b) Weak: doesn't define political players or explain why the decisions aren't theirs.
❼ 3D printers could be so advanced by 2040 that they could be used to create small unmanned aircraft.	a) Strong: it seems the natural way things will happen. b) Weak: the prediction is not backed by evidence.
❽ Those who don't know history are destined to repeat it.	a) Strong: people always make the same mistakes. b) Weak: a quote without support.

Academic
Survival Skill

Applying Critical Thinking Techniques

Critical thinking means questioning what you read, deciding whether the text contains reliable information and whether it presents a convincing argument. Critical thinking also means deciding if the information in the text is important to you or the task at hand.

Critical Thinking: One technique is to become "devil's advocate," which means taking the opposite point of view. This technique can help you spot flaws in an argument.

A. Apply critical thinking techniques to this paragraph. Then, complete the table by writing examples.

> Biomimicry is the latest of many ideas that everyone believes in but no one understands. Suddenly, businesses are eager to use biomimicry principles but don't know how to apply them to products. It's great to say that there is a natural solution to the problem of carbon dioxide pollution, but any such solution may have developed over billions of years. Yes, trees may be able to filter carbon dioxide and use it for food, but that fact doesn't mean we who work in the coal industry can quickly design an inexpensive machine to do the same.

TECHNIQUES	WHAT TO DO	EXAMPLE
CLASSIFY	Identify the type of writing. Is it formal or informal? Is it descriptive or persuasive, or a combination of something else?	The writing is *informal and persuasive*.
IDENTIFY BIAS	If the text is persuasive, decide if it is in favour of a particular point of view. If possible, identify how the writer might benefit in some way.	The bias is ...
QUESTION THE THESIS	Identify the main argument or arguments. Does the thesis present a new way of examining or explaining something?	The main argument is...
QUESTION SUPPORTING IDEAS	Does the thesis have supporting ideas along with examples and explanations?	One supporting idea is ...
QUESTION EVIDENCE	Are there references to support the idea? Is the evidence current and authoritative?	References ...
APPLY FINDINGS	Are the findings (conclusions) of the argument meaningful to you? Can you apply them to your existing knowledge or needs (e.g., in writing an essay)?	I (can/can't) apply the information to my existing knowledge or needs.

B. Write the skill you would use to critically evaluate each of these statements.

1. Everyone knows that an asteroid killed the dinosaurs. _____

2. As a bus driver, I know bus drivers should be paid more. _____

3. Callison and Quimby (1984) ask whether tiny dinosaurs were actually fully grown. _____

4. Teachers who are generally happy are also happy on the job. _____

C. Discuss each of the statements in task B with a partner. In terms of thinking critically about the statements, what questions might you have?

FINAL ASSIGNMENT
Write an E-mail Request for Information

Use what you learned in this chapter to write a formal request for information from one of the authors in the readings.

A. Choose a topic. Review the chapter to find one point of information that you would like to research in greater detail; for example, a topic related to printing blood vessels, measuring pressure with artificial knees or how biomimicry could be applied to something of personal interest to you in your field of study, or a sport or hobby.

MY TOPIC: _____

B. Speak with your teacher. Ask for approval of your choice of topic.

C. Using the e-mail format you learned in Focus on Writing, write your e-mail. Ask three questions. Use the paragraph format for the body of your message. Include a topic sentence that explains the reason you are writing and a closing sentence that summarizes your request. Or you could ask how you might find further information on the topic: books to read, websites to visit and people to consult.

D. Vary the sentence structure to include at least one example of each type: simple, compound and complex. Review Focus on Grammar on page 102. Ensure that your e-mail uses proper tone and register (see Focus on Writing, page 107). Refer to the Models Chapter (page 194) to see an example of a formal e-mail and to learn more about how to write one.

E. Proofread your e-mail. Then, share it with a partner and ask for feedback.

F. Make corrections and write a final copy.

How confident
are you?

Think about what you learned in this chapter. Use the table to decide what you should review.

I LEARNED ...	I AM CONFIDENT	I NEED TO REVIEW
vocabulary related to 3D printing and biomimicry;	☐	☐
how to evaluate research sources;	☐	☐
different sentence structures;	☐	☐
about register and tone in writing;	☐	☐
how to apply critical thinking techniques;	☐	☐
how to write formal e-mails.	☐	☐

VOCABULARY
Challenge

Think about the vocabulary and ideas in this chapter. Use these words to write two sentences that summarize 3D printing technology.

diminished	evident	evolve	functional	inevitable	procedure

_____

_____

_____

_____

_____

_____

Visit My eLab to build on what you learned.

CHAPTER 6

A View of the Future

Instead of bringing a travel guide on a trip to Paris, imagine using an augmented reality (AR) device. You can gaze through special AR glasses or point a phone: both overlay information on the object or place you are interested in. From your hotel room, your view of the Eiffel Tower prompts the AR device to supply notes on the Tower's history, ticket prices, elevator wait times, restaurant reviews and booking information. Looking at the streets, interactive maps guide you there.

What else in the world could AR help you learn?

In this chapter, you will

- learn vocabulary related to augmented reality and artificial intelligence;

- identify organizational patterns;

- use transitions to ensure unity and coherence;

- review the correct use of articles;

- paraphrase and summarize to avoid plagiarism;

- write summaries.

GEARING UP

A. Look at the photo and then answer the questions.

An example of how augmented reality (AR) could be used is overlaying dinosaur animation and information on a forest scene.

Source: *A Day Made of Glass.* (2014). Image provided by Corning Incorporated.

1 What advantages might an AR approach have over the same information in books? What disadvantages?

_____

_____

2 AR commonly labels maps with information about locations, including homes. How might this lead to privacy concerns?

_____

_____

3 Facial recognition software identifies people according to features on their face. Why might you want to use this technology? What disadvantages could result from others using it?

_____

_____

_____

4 Using AR, a doctor could overlay a picture of your X-ray on a recent injury. How could this be more helpful than simply holding an X-ray in one's hand?

_____

_____

B. Discuss the questions and your answers, first with a partner, then in a group.

Identifying Organizational Patterns

Being able to recognize organizational patterns in academic writing will help you understand and evaluate the text that is being presented. One way to spot a pattern is to look for commonly used signal words and phrases that are related to a particular organizational pattern. This same skill will also help you when you take notes. For example, if you recognize a chronological pattern, you can take notes on a timeline or on a Venn diagram when you see a compare and contrast pattern.

A. Read about organizational patterns and then choose the kind of information best suited for each pattern.

ORGANIZATIONAL PATTERNS	EXPLANATION	SIGNAL WORDS/PHRASES	KIND OF INFORMATION
CLASSIFICATION	Organizes text in relation to a group with shared characteristics; often used in definition paragraphs and essays.	*for example, for instance, defined as, classified as, part/group*	a) various AR technologies b) map of Canada c) description of oxygen
CHRONOLOGICAL	Arranges events according to when they occur in time.	*before, initially, then, after, first, second, third, ..., finally*	a) places in a town b) history of buildings c) future of bicycles
COMPARE AND CONTRAST	Discusses how two or more things are similar or different.	*same as, similarly, different than, as opposed to, instead of, however, compared with, although*	a) leader in AR b) leader's achievements c) one decision by a leader
CAUSE AND EFFECT	Shows the relationship between two or more things: the cause or causes and the resulting effect or effects.	*because, as a result, for this reason, this led to, consequently, may be due to*	a) directions to a fire b) history of painting c) how accidents happen
PROBLEM/ SOLUTION	Introduces a problem and then offers one or more solutions.	*the problem is, the question is, one solution/answer is*	a) Nobel Prize winners b) basic singing lessons c) how to avoid an illness

B. Read these excerpts. Which organizational pattern does each use?

ORGANIZATIONAL PATTERN

1 Augmented reality is hidden content, most commonly hidden behind marker images, that can be included in printed and film media, as long as the marker is displayed for a suitable length of time, in a steady position for an application to identify and analyze it. Depending on the content, the marker may have to remain visible.

_____

2 Augmented reality has its origins as early as the 1950s and has progressed with virtual reality since then, but its most significant advances have been since the mid 1990s.

_____

3 The idea of having a great deal of information available to you at anytime and in anyplace is inherently appealing in some ways but might be overwhelming in others.

_____

VOCABULARY BUILD 1

A. Below are words from the Academic Word List that you will find in Reading 1. Highlight the words you understand and then circle the words you use.

accessible
initial
potential
visible

adjectives

augmented reality

noun — simulation

verbs — enabling
indicating
superimposing

B. Choose the phrase that best completes each sentence. Key words are in bold.

1 By **superimposing** the engine diagram on the car engine, _____.

   a) it was easier to see what was missing

   b) the customer left a sticky mess

   c) it became impossible to start the car

2 A mobile phone is more **accessible** than a traditional phone _____.

   a) once you have given your friends your number

   b) as long as you remember to charge it

   c) because you can carry it around with you

3 The image became **visible** when _____.

   a) we looked away

   b) light shone on it

   c) shadows fell on it

4 After **indicating** her preference, she asked _____.

   a) which one she should choose

   b) the clerk to package her virtual glasses

   c) whether one was better than the other

C. Fill in the blanks with the correct words to complete the sentences.

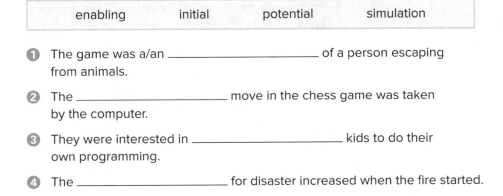

enabling	initial	potential	simulation

1 The game was a/an _____ of a person escaping from animals.

2 The _____ move in the chess game was taken by the computer.

3 They were interested in _____ kids to do their own programming.

4 The _____ for disaster increased when the fire started.

READING 1 | **Guide to Augmented Reality**

A Boeing 747 airplane contains more than four hundred kilometres of wiring connecting countless devices. When something goes wrong, carrying around heavy repair manuals can be a great challenge. In the early 1990s, Boeing engineers met this challenge by creating computer-screen glasses that overlay instructions and wiring diagrams onto the parts of the plane. One of the engineers, Thomas Caudell, was the first to call this "augmented reality."

A. An old proverb says, "Necessity is the mother of invention." What does this mean and how does it relate to augmented reality?

_____

_____

B. Augmented reality glasses have become controversial because of fears that users might be spying on others around them or recording images and videos. How might this differ from using a phone to do the same thing?

_____

_____

C. Reading 1 mixes organizational patterns. While you read, note in the margin the different patterns the writer uses. For example, the first paragraph uses classification.

Guide to Augmented Reality
What is AR?

rendered (adj.): drawn by a computer program

marker images (n.): graphics recognized by a computer for positioning purposes

AR is the process of superimposing digitally **rendered** images onto our real-world surroundings, giving a sense of an illusion or virtual reality. Recent developments
5 have made this technology accessible using a smartphone.

How is it used?

Augmented reality is hidden content, most commonly hidden behind **marker images**, that can be included in printed and film media, as long as the marker is displayed for a suitable length of time, in a steady position for an application to identify and
10 analyze it. Depending on the content, the marker may have to remain visible.

It is used more recently by advertisers where it is popular to create a 3D render of a product, such as a car or football boot, and trigger this as an overlay to a marker. This allows the consumer to see a 360-degree image (more or less; sometimes the base of the item can be tricky to view) of the product. Depending on the quality of
15 the augmentation, this can go as far as indicating the approximate size of the item, and allow the consumer to "wear" the item, as viewed through their phone.

Alternative set-ups include printing out a marker and holding it before a webcam attached to a computer. The image of the marker and the background as seen by the webcam is shown on screen, enabling the consumer to place the marker on places such
20 as the forehead (to create a mask) or move the marker to control a character in a game.

In some cases, a marker is not required at all to display augmented reality.

How does it work?

barcode image (n.): black and white graphic that alerts the computer or phone to display information

origins (n.): beginnings

CAD (n.): computer-aided design, used with 3D objects

mocked up (v.): drawn or created as a model

demographic (n.): particular group of people

Using a mobile application, a mobile phone's camera identifies and interprets a marker, often a black and white **barcode image**. The software analyzes the marker 25 and creates a virtual image overlay on the mobile phone's screen, tied to the position of the camera. This means the app works with the camera to interpret the angles and distance the mobile phone is away from the marker.

Due to the number of calculations a phone must do to render the image or model over the marker, often only smartphones are capable of supporting augmented reality 30 with any success. Phones need a camera, and if the data for the AR is not stored within the app, a good 3G Internet connection.

Background

Augmented reality has its **origins** as early as the 1950s and has progressed with virtual reality since then, but its most significant advances have been since the mid-1990s.

35 The technology has been around for many years, used in **CAD** programs for aircraft assembly and architecture, simulation, navigation, military and medical procedures. Complex tasks including assembly and maintenance can be simplified to assist in training and product prototypes can be **mocked up** without manufacturing.

Augmented reality has been proven very useful on a day-to-day basis when tied with 40 location-based technology. Several apps are available that will show consumers their nearest food outlets or subway transport stations when they raise the app and view their surroundings through the camera.

Their use in marketing is particularly appealing, as not only can additional, detailed content be put within a traditional 2D advert, [but] the results are interactive, cool, 45 engaging and due to the initial novelty—have high viral potential. Consumers react positively to fun, clever marketing, and brands become memorable.

The potential audience varies depending on the application of AR. Through a smartphone, it is limited to an audience with suitable handsets and those willing to download an app. With printing a marker for use with a webcam, it is limited to those willing 50 to follow through these steps, though this often opens a wide **demographic**, including children (printing an AR code on a cereal box to play a game, for instance).

conventional (adj.): what
is usually done

What is certain is that the smartphone population is rising, and with this, the level of processing power is too. More and more consumers
55 are carrying phones capable of displaying
augmented reality, and once an app is down-
loaded and they have scanned their first
code, they are far more receptive to future
appearances of a code—driven by curiosity.
60 As long as the resulting augmented content
remains engaging and innovative, consumers
will certainly adopt augmented reality as a
new and fun twist to **conventional** marketing
and services.   (713 words)

Onvert. (2014). What is augmented reality? Retrieved from http://onvert.com/guides/what-is-augmented-reality/

D. Based on your understanding of Reading 1, explain the following phrases.

1 augmented reality is hidden content: _____

_____

2 a 3D render of a product, such as a car: _____

_____

3 place the marker on places such as the forehead (to create a mask):

_____

_____

E. Write about the significance of each of these concepts to augmented reality.
Then, discuss with a partner.

1 interpret angles and distance: _____

_____

2 a good 3G connection: _____

_____

3 view their surroundings through the camera: _____

_____

4 AR on a cereal box: _____

_____

5 phones capable of displaying AR: _____

_____

F. According to Reading 1, AR and virtual reality applications have been used in the following areas. In a group, think of one or more examples for each and write them in the table.

TECHNOLOGY USED FOR ...	EXAMPLES
1 aircraft assembly	*AR can replace heavy manuals but also teach procedures of how to install different components.*
2 architecture	
3 navigation	
4 military purposes	
5 medical procedures	

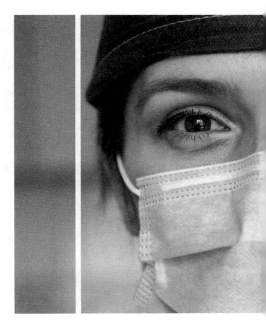

FOCUS ON WRITING

Ensuring Unity and Coherence

Sometimes you read a paragraph that doesn't seem to make sense. The writer begins on one topic then switches to an unrelated one. This demonstrates a lack of unity. *Unity* means that the parts of a paragraph need to fit together: a topic sentence with supporting sentences that directly relate to it. *Coherence* is achieved when the supporting sentences are organized in a logical way, and are connected.

A. Read this topic sentence. Then, choose those sentences that would give it unity as a paragraph.

> Having a great deal of information available anytime and anyplace is appealing in some ways but might be overwhelming in others.

☐ Although Alexander Graham Bell got a patent in 1876 for the first practical telephone, other researchers before him did important work.

☐ Arbitrary information might even be a dangerous distraction, particularly when you are engaged in other tasks, such as driving.

☐ In other cases, you might simply be exhausted at having advertisements intrude on your thoughts.

☐ Libraries have existed since ancient times and one of the great losses in history was the destruction of the Library of Alexandria, in Egypt.

☐ Sometimes people talk too much and it is not particularly interesting to anyone and can be damaging, particularly in a business context.

☐ While it could be helpful to know the best route to take or be warned of poor weather conditions, if such information takes your attention from the road, it might cause an accident.

Stuttgart City Library

B. Coherence can be achieved through techniques that connect ideas between sentences. Read the different techniques and then think of new examples that follow the patterns of the explanations.

TECHNIQUES	EXPLANATION	EXAMPLE
REPETITION	Key words or phrases from the first sentence are repeated in the next sentence.	AR is **new**. **New** ideas scare some people.
SYNONYMS	Synonyms (words with the same meaning) are used to connect similar ideas.	AR is **new**. **Original** ideas scare some people.
ANTONYMS	Antonyms (words with the opposite meaning) are used to show contrast.	AR is **new**. **Old** ideas comfort some people.
NUMBERING	Numbers (or letters) signal different points, usually within a sentence. Numbered items may be developed in following sentences or paragraphs.	There are three reasons AR scares Erica: **1)** loss of privacy; **2)** the expense; and **3)** the learning curve.
PRONOUNS	Pronouns refer to the noun in the previous sentence.	AR is new to **Conrad**. New ideas scare **him**.
TRANSITION WORDS	Signal words (see Focus on Reading, page 120) can be used to provide transitions between sentences.	AR is becoming popular. **For example**, the global AR market is expected to grow 132 percent in the next five years.

C. Read each sentence and then write a second one. Use a different technique to achieve coherence between each pair of sentences. Then, write the technique you used.

TECHNIQUE USED

1 Increasing and maintaining visitor numbers is a challenge for museums.

They are trying to identify new visitors in different ways.   pronoun

2 The system constantly adapts to a visitor's preferences.

_____   _____

_____

_____

3 Storytelling is certainly not absent from museums.

_____   _____

_____

_____

4 It's edutainment.

_____   _____

_____

_____

5 Interactive tours can be created by museum curators.

_____   _____

_____

_____

VOCABULARY BUILD 2

A. Below are words and phrases from the Academic Word List that you will find in Reading 2. Highlight the words you understand and then circle the words you use.

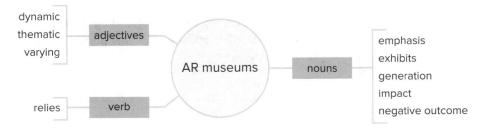

dynamic
thematic — adjectives
varying

AR museums

nouns — emphasis
exhibits
generation
impact
negative outcome

relies — verb

Hagia Sophia Museum, Istanbul

B. Fill in the blanks with the correct words to complete the paragraph.

emphasis	generation	impact	negative outcome	relies

The latest _____ of computer users has put a new

_____ on the everyday use of technology. The group

_____ on constant communication, so ownership of a mobile

phone has a major _____ on social life. The group also fails

to see any _____ from being available anytime, anyplace.

C. Highlight the word or phrase in parentheses that best completes each sentence. Key words are in bold.

① The museum's **thematic** approach meant dinosaurs were (separate from / included with) recent inventions.

② Their **varying** objections made up (one point / seven points) against the proposal.

③ The public **exhibits** were in the city's new (home / gallery).

④ The **dynamic** business leader was known for her great (energy / laziness).

READING ②

Tell Me a Story: Augmented Reality Technology in Museums

When you visit a museum, exhibits are explained at a level that allows everyone to understand them. In a setting such as a university class, students have similar educational backgrounds so explanations can be at the same level. But at a museum, everyone from young children to adult experts would see the same exhibits but might require different levels of explanation. By using augmented reality, museums are able to adapt to the needs of different visitors.

A. A natural history museum might display a whale skeleton along with a written explanation. How would augmented reality, using images, sound and video, allow a museum to do a better job in explaining a whale exhibit? Discuss in a group.

_____

_____

B. Read the first paragraph of Reading 2. Why do the writers reference a children's picture book to introduce ideas about museum exhibit presentation?

_____

_____

C. While you read, take notes on the techniques used to achieve cohesion in paragraphs 2, 4 and 10. For example, in paragraph 1, "the story" is a synonym technique to transition from "the children's book" and "although" is a contrast technique that indicates an exception.

Critical Thinking: Use topic sentences to help organize your note-taking. Ask yourself how the writer's ideas and evidence support each topic sentence.

Tell Me a Story: Augmented Reality Technology in Museums

premise (n.): basis of an argument

dedicated (adj.): devoted to a particular purpose

The Night at the Museum is a children's picture book by Milan Trenc—later, a Hollywood blockbuster—that told the story of a New York museum night watchman discovering, to his horror, that at night the building's exhibits came to life. The basic **premise** of
5 the story, however far-fetched, is that this dusty museum suddenly became even more interesting if the exhibits were telling their own story, although it did still involve being chased by a Tyrannosaurus Rex.

Museums around the world today face the challenge of increasing and maintaining visitor numbers, especially with younger audiences. A fall in visitors is seen by most
10 as a negative outcome, both financially and in terms of wider social and educational impact. It can happen due to a range of factors, but one of the most important is that museums can often find themselves competing with the products of the entertainment industry, which at its heart is in the business of telling a good story.

Don't get us wrong; storytelling is certainly not absent from museums. It's one of the
15 most important factors behind the emergence of the so-called new museology doctrine, which brought storytelling to the forefront of the museum experience through audio guides, video and by placing more emphasis on thematic organization and different perspectives, such as varying cultural interpretations.

Taking this trend further is the emergence of interactive digital storytelling, which
20 combines participation with automatic story generation and narration to focus in on making storytelling more personal and mobile. It's edutainment—something that both educates and entertains for a more engaging, adaptive and fundamentally enjoyable visitor experience.

One of the most successful real world uses of interactive digital storytelling is aug-
25 mented reality (AR), such as that employed to great effect at the British Museum. The technology transformed the museum experience for a child into a story puzzle using a **dedicated** tablet app. The app sets up a game, A Gift for Athena, which rewards the visitor for finding certain statues from their outlines by telling them more about the exhibit and directing them into the next stage of the game.

EU (n.): European Union

constitute (v.): make up part of a whole

ethnographic observations (n.): studies of peoples or cultures

IT (n.): information technology

30 The **EU**-funded Chess project (a shorter name for a much longer Cultural Heritage Experiences through Socio-personal interactions and Storytelling) takes digital storytelling much further and plans to make interactive content such as games and augmented reality available to the entire museum sector.

The project relies on visitor profiling, matching visitors to pre-determined "personas"
35 —which are designed as a representative description of the various people that **constitute** a given museum's visitor base. These are created through data from surveys, visitor studies and **ethnographic observations**. A given visitor is matched initially through a visitor survey to one of several representative personas, which in turn influences fundamentally the experience delivered by the Chess system.

40 Doing this makes the visitor experience non-linear. The system constantly adapts to a visitor's preferences. For example, if a visitor fails in a game or stays longer in front of certain artefacts, the system can adapt the storyline. It makes the experience more dynamic and relevant, so instead of sending the visitor to X exhibit, the system might instead choose to send you to Y exhibit, where you will get more information that's
45 relevant to what you've shown an interest in.

> The letters "X" and "Y" are used to illustrate two choices between similar types.

Interactive tours can be created by the museum curators themselves rather than by **IT** programmers. It gives museums the chance to constantly create new experiences to try to get people to visit more than once.

We've been testing the project at the Acropolis Museum in Athens, Greece,
50 where the team used the technology to bring a collection of architectural and sculptural remains to life by using AR to restore colours and lost features. Similarly, at the Cité de l'Espace in Toulouse, France, the project has been used to bring space flight and the layout of the universe to life.

…

55 Storytelling is at the heart of an engaging experience.

(651 words)

Ioannidis, Y., Balet, O., & Pandermalis, D. (2014, April 4). Tell me a story: Augmented reality technology in museums. *The Guardian*. Retrieved from http://www.theguardian.com/culture-professionals-network/culture-professionals-blog/2014/apr/04/story-augmented-reality-technology-museums

D. Scan the article and write information about each museum.

MUSEUMS	INFORMATION
NEW YORK MUSEUM	*According to the children's book, the building's exhibits came to life at night.*
BRITISH MUSEUM	
ACROPOLIS MUSEUM	
CITÉ DE L'ESPACE	

E. Indicate whether these statements are true or false, according to the text.

STATEMENTS	TRUE	FALSE
❶ Maintaining visitor numbers, especially with younger audiences, impacts finances and educational opportunities.	☐	☐
❷ Museums compete with the entertainment industry in terms of good storytelling.	☐	☐
❸ Digital storytelling makes museum experiences less personal and mobile.	☐	☐
❹ A Gift for Athena is a computer-based game to explore the museum.	☐	☐
❺ The Chess project profiles people to make the museum experience the same for everyone.	☐	☐
❻ Using the Chess project, interactive tours can only be created by IT programmers.	☐	☐
❼ The writers feel that storytelling is at the heart of an engaging experience.	☐	☐

FOCUS ON GRAMMAR

Articles

When you write, using the wrong articles can significantly alter your meaning. It's important to understand articles and use and interpret them correctly. Although there are only two kinds of articles, the definite article *the* and the indefinite article *a* (*an* in front of words beginning with *a, e, i, o, u* sounds), the rules are surprisingly complicated.

An article gives information about a noun. The definite article *the* indicates that one particular item is being discussed. Compare the use of *the* and *a* in these examples.

ARTICLE USE	EXPLANATION
The project is interesting.	*The* refers to a particular project, one that can be seen or is already known. In this case, it is a definite project, so the definite article is the term for *the project*.
A project is fun.	*A* changes the meaning of project, shifting it to a general category; the meaning is that all projects are fun. In this case, there is not a definite project being discussed, so the indefinite article is used.
I have **a** project.	In this case, *a* indicates the singular. You could also say, I have *one* project, which emphasizes the number, e.g., I do *not* have *two* projects.
I like projects.	In this case, no article is used because the noun *projects* is general. Adding an unnecessary article is a common grammatical error.
A student has **a** project. **The** student likes **the** project.	In this two-sentence passage, the indefinite *a* is used when describing the student and project the first time they appear, but as the discussion continues, the student and the project are known and therefore definite.
All of/Most of/None of/Some of **the** projects are finished.	The definite article follows *all of, most of, none of* and *some of*.
All/Most/No/Some projects are interesting.	With *all, most, no* and *some*, no article is necessary.

Fill in the blanks with the correct articles to complete the sentences: *a*, *an*, *the*, or *X* if no article is needed. Then, discuss your answers with a partner.

1. Your AR simulates _____ X-ray view of your car.

2. Imagine _____ day with augmented reality combined with _____ artificial intelligence.

3. On _____ way to work, you get _____ flat tire and have to fix _____ tire before anything else.

4. If such information takes your attention from the road, it might cause _____ accident.

5. In _____ future, if you could access _____ knowledge so easily you would be motivated to learn.

> Use what you learned about articles when you write assignments.

Academic
Survival Skill

Avoiding Plagiarism

Plagiarism is using the words or ideas of others as your own. In an academic context, plagiarism is a serious offence and can lead to being expelled from a course or an institution. In the digital age, it's easy to plagiarize (copy and paste) but it's also easy to detect plagiarism (copy and search). Three ways to avoid plagiarism are to quote with citations, to paraphrase and to summarize.

When you quote the words of another, the quote is set off by quotation marks, followed by an in-text citation, including a page or paragraph number and a full reference at the end. When you quote the ideas of another, the ideas are paraphrased, followed by an in-text citation and a full reference, but you do not need to provide a page or paragraph number.

This excerpt is from page 137 of this book, Beatty, K. (2015). *LEAP Intermediate: Reading and Writing*. Montreal: Pearson. Write it as a quote.

> It may be fine to recognize a friend, but would it be okay for facial recognition software to identify you to strangers, sharing details of your life? How much do you want a stranger to know about you?

IDENTITY PROTECTION

_____

_____

_____

_____

_____

_____

When you paraphrase, you are expressing another's words or ideas in your own words. A paraphrase is similar to a summary, but unlike a summary, it does not necessarily shorten the text. A paraphrase takes the original sentence, or sentences, and states them in another way, making the meaning clearer. When you paraphrase, do not simply use a series of synonyms to replace key words.

Read this excerpt from Reading 3 and then read the example paraphrase.

ORIGINAL EXCERPT	PARAPHRASE
Social media tools already track your preferences and use them to tailor **advertisements** on the websites you skim. But tracking your location and the things you glance at in the real world could be an enormous invasion of your and others' **privacy**.	Beatty (2015) writes that when you use **social media**, the Web notes your interests and delivers **advertisements** accordingly. If you use AR outside, the things you look at may also be noted. This might lead to **privacy** concerns.

As with a paraphrase, a summary conveys the words or ideas of another, but unlike a paraphrase, a summary is much shorter than the original text, approximately one quarter to one third the length of the original text. Before you summarize, read the entire text and try to understand its overall meaning. While you read, take notes or highlight key points. Then, write the summary in your own words. Keep a copy of the original, with references, and refer to it when you finish, ensuring that your summary has not accidentally plagiarized original content.

To write a summary, follow these steps.

- Skim the text to get a general understanding. Then, read it in detail, asking yourself *who, what, when, where, why* and *how* questions. Highlight key points.
- If the text is long, write notes on different sections, for example, sections with subheadings. Write notes in your own words. Keep in mind why the information is important or worth knowing, but don't add personal opinions.
- Ignore unimportant details.
- Write a topic sentence that explains what the summary is about. Include the author's name as well as the title and the source of the text.
- Review your summary to ensure you have achieved unity and coherence. Refer to Focus on Writing, page 125.

WARM-UP ASSIGNMENT
Write a Short Summary

Write a short summary of the article below, titled "HUDs in Your Future."

A. Read the article and, using information from Academic Survival Skill, write a summary. Ensure your summary avoids plagiarism by citing author, date and page number and by paraphrasing main ideas. Refer to the Models Chapter (page 195) to see an example of a summary and to learn more about how to write one.

HUDs in Your Future

One area where augmented reality has been used for some time is in heads up displays (HUDs) in military aircraft. The displays appear on the windshield before the pilot's eyes so there is no need to look down at a set of control indicators, such as those for speed, direction and fuel. For a jet fighter, this is important because a target, such as an enemy jet, may be in front of the pilot and moving quickly out of range in the space of a distracted glance.

Source: TechMASH. (2014). Car HUDs from Microvision. Photo Courtesy of MicroVision Incorporated.

The same technology is now being adapted for use in cars, allowing drivers to see fuel levels and speed as well as global positioning system (GPS) data mapping routes
10 to drive. The system can also indicate important traffic information: speed zones, stop signs or updates on roads that are closed or busy.

_____

McLean, M. (2015). *Focused forward: Heads up display applications* (p. 88). Halifax, NS: RareLeaf Press.

B. Compare summaries with a partner. Did you write a topic sentence that explains what the summary is about? Did you include the author's name as well as the title and the source of the text? Did you paraphrase the original text? Is your summary coherent?

C. Make corrections and write a final copy.

VOCABULARY BUILD 3

A. Below are words and phrases from the Academic Word List that you will find in Reading 3. Highlight the words you understand and then circle the words you use.

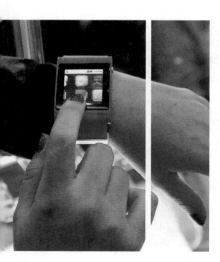

approximate
arbitrary
crucial
→ **adjectives** →

augmented reality + artificial intelligence

→ **nouns** →
artificial intelligence
paradigm shift

→ **verbs** →
allocate
orients

B. Write a definition for each of these words. For words you are not sure of, look at their context in the reading. Use a dictionary to check your answers.

❶ orients: _____

_____

❷ arbitrary: _____

_____

③ artificial intelligence: _____

_____

④ paradigm shift: _____

_____

C. Highlight the word or phrase in parentheses that best completes each sentence. Key words are in bold.

① The **approximate** time she arrived was (12:01 a.m. / around midnight).

② The **crucial** decision they had to make was whether or not to (go to university / eat lunch).

③ It was the manager's job to **allocate** enough time for (sleep / the meeting).

D. VOCABULARY EXTENSION: Like augmented reality, the phrases *artificial intelligence* and *paradigm shift* are collocations—commonly associated words. Use these words to construct pairs of words that naturally go together. Use each word only once. Check your answers in Reading 3.

arrival	frequency	information	radio	speech	time
commands	identity	list	shopping	theft	weather

My eLab ✎

Visit My eLab to complete Vocabulary Review exercises for this chapter.

① ___*shopping list*___   ④ _____

② _____   ⑤ _____

③ _____   ⑥ _____

READING ③   AR + AI = New Life

❗ *Develop Your Vocabulary: Keep a list of short forms (acronyms and initialisms) and their meanings. Review them regularly until memorized.*

Like many other inventions, AR was predicted in science fiction. After finishing *The Wizard of Oz*, Frank L. Baum (1856–1919), in 1901, wrote a novel about a Demon of Electricity who gives a boy a pair of glasses that he explains will overlay symbols for the qualities of anyone the boy looks at: G for good, E for evil, W for wise and so on. Today, we would call this technology *facial recognition software*. Although we can't yet use technology to measure people's characters, we can overlay Web-based information about them.

A. In Baum's story, the boy who receives the glasses decides not to use them to examine his family members, fearing the glasses might reveal qualities that go against the goodness he sees in his loved ones. What message does this story send about augmented reality?

_____

_____

B. Reading 3 begins with a fictional day in which one person uses AR and AI extensively. Discuss with a partner how you each might use AR and AI on a typical day.

C. While you read, note the organizational pattern in the complete text, as well as in each paragraph.

AR + AI = New Life

Imagine a day with augmented reality (AR) combined with artificial intelligence (AI). You wake up and immediately put on AR glasses that show a ghostly image of your schedule. A global positioning system (GPS) sensor recognizes your window and
5 overlays the day's crucial weather information. It's going to be cool and rainy. As you decide what to wear, miniature radio frequency identification tags (RFID) embedded in your clothes work with your AI to transmit information about sales at two of your favourite stores. As you decide what to have for breakfast, your glasses scan barcode images on your cereal package and milk container and list calories and other nutri-
10 tional information. The milk is almost past its shelf life so your AI program asks if you want to add milk to your shopping list. "Yes." The AI in your glasses recognizes speech commands.

It is time to go to work but you are unsure whether to take your car or allocate extra time for the bus. A **glance** at your bus pass alerts your AI to consult with your calendar
15 and local road maps and estimate your approximate arrival time. Your AI discovers your bus has broken down so you decide to take the car. But, on the way to work, you get a flat tire and have to fix it. You have never done this before but your AR glasses see the tire and the AI program recognizes that it is flat. Your AR simulates an X-ray view of your car so you can see the location of the spare tire and tools. A
20 short Web video lets you begin the tire replacement process and soon you arrive at work. Along the way, the AI program orients you to the best route to take but does not display sales at the stores you pass because your AI recognizes you are late.

Arriving at work, you see a colleague and the AI's facial recognition program tells you that not only has your friend been promoted recently but also today is her
25 birthday. You congratulate her and suggest lunch to celebrate. Your AI hears the word *lunch* and explores price and location parameters to display local restaurant sugges-tions. You agree on a place and as you walk to your desk, your AR glasses are already displaying your work e-mails.

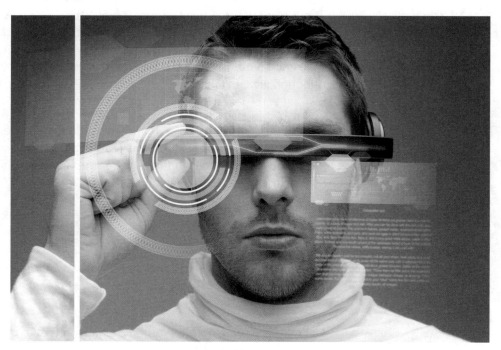

glance (v.): look quickly

barriers (n.): obstacles that prevent movement or access

information overload (n.): exposure to too much information

intrude (v.): enter uninvited or unwelcome

invasion (n.): entry and attack on another's area

identity theft (n.): illegal use of another person's personal information

hacked (v.): access another's computer without permission

This start of an AR and AI-enabled day is not all
30 science fiction. Many of these ideas are already
in use and some are likely to become common-
place in coming years (Bonsor, 2014; Hill, 2014;
Widder, 2014). But, as with any technology,
barriers stand in the way including **information**
35 **overload**, privacy and security.

The idea of having a great deal of information
available to you anytime and anyplace is inherently appealing in some ways but might be overwhelming in others. Arbitrary information might
40 even be a dangerous distraction, particularly
when you are engaged in other tasks, such as
driving. While it could be helpful to know the best
route to take or be warned of poor weather conditions, if such information takes your attention
45 from the road, it might cause an accident. In
other cases, you might simply be exhausted at
having advertisements **intrude** on your thoughts.

Social media tools already track your preferences
and use them to tailor advertisements on web-
50 sites you skim. But tracking your location and the things you glance at in the real
world could be an enormous **invasion** of your and others' privacy. It may be fine to
recognize a friend, but would it be okay for facial recognition software to identify you
to strangers, sharing details of your life? How much do you want a stranger to know
about you?

55 These questions are particularly important in terms of security. If your face can be
matched to your home or place of work, thieves not only know where you are but
might also be able to engage in **identity theft**, falsely making purchases using your
financial information. What if such AI and AR systems are **hacked** and trusting individuals given false and dangerous travel information?

60 Samuel Johnson (1709–1784) described two kinds of knowledge, knowing something
or knowing where you could find information about it. In the future, if you can access
knowledge so easily, will you be motivated to learn and to think and to remember?

What is without question is that an inevitable combination of AI and AR will create
a paradigm shift that will disrupt your life from the moment you wake until the
65 moment you fall asleep. (765 words)

References

Bonsor, K. (2014). How augmented reality works. *How Stuff Works*. Retrieved from http://computer.
howstuffworks.com/augmented-reality.htm

Hill, S. (2014, March 15). Get past the gimmicks and gaze upon the future of augmented reality apps.
Digital Trends. Retrieved from http://www.digitaltrends.com/mobile/future-ar-mobile/#ixzz
376wQUWz6

Widder, B. (2014, March 14). Best augmented reality apps. *Digital Trends*. Retrieved from http://
www.igitaltrends.com/mobile/best-augmented-reality-apps/#!bcOjV0

D. Read the events and predict when they are likely to happen. Write the numbers on the timeline. Then, discuss in a group.

NOW   IN A YEAR   IN FIVE YEARS   IN TEN YEARS   IN A CENTURY   NEVER

1   AI adds items to your shopping list.

2   AI makes suggestions for your daily travel plans.

3   AR programs scan barcode images on your food packages.

4   AR/AI gives X-ray views of your car and other appliances.

5   Facial recognition software provides information about friends and colleagues.

6   GPS-based weather reports are available for your exact location.

7   Most people wear AR glasses.

8   RFID tags report on store sales.

9   False travel instructions cause accidents.

10   Thieves steal AR and AI data.

E. Reading 3 ends with the suggestion that "the inevitable combination of AI and AR will create a paradigm shift that will disrupt your life from the moment you wake until the moment you fall asleep." In what ways might artificial intelligence and augmented reality become bigger parts of your life? Discuss in a group.

FINAL ASSIGNMENT
Write a Summary

Use what you learned in this chapter to write a summary of one of the readings.

A. Choose which reading you will summarize.

☐ Reading 1 Guide to Augmented Reality

☐ Reading 2 Tell Me a Story: Augmented Reality Technology in Museums

☐ Reading 3 AR + AI = New Life

B. Review the reading and its exercises.

C. Follow the steps for summarizing found in Academic Survival Skill on page 132.

D. Write your summary. Paraphrase at least two important points and give in-text citations. Refer to the Models Chapter (page 195) to see an example of a summary and to learn more about how to write one.

E. Proofread your summary. Make sure your paragraphs are unified and coherent. Check your use of articles. Then, share your summary with a partner for feedback.

F. Make corrections and write a final copy.

How confident
are you?

Think about what you learned in this chapter. Use the table to decide what you should review.

I LEARNED ...	I AM CONFIDENT	I NEED TO REVIEW
vocabulary related to augmented reality and artificial intelligence;	☐	☐
organizational patterns in texts;	☐	☐
transitions to ensure unity and coherence;	☐	☐
the correct use of articles;	☐	☐
how to paraphrase and summarize avoid plagiarism;	☐	☐
how to write summaries.	☐	☐

VOCABULARY
Challenge

Think about the vocabulary and ideas in this chapter. Use these words to write two sentences that summarize the future of augmented reality.

allocate	approximate	impact	potential	relies	simulation

_____

_____

_____

_____

_____

Visit My eLab to build on what you learned.

CHAPTER 7

Education for All

Many people enter the workforce without a college or university degree but, increasingly, those who attend academic institutions are finding that they need not just one but two degrees to get the best jobs. These students either extend the years they spend at school or find alternative programs to complete a second degree while they work. As has always been the case, some people study purely for personal interest, without intending to pursue a job in the field. All of this is creating opportunities for online education providers.

What would you like to study for your own interest?

In this chapter,
you will

- learn vocabulary related to technology-enhanced education;

- interpret visual elements;

- review pronoun-antecedent agreement;

- learn steps in a process;

- explore ways to work in a group;

- write a process paragraph and give a presentation.

GEARING UP

A. Look at the map and then answer the questions.

Territory size by the proportion of those enrolled in tertiary education

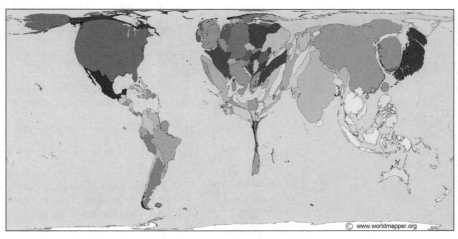

Source: Worldmapper. (2014). *Tertiary Education*. Retrieved from http://www.worldmapper.org/
display.php?selected=203 © Sasi Group (University of Sheffield) and Mark Newman (University of Michigan).

1 Name three countries that are well represented in terms of tertiary
(i.e., college level) education. Why is this so?

_____

_____

2 Which parts of the world are poorly represented in terms of tertiary
education?

_____

_____

3 How might technology be used to create educational opportunities
in parts of the world where such opportunities are most needed?

_____

_____

B. Discuss the questions and your answers, first with a partner, then in a group.

Interpreting Visual Elements

Reading refers to more than interpreting text. You also interpret various visual elements, including charts, graphs and tables. You have already encountered mind maps that show relationships between ideas, timelines that record events over time, and Venn diagrams that reveal what different ideas have in common. Other visual elements help explain different ideas and relationships.

A. Read the information in the table. Write an example of a kind of data commonly reported with each visual element. Then, discuss with a partner.

VISUAL ELEMENTS	EXPLANATION AND PURPOSE
BAR CHART	Bar charts illustrate comparative amounts: display numerical data in vertical or horizontal bars with lengths proportional to amounts. Example: *money budgeted for education in different countries*
FLOW CHART	Flow charts show a sequence of related events and consequences connected by lines and/or arrows. Example: _____
GANTT CHART	Gantt charts schedule project tasks on a timeline that shows where tasks start and stop and how they overlap other tasks. Example: _____
ILLUSTRATION	Illustrations are pictures or diagrams that help explain or demonstrate ideas in a text. Illustrations are less likely to be based on numerical data. Example: _____
LINE GRAPH	Line graphs connect data points that represent changes in amounts over time between two or more factors. Example: _____
MAP	Maps show geographical information and symbols (usually explained in a legend) that highlight how certain features are distributed. Example: _____
PIE CHART	Pie charts are circles divided into sections that represent amounts that are relative percentages of the whole. Example: _____

B. Which visual element would you use to represent each kind of information?

① number of female versus male university students entering college each year for ten years

_____

② current distribution of universities in South America

_____

③ increase in spending on computers and phones over the last ten years

_____

④ steps involved in enrolling in several college programs

_____

⑤ comparison of several features of two online learning courses

_____

⑥ time necessary for students to complete different jobs to finish a project

_____

VOCABULARY BUILD 1

A. Below are words from the Academic Word List that you will find in Reading 1. Highlight the words you understand and then circle the words you use.

ignored
utilizes — **verbs**

Massive Open Online Course (MOOC) — **nouns** — diversity retention trend

consistent
reliable — **adjectives**

B. Draw an arrow (↓) to indicate where in each sentence the word in parentheses should be placed.

① (ignored) The student the party invitation to finish her project instead.

② (trend) A recent has seen students using only computers to take notes in class.

③ (retention) Reading appears to be higher with paper books than with e-books.

C. Choose the phrase that best completes the sentence. Key words are in bold.

① A scientist **utilizes** a variety of _____ the spread of viruses.

a) ways to encourage

b) books to ignore

c) tools to investigate

② By promoting **diversity** in the workplace, governments _____.

a) can restrict the number of job applicants

b) encourage the best people to get jobs

c) frequently ignore the contributions of others

③ In order to be **consistent**, the teacher _____.

a) marked all the mid-term exams in the same way

b) developed a different approach for each student

c) applied a variety of approaches when marking

④ The computer was not **reliable** _____.

a) so everyone bought one

b) and was replaced

c) but only when used

READING ❶

To Adapt MOOCs, or Not? That Is No Longer the Question

A Massive Open Online Course (MOOC) is another way of teaching and learning. Although there are different forms, the basic idea involves professors recording a set of lectures and setting discussion questions and computer-based tests. Students watch the lectures, participate in discussion forums with other students, and then complete the automatically marked tests or peer mark assignments, without any contact with the professor. Students are not given traditional university credit, in part because professors cannot guarantee that the student writing the test is the same student who took the course.

A. One commercial MOOC provider, Coursera, approached Princeton University professor Mitchell Duneier about licencing his course so other colleges could use the content to save money. Why do you think he refused?

_____

_____

_____

_____

B. According to Yvonne Belanger (2012), although many students sign up for MOOCs, a surprising number fail to complete their studies. Look at the student participation numbers for a Duke University course on bioelectricity and then discuss with a partner why the completion rate might be so low.

STUDENTS WHO ...	NUMBER
enrolled	12,461
watched a video	7593
answered at least one question correctly on both week 1 quizzes	1267
attempted the final exam	358
passed, earning a certificate	313

Reference

Belanger, Y. (2012, December 4). Duke's first MOOC: A very preliminary report. Duke Center for Instructional Technology. Retrieved from http://cit.duke.edu/blog/2012/12/bioelectricity-preliminary-report/

C. While you read, highlight information that could be represented using a visual element. Indicate which visual element would be the most suitable.

To Adapt MOOCs, or Not? That Is No Longer the Question

Online education is certainly not a new approach for learning and teaching in globally disparate environments; it is an approach that has been steadily evolving for years. Massive Open Online Courses (MOOCs) are a logical product of this evolution. Online
5 course offerings are one of the most effective and efficient delivery methods for contents and skills globally. There are many commonsense advantages to the online course approach, including the wide flavour of degree programs and classes offered, flexible study times and the ability for students to balance between a career and education. Although the online movement is growing dramatically, leading to more
10 creative philosophies such as MOOCs, it cannot be considered a true revolution. Yet it cannot be ignored for the simple reason that it promotes sharing information worldwide and has created many opportunities for teaching and learning in a variety of disciplines [1, 19, 20, 21].

According to a recent worldwide survey, the adoption of MOOCs is on the rise [2, 3].
15 Here are a few important responses to the trend that should cause universities to seriously pay attention to MOOCs:

- 90 percent of schools offer or plan to offer online courses in the next three years —74 percent offer them today.

- 2013—Only 13 percent of schools offer MOOC; but 43 percent plan to offer MOOCs
20 by 2016.

- Only 44 percent of schools are planning to offer MOOC credits.

- 83 percent of schools would consider joining an online education group such as edX, Coursera or Udacity.

- 67 percent of schools believe that MOOCs will never replace traditional, resi-
25 dential classes; 5 percent said yes within five years [quoted directly from the survey results 3].

elite (adj.): highest level group

ego (n.): sense of self-esteem

intimidating (adj.): frightening or worrying

boon (n.): something helpful

anecdotal (adj.): based on personal experience

magnitude (n.): great size or extent

Thus, "To adopt MOOCs or not?" is no longer a question. It is a logical outcome of the ongoing evolution of distance learning.

…

30 Advantages and disadvantages

1. *Motivation.* MOOCs currently and generally are developed by **elite** universities using prominent professors [5]. The consequences of this approach are two-fold: (i) it serves as a great global marketing technique for universities and (ii) provides opportunities for faculty involved to sell course materials, textbooks and other 35 related items. On the other hand, student motivation to take these types of courses includes curiosity or getting certificates from the elite universities, boosting their **ego** and possibly their resumes.

2. *Enormous enrollment.* MOOCs have the potential to engage a large number of students—thousands—to take a single course. For instance, Stanford's course on 40 artificial intelligence, taught by two "celebrity professors," attracted 150,000 students. The class size may be **intimidating** to instructors, and the common tasks of regular interaction and evaluation are almost impossible; however, a recent report demonstrates the massiveness of MOOCs is a net **boon**, because it can energize students and faculty experiences [19, 20].

45 3. *Retention.* One of the major challenges of MOOCs is drop rate [9]. Since students do not invest any financial resources, it is easy for them to drop a course at any time without any of the consequences that they would have faced with traditional courses. Courses commonly only have a 10–20 percent completion rate [7, 22]—a few **anecdotal** reports denote as low as 2 percent completion rate.

50 4. *Diversity and disparity.* Students who are taking MOOC courses inherently represent wider and larger diversity compared with traditional structured curriculum courses. MOOCs experience a wider variety of elements such as background education, specific knowledge and skills, just to list a few. While like the traditional online courses, students geographically present disparity, naturally the **magnitude** is much 55 larger with the MOOCs offerings [20].

5. *Interaction and feedback.* Almost no one in a MOOC receives individual interaction or attention from an expert. Lack of consistent review and grading system further weakens the already non-existent interaction, which ultimately provides unacceptable feedback compared with traditional learning [8]. Generally, the evaluation of 60 students' work utilizes guided peer assessment, which, in turn, opens up new safety and privacy issues [19].

…

6. *Success rate.* While thousands enroll for the MOOC courses, the completion rate is extremely low; this makes it challenging to determine whether MOOCs are success-65 ful [5, 7]. Studies report completion rates of between 10 percent and 20 percent (80–90 percent non-completion rate), and an even smaller rate of students actually receive certificates. It must be noted that "completion" is different from "learning," and yet there are no reliable data to support the MOOCs learning outcomes.

70 While MOOCs are in their infancy and need resources and time to evolve into a fully effective and efficient educational platform, their potential and movement cannot be ignored.

(740 words)

References

[1] Martin, F.G., Will massive open online courses change how we teach? *Communications of the ACM*, August 2012, 55(8), 26–28.

[2] Vihavainen, A., Luukkainen, M., Kurhila, J., Multi-faceted Support for MOOC in Programming, *ACM Joint Conference SIGITE/RIIT,* Canada, Alberta, 2012.

[3] Afshar, V., Adoption of Massive Open Online Courses [Worldwide Survey], Retrieved on June 20, 2013: http://www.huffingtonpost.com/vala-afshar/infographic-adoption-of-m_b_3303789.html

[5] Sahami, M., Martin, F. G., Guzdial, M., Parlante, N., The Revolution Will Be Televised: Perspectives on Massive Open Online Education, *ACM-SIGCSE'13*, Denver, Colorado, USA, March 2013, 457–458.

[7] Malan, D.J., Implementing A Massive Open Online Course (MOOC), *Tutorial Presentation, Journal of Computing Sciences in Colleges*, June 2013, 28(6), 136–137.

[8] Carlson, R., Assessing Your Students: Testing in the Online Course, Syllabus, 12(7), 16–18, 2000.

[9] To MOOC or Not to MOOC? What's In It For Me? Retrieved on June 20, 2013: http://edwired.org/2013/05/07/to-mooc-or-not-to-mooc-whats-in-it-for-me/

[19] Head, K., Massive Open Online Adventure, The Digital Campus-Chronicle of Higher Education, Retrieved on June 18, 2013: http://chronicle.com/article/Massive-Open-Online-Adventure/138803/

[20] Roth, M., My modern experience teaching at MOOC, Retrieved on June 20, 2013: http://chronicle.com/article/My-Modern-MOOC-Experience/138781/

[21] The Digital Campus 2013, Major Players in the MOOC Universe, *The Chronicle of Higher Education*, June 22, 2013. http://chronicle.com/article/The-Major-Players-in-the-MOOC/138817/ MOOC Universe

[22] MOOC Completion Rates: The Data. Retrieved on June20, 2013: http://www.katyjordan.com/MOOCproject.html

North, S.M., Richardson, R., & North, M.M. (2014). To adapt MOOCs, or not? That is no longer the question. *Universal Journal of Educational Research, 2*(1), 69–72. doi: 10.13189/ujer.2014.020108

D. Answer the questions and then compare answers with your partner.

1. What do the writers believe are the advantages of online learning?

_____

_____

2. Why do the writers feel there is no question that MOOCs will be adopted?

_____

_____

3. When MOOCs are free, how can universities make money from them?

_____

_____

4. MOOC courses are often not accepted as credit courses because students cannot be properly assessed. What problems with assessment do the writers point out?

_____

_____

E. Write sentences to explain the significance of each number.

1 150,000 _____

_____

_____

2 2 percent _____

_____

_____

3 43 percent _____

_____

_____

4 5 percent _____

_____

_____

5 between 10 percent and 20 percent _____

_____

_____

FOCUS ON GRAMMAR

Pronoun-Antecedent Agreement

When you read a text, notice when a pronoun takes the place of a noun. The most common pronouns are personal pronouns and can replace the subject or the object of a sentence. The noun to which a pronoun refers is called the *antecedent*. Pronoun and antecedent must agree in gender (male, female or neutral), case (subject, object or possessive) and number (singular or plural).

A. Look at the table and fill in the missing pronouns.

	SUBJECT	OBJECT	POSSESSIVE ADJECTIVES	POSSESSIVE PRONOUNS
first person singular	I		my	mine
second person singular		you	your	yours
third person singular	he/she/it	him/her/it	his/_____ /its	his/hers/its
first person plural	we	us		ours
second person plural	you	you	your	
third person plural	they		their	theirs

Note: two singular subjects connected by a conjunction are treated as plural. The teacher **and** the student wrote **their** ideas on the board.

B. Highlight the pronoun in parentheses that best completes each sentence.

1. John found (my / me / mine) book and put (its / it / us) on (you / your / yours) desk.

2. People freely give (they / them / their) time and expertise to share what (he / they / them) know.

3. When students solve problems, (our / they / us) are rewarded with harder problems.

4. The just-in-time learning model implies (you / me / them) can wait to learn something until just before (us / you / their) need to use (them / it / theirs).

5. Millions experience Internet-based learning in informal ways when (we / they / us) use online tutorial videos.

Indefinite pronouns

An indefinite pronoun does not refer to any person or thing in particular. Indefinite pronouns can be singular or plural, or both. Plural indefinite pronouns include: *several, both, few* and *many*. Singular indefinite pronouns include: *anybody, anyone, everybody, everyone, no one, nobody, somebody, someone, either, neither.*

Gender

Although we consider it sexist, *his* and *he* are often used in situations where the gender might be either male or female.

Every girl and boy should pick up **his** book and decide where **he** can keep it.

Male and female pronouns can be used to avoid offence but can sound awkward, and the traditional order of pronouns (his/her and he/she) can also appear sexist.

Every girl and boy should pick up **his** or **her** book and decide where **he** or **she** can keep it.

Find ways to avoid gender-biased writing. Change *his* or *her* to *a* if no meaning is lost. Note changes in the pronouns as well as the plural of some nouns.

Students should pick up **their** book**s** and decide where **they** can keep **them**.

C. Rewrite these sentences to make them gender-neutral. Change pronouns and make nouns plural where necessary.

1. Each classmate can sign his name to join the debate team.

   _____

   _____

2. Everybody should choose his seat at the table.

   _____

   _____

3. Each student should write his name.

   _____

   _____

Use what you learned about pronoun-antecedent agreement when you write assignments.

My eLab

Visit My eLab Documents to review other types of pronouns: demonstrative, interrogative, relative, reflexive and intensive.

Develop Your Vocabulary: Phrases like "military-industrial machine" are compound nouns whose meaning is unclear from the individual words. Look for definitions in a dictionary.

A. Below are words and phrases from the Academic Word List that you will find in Reading 2. Highlight the words you understand and then circle the words you use.

conducted
ensure
merges
philosophized
transforming
→ **verbs** → self-organized learning environment (SOLE)

nouns →
implications
military-industrial machine
resourcefulness

adjectives →
contemporary
unmediated

B. Fill in the blanks with the correct verbs to complete the sentences.

❶ A new educational model _____ technology with students' natural creativity.

❷ Just as computers once did, mobile phones are _____ educational opportunities.

❸ Experiments have been _____ to find the best ways to help students remember.

❹ It is important to _____ that students' needs are met, regardless of teaching style.

❺ Many have _____ about the best way to teach, but in the end it may be personal.

C. Highlight the word or phrase in parentheses that best completes each sentence. Key words are in bold.

❶ Preschool education may be largely **unmediated** if parents (make / don't make) decisions about their child's learning.

❷ **Implications** of creating a new school curriculum are likely to be (serious / trivial).

❸ **Contemporary** thinking on education tends to focus on (innovations / traditions).

❹ The **military-industrial machine** suggests that armies and large companies have (no / many) common goals.

❺ Poor nations must rely on **resourcefulness** to overcome what they cannot (afford / waste) in their schools.

READING ❷ The SOLE of a Student

SOLE = Self-Organized Learning Environment

A *polymath* is someone with knowledge in a variety of areas. Sugata Mitra has been called a polymath because of his work in adding to the understanding of molecules, semiconductors, sense organs, computer networking and Alzheimer's disease. His work has led him to an interest in what he calls "minimally-invasive education," where students are largely left to learn by themselves.

A. You have learned many things on your own or without a formal teacher. Write a list and compare it with a partner's list. Which techniques have you used to learn on your own?

B. Read this excerpt from Reading 2 and consider the approach used in the experiment. Then, write three benefits and three problems on a separate page. Discuss your answers in a group.

> I conducted an experiment called the "hole in the wall." By installing Internet-equipped computers in poor Indian villages and then watching how children interacted with them, unmediated, I first glimpsed the power of the cloud [i.e., the Internet]. Groups of street children learned to use computers and the Internet by themselves, with little or no knowledge of English and never having seen a computer before. Then they started instinctually teaching one another.

C. In the first paragraph of Reading 2, Mitra sets up the ideas that follow by asking "How do we spark creativity, curiosity and wonder in children?" While you read, take notes on how Mitra tries to answer that question in each paragraph and in the flow chart.

The SOLE of a Student

pedagogical (adj.): educational

zenith (n.): top point or peak

Victorians (n): people who lived under Queen Victoria's rule (1837–1901)

churned (v.): mixed

robust (adj.): strong

relics (n.): objects from the past

From Plato to Aurobindo, from Vygotsky to Montessori, centuries of educational thinking have vigorously debated a central **pedagogical** question: how do we spark creativity, curiosity and wonder in children? But those who philosophized pre-
5 Google were prevented from wondering just how the Internet might influence the contemporary answer to this age-old question. Today, we can and must; a generation that has not known a world without vast global and online connectivity demands it of us.

But first, a bit of history: to keep the world's military-industrial machine running
10 at the **zenith** of the British Empire, **Victorians** assembled an education system to

mass-produce workers with identical skills. Plucked from the classroom and plugged instantly into the system, citizens were **churned** through an edu-
15 cational factory engineered for maximum productivity.

Like most things designed by the Victorians, it was a **robust** system. It worked. Schools, in a sense, manufac-
20 tured generations of workers for an industrial age.

But what got us here won't get us there. Schools today are the product of an expired age; standardized cur-
25 ricula, outdated pedagogy and cookie cutter assessments are **relics** of an earlier time. Schools still operate as if

salient (adj.): most noticeable

democratizing (adj.): making equal for all

agency (n.): action or intervention

all knowledge is contained in books, and as if the **salient** points in books must be stored in each human brain—to be used when needed. The political and financial
30 powers controlling schools decide what these salient points are. Schools ensure their storage and retrieval. Students are rewarded for memorization, not imagination or resourcefulness.

Today we're seeing institutions—banking, the stock exchange, entertainment, news-papers, even health care—capture and share knowledge through strings of zeros and
35 ones inside the evolving Internet ... "the cloud." While some fields are already far advanced in understanding how the Internet age is transforming their structure and substance, we're just beginning to understand the breadth and depth of its implica-tions on the future of education.

Unlocking the power of new technologies for self-guided education is one of the
40 twenty-first century superhighways that need to be paved. Profound changes to how children access vast information is yielding new forms of peer-to-peer and individual-guided learning. The cloud is already omnipresent and indestructible, **democratizing** and ever changing; now we need to use it to spark the imaginations and build the mental muscles of children worldwide.

45 This journey, for me, began back in 1999, when I conducted an experiment called the "hole in the wall." By installing Internet-equipped computers in poor Indian villages and then watching how children interacted with them, unmediated, I first glimpsed the power of the cloud. Groups of street children learned to use computers and the Internet by themselves, with little or no knowledge of English and never having seen
50 a computer before. Then they started instinctually teaching one another. In the next five years, through many experiments, I learned just how powerful adults can be when they give small groups of children the tools and the **agency** to guide their own learning and then get out of the way.

Learning dynamics

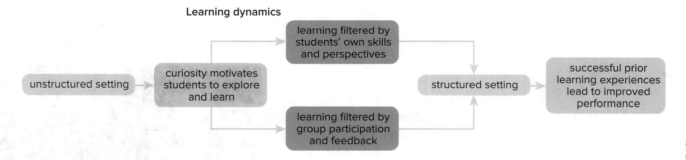

It's not just poor kids that can benefit from access to the Internet and the space and
55 time to wonder and wander. Today, teachers around the world are using what I call "SOLEs," "self-organized learning environments," where children group around Internet-equipped computers to discuss big questions. The teacher merges into the background and observes as learning happens.

I once asked a group of ten-year-olds in the little town of Villa Mercedes in Argentina:
60 Why do we have five fingers and toes on each limb? What's so special about five? Their answer may surprise you.

The children arrived at their answer by investigating both **theology** and evolution, discovering the five bones holding the web on the first **amphibians'** fins, and studying geometry. Their investigation resulted in this final answer: the strongest web that
65 can be stretched the widest must have five supports.

…

We need a curriculum of big questions, examinations where children can talk, share and use the Internet, and new, peer-assessment systems. We need children from a range of economic and geographic backgrounds and an army of visionary educators.
70 We need pedagogy free from fear and focused on the magic of children's innate quest for information and understanding.

(696 words)

> **Critical Thinking:** Mitra's success comes in part because he has investigated a number of different fields. To think critically, read and learn outside your discipline.

Mitra, S. (2013). The SOLE of a student. *NDTV*. Retrieved from http://www.ndtv.com/article/world/the-sole-of-a-student-ted-winner-sugata-mitra-s-blog-336014

D. Correctly number the sentences to make a summary of Reading 2.

_____ A computer placed in a public space showed how children used it and interacted to learn.

_____ Example: Children determined that the norm of five fingers is based on building the strongest webs.

___1___ Debate: How do we spark creativity, curiosity and wonder in children?

_____ In self-organized learning environments (SOLEs), children group around Internet-equipped computers to discuss big questions, and the teacher observes.

_____ Many non-educational institutions are being transformed by the Internet.

_____ People are exploring how an Internet-enabled world can help learning.

_____ School pedagogy is outdated.

_____ Children access vast information through peer-to-peer and individual-guided learning.

_____ Schools still operate as if all knowledge is contained in books, and students are rewarded for memorization, not imagination or resourcefulness.

_____ Victorians' education system mass-produced workers with identical skills.

E. Draw a Venn diagram on a separate page with OLD SCHOOLS as the label for one circle and NEW SCHOOLS as the label for the other. Decide where each sentence in task D belongs and write the number in the appropriate circle, including the overlap between the two circles.

Explaining Processes

You may have noticed the flow chart on page 152. A process paragraph, with or without a flow chart, is a descriptive way to explain how something is done or how something happened. For example, a process paragraph might explain developments in the evolution of computers or the steps for what to do if one is not working. Writing about process involves a sequence of steps along with definitions of any technical terms.

A. Read the steps required to write a process paragraph.

STEPS	EXPLANATION	EXAMPLE
CHOOSE A TOPIC	Choose a topic that you understand well and write it in your title.	*How to Brainstorm*
CONSIDER YOUR AUDIENCE	Consider who will be reading your process paragraph and decide how much background information you will need to give.	*college students*
BREAK THE PROCESS INTO STEPS	Use a flow chart to briefly outline the steps.	*define problem → appoint reporter → each member speaks → review ideas → discuss → decide*
WRITE A TOPIC SENTENCE	A topic sentence should state what you are going to explain, and why.	*Brainstorming is a skill for generating new ideas that will help you solve problems creatively.*
DEFINE KEY TERMS	Technical terms might need to be defined at the beginning or as part of the step where they appear.	*Brainstorming is a group-thinking activity based on not rejecting others' ideas.*
WRITE THE STEPS IN A LOGICAL ORDER	Write the steps in the correct order. Use transition words to signal the order of steps: *first, begin by, before, next, then, as soon as, finally*. Review the steps to make certain you are not missing any.	*First, define the problem being discussed. Next, appoint a reporter who will record everyone's ideas. Then, let each person offer ideas without interruption or criticism. Finally, when everyone has offered ideas, review and discuss how practical each one is for solving the problem.*
CONCLUDING SENTENCE	Process paragraphs do not need a concluding sentence. However, sometimes a concluding sentence is used to offer encouragement or to give a suggestion of where to find additional information on the topic.	*This is only one of many ways to brainstorm. Look online for others and make brainstorming part of your future group-thinking process.*

B. Number these steps in the correct order to form a process paragraph on how to solve a problem with creative thinking. Highlight the transition words.

_____ After you have had enough time to reflect, be open to surprising ideas and make sure you write them down to study after.

_____ Begin by immersing yourself in the problem you are trying to solve. Find out as much as possible about the problem.

_____ Creative thinking is a way to solve problems that everyone should practise.

_____ Finally, become critical. Challenge your ideas and look for errors; this process can help you spot problems and develop solutions.

___*1*___ How to Solve a Problem with Creative Thinking

_____ Next, step away, giving yourself time to reflect on what you learned.

C. Write a concluding sentence for the process paragraph in task B.

_____

_____

_____

_____

WARM-UP ASSIGNMENT
Write a Process Paragraph

Write a process paragraph that describes the steps needed to teach someone something new, such as those involved in learning a special skill in your academic discipline, a sport, a game, how to fix something or how to cook something. Follow the steps outlined in Focus on Writing.

A. Choose a topic—something you know about that you can easily explain. Your audience will be your class. Use this flow chart to briefly outline the steps.

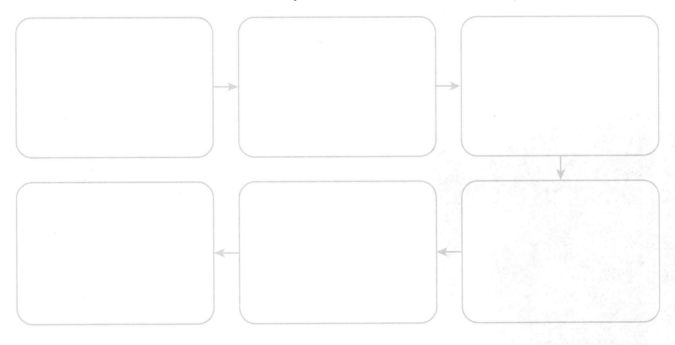

B. Write your paragraph. Use transition words to signal the order between steps. Pay attention to your use of pronoun-antecedent agreement. Refer to the Models Chapter (page 197) to see an example of a process paragraph and to learn more about how to write one.

C. Add a title and a concluding sentence explaining where students can find more information on your topic.

D. Proofread your paragraph to make sure you have not missed any steps. Then, share your paragraph with a partner and ask for feedback.

Use feedback from your teacher and classmates on this Warm-Up Assignment to improve your writing.

A. Below are words from the Academic Word List that you will find in Reading 3. Highlight the words you understand and then circle the words you use.

criteria
hierarchy — **nouns**

adjectives — authoritative
crowdsourced
unspecified

future of
education

administer
compensated
implies — **verbs**

adverbs — explicitly
implicitly

B. Fill in the blanks with the correct words to complete the paragraph.

| criteria crowdsourced explicitly hierarchy implicitly unspecified |

The use of _____ content for computer-based textbooks means a change to the traditional _____ of textbook writer, teacher and student. While not _____ stated in any official guidelines, _____ are _____ based on who has the best ideas, not on who has the most experience. What remains _____, however, is whether teachers will reserve the right to make final edits on content and style.

C. Read each sentence and use the context to help you choose the best definition for the word in bold.

❶ The **hierarchy** remains teacher-centred in countless class-rooms that still feature students quietly listening to lectures.
  a) arrangement of things according to relative importance
  b) system of organization in which people are ranked one above the other

❷ The challenge with digital textbooks is finding ways to ensure writers, illustrators and other textbook contributors and publishers are fairly **compensated** for their work.
  a) given something, typically money
  b) made up for something unwelcome or unpleasant

❸ Professionally published texts tend to be more **authoritative** than unedited e-books or volunteer postings on websites.
  a) able to be trusted as being accurate or true
  b) commanding and self-confident

❹ In contrast, a just-in-time learning model **implies** you can wait to learn until just before you need to use the information.
  a) suggests something as a logical consequence
  b) suggests something is true, though not expressly stated

⑤ Millions experience Internet-based learning in informal ways when they use online tutorial videos to help them solve problems, from how to bake a cake to how to **administer** first aid.

a) manage or be responsible for the running of a business

b) dispense or apply

D. VOCABULARY EXTENSION: For the words *implicitly* and *explicitly*, the prefix *im-* (or *in-*) often refers to *inside* while the prefix *ex-* often refers to *outside*. Write short definitions for the following words. Look up those you don't know in a dictionary. Then, indicate which pairs of terms are antonyms (opposites).

WORDS	DEFINITIONS	ANTONYMS
❶ inhale exhale	*breathe in*	☐
❷ inhibit exhibit		☐
❸ introvert extrovert		☐
❹ inspire expire		☐
❺ implore explore		☐

Visit My eLab to complete Vocabulary Review exercises for this chapter.

READING ③   **The Future of Education**

For much of history, getting an education has been about the memorization of facts. American anthropologist Margaret Mead (1901–1978) suggested that children should be taught *how* to think, instead of *what* to think. In a rapidly changing world, this advice seems more important than ever. A child—or adult— who can think independently has an advantage when facing new situations or problems.

A. Compare one important thing you have learned in a traditional way, either in school or outside of school, with one important thing you learned in a non-traditional way. Discuss the advantages and disadvantages of traditional and non-traditional learning with a partner.

B. The first paragraph of Reading 3, on page 158, points out the historical contrast between doctors' and teachers' jobs. Is the comparison a fair one? Why might doctors' jobs have changed so much and teachers' jobs so little?

_____

_____

_____

_____

C. Look at the illustration. Why do you think the information was organized as an illustration instead of another kind of visual element? What problems does it present?

_____

_____

_____

The Future of Education

reassuringly (adv.): removing doubt or fear

A doctor from one hundred years ago, visiting a modern hospital, would be completely lost. The tools, procedures, medicines and the criteria for the doctor's role would all differ. In contrast, a teacher returning from one thousand years ago would find many classrooms **reassuringly** familiar. The hierarchy remains teacher-centred in countless classrooms that still feature students quietly listening to lectures. However, education is undergoing massive change, fuelled by technology, research and private and public innovation.

Gamification

Lee and Hammer (2011) describe gamification in education as using the interactive aspects of video games to allow students "to experiment with rules, emotions and social roles" (p. 2). Essentially, gamification creates computer-based educational opportunities. An interactive science fiction novel, for example, might be adapted into a game where the reader takes on the role of each character, exploring plot choices. When students solve problems, they are rewarded with harder problems that encourage development of comprehension, strategies and other abilities. Gamification improves motivation for learning but, at the same time, faces criticism for making education about being entertained rather than true learning and problem solving.

Source: Sorsa, L. (2014). *Students imagine the future.* Thinklink Graphics. Retrieved from http://www.thinklinkgraphics.com/2013/08/students-imagine-the-future-of-ontarios-education-system/

prominent (adj.): important

forging (v.): making or shaping something

wikis (n.): websites that allow collaborative editing

dispense with (v.): manage without

apprenticeship (n.): learning while working at a skill, trade or profession

The flipped classroom

20 The flipped classroom presents most learning experiences online in the form of video lectures and tutorials. Students review them, and when they meet their teachers, 25 problems the students have encountered are discussed in depth. Among the most **prominent** examples of the flipped classroom are courses in mathematics and other 30 subjects offered by Khan Academy. Students appreciate opportunities to review the materials over and over, progressing at their own pace. However, the flipped classroom requires discipline: students work on their own and they decide when to return to class; a teacher will 35 not always have time to give each student personal attention.

Crowdsourced knowledge

Wikipedia is one of countless websites where people freely offer their time and expertise to share what they know. This crowdsourced knowledge is modified as people edit and update existing entries and add new ones, **forging** mind map-like links. 40 Online newspapers have adopted the model, asking readers for their stories, pictures and videos, and inviting extensive reader comments. In educational settings, students and teachers create **wikis** of mind-mapped information that others build on and edit. But this approach ignores the expertise of professional materials developers; a student's opinions are not more important than a professor's facts.

45 E-texts

Whether or not crowdsourced materials and wikis eventually replace textbooks, what is certain is that students are likely to **dispense with** traditional paper textbooks and read digital versions instead. These may be more expensive initially, but are more convenient to carry and more interactive. Waller (2013) points out:

50 With e-textbooks, you can perform a word or phrase search easily with a screen touch, and some readers have the capability of highlighting and ability to take notes. Another advantage of e-textbooks is that they update more easily than traditional paper textbooks, which have to be reprinted. (p. 4)

55 A curious concern with e-texts is that they make searching for explanations too easy; if readers never face problems in trying to understand something, they never learn to think.

"Just-in-time" learning

The **apprenticeship** system has long allowed novices to learn with a master of a par- 60 ticular craft. This is still an educational model for some. Aspects of it are also implicitly part of the conventional school system that assumes most knowledge should be absorbed and tested for some unspecified future use.

In contrast, the just-in-time learning model implies you can wait to learn until you need to use the information. Tutorial videos have become just-in-time learning solu-
65 tions for a range of topics, such as how to deliver a speech. For many, this is preferable to going to class to learn the skill, but online tutorials are not interactive; when you don't understand or something goes wrong, the video cannot remedy the situation.

A perfect future?

Will these educational innovations collectively change the nature of schools? Other
70 technologies like radio correspondence courses showed great initial promise but did not explicitly have much lasting value in driving major changes in education. Many of today's technological innovations will turn out the same way.   (681 words)

References

Lee, J.J. & Hammer, J. (2011). Gamification in education: What, how, why bother? *Academic Exchange Quarterly, 15*(2). Retrieved from http://www.gamifyingeducation.org/files/Lee-Hammer-AEQ-2011.pdf

Waller, D. (2013). Current advantages and disadvantages of using e-textbooks in Texas higher education. *Focus on Colleges, Universities, and Schools, 7*(1), 1–6.

D. What advantages and disadvantages does each educational innovation have? Write your answers and then discuss them with your partner.

EDUCATIONAL INNOVATION	ADVANTAGES	DISADVANTAGES
gamification	*motivating*	
flipped classroom		
crowdsourced knowledge		
e-texts		
just-in-time learning		

E. The concluding paragraph of Reading 3 suggests that some current educational innovations may disappear. Why? Which of the new learning technologies and approaches are likely to still be around in twenty years? Which might disappear, and why? Discuss in a group.

Academic
Survival Skill

Working in a Group

Being able to work effectively as a group is a valuable achievement. Group work skills are always useful, whether organizing projects with friends, fellow students, volunteers or co-workers. Part of working in a group is making sure all share a common goal and have a plan for reaching it. Group members may sometimes have personal priorities that interfere with the goal. Good group members learn to manage each other, ensuring that conflict is recognized and quickly handled.

A. Read the steps with a partner. Compare them with a group project you may have participated in. Discuss similarities and differences and add to the questions.

STEPS IN A GROUP PROJECT	QUESTIONS
Define the assignment; make sure everyone has a common understanding.	What exactly is the teacher asking for in this assignment? What additional information does the group need?
Negotiate to divide the work into smaller equal tasks.	What is a fair way to divide the work?
Define roles for each group member based on interests, strengths and skills.	Who will do which task? Do any of the group members have special skills?
Organize a timeline to get the work done in a sequential manner.	Is there an order in which things need to be done? Do some tasks need to be finished before other tasks can be started?
Keep track of progress and report to the group, dealing with conflicts promptly.	Are you using a Gantt chart or some other way to organize your schedule? Do you need help from another group member or do other group members need more help or time?
Evaluate how well you worked together to improve for next time.	Was the process of working together efficient and effective for everyone? What should be changed? What could have been done to make working together better?

B. Use the information in this paragraph to complete the Gantt chart.

> We will begin the project on April 23 and spend four days designing the questionnaire. As soon as the questionnaire is finished, we will spend two days using it to collect information. Then, on the 29th, we can begin work on the computer presentation. This work will continue until May 5, but during this time, from April 30 to May 3, work can be done on the handouts. While the handouts are being made, the poster should be designed. Poster design will also go on from April 30 to May 3, but the person who makes the posters should put them up on May 5. We will have a meeting to practise the presentation on the evening of May 5. The presentation is on May 6. A meeting to evaluate how our working together went will be held on May 7.

ACTIVITIES	APRIL								MAY						
	23	24	25	26	27	28	29	30	1	2	3	4	5	6	7
DESIGN QUESTIONNAIRE	▓	▓	▓	▓											
COLLECT INFORMATION															
WORK ON COMPUTER PRESENTATION															
PREPARE HANDOUTS															
DESIGN AND PLACE POSTERS															
PRACTISE PRESENTATION															
PRESENTATION															
EVALUATION MEETING															

C. Discuss the Gantt chart in a group. Which tasks would be the easiest to complete? Which tasks would be the hardest? Decide who in your group would take on which task based on individual strengths or skills.

FINAL ASSIGNMENT

Write a Process Paragraph and Give a Presentation

Working in a group, use what you learned in this chapter to write two (or more) paragraphs outlining a process. Then, present the process to the class.

A. Form a group of three or four students and, as a group, choose a topic related to education.

☐ How do students choose a discipline or program to study?

☐ How were the first universities established?

☐ How do different students plan their study schedules?

☐ How does a particular type of book organize information?

☐ ANOTHER TOPIC: _____

B. Ask your teacher for approval of your choice of topic.

C. Follow the steps in Academic Survival Skill: assign roles, divide work among group members and prepare a Gantt chart to schedule task times and deadlines, with the start date and the presentation date. Tasks might include research, writing, visual elements, preparation of the presentation and giving the presentation in front of the class.

D. For the written work, review Focus on Writing (page 154) and Focus on Grammar (page 148). For visual elements, review Focus on Reading (page 142). Refer to the Models Chapter (page 197) to see an example of a process paragraph and to learn more about how to write one.

E. Work to complete assigned tasks and monitor progress as a group.

F. Practise your presentation, and then deliver it to the class.

G. After the presentation, meet as a group to discuss feedback from the class and your teacher and to evaluate how well you worked together as a group and what could be improved for next time.

How confident are you?

Think about what you learned in this chapter. Use the table to decide what you should review.

I LEARNED ...	I AM CONFIDENT	I NEED TO REVIEW
vocabulary related to technology-enhanced education;	☐	☐
how to interpret visual elements;	☐	☐
pronoun-antecedent agreement;	☐	☐
steps in a process;	☐	☐
how to work in a group;	☐	☐
how to write and present a process.	☐	☐

VOCABULARY Challenge

Think about the vocabulary and ideas in this chapter. Use these words to write two sentences that summarize ideas about education.

consistent	ensure	explicitly	implications	implicitly	reliable

_____

_____

_____

_____

_____

My eLab ✐
Visit My eLab to build on what you learned.

CHAPTER 8

Rights and Obligations

The basic obligation of a government is to care for its citizens. But the mistreatment of minorities by their own governments is both an old issue and one that continues to be a problem around the world. Such inequality is often criminal in nature, but it can take decades—or even centuries—for injustices to be universally recognized and addressed.

Although justice may be too late for those who have lost their lives, every time a wrong is recognized and an effort made to make it right, civilization moves forward.

What rights are important to you?

In this chapter, you will

- learn vocabulary related to human rights;

- distinguish fact from opinion;

- use the active and passive voice;

- explore the compare and contrast essay format;

- learn how to prepare for an exam;

- write a compare and contrast essay.

GEARING UP

A. Look at the diagram and then answer the questions.

Nine aspects of human rights

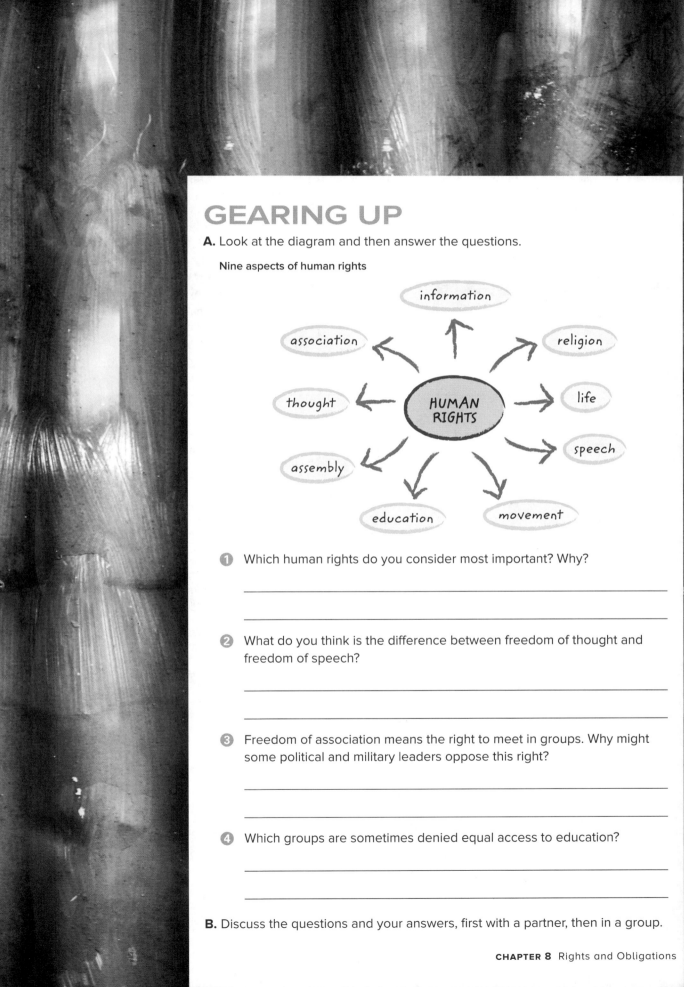

1 Which human rights do you consider most important? Why?

_____

_____

2 What do you think is the difference between freedom of thought and freedom of speech?

_____

_____

3 Freedom of association means the right to meet in groups. Why might some political and military leaders oppose this right?

_____

_____

4 Which groups are sometimes denied equal access to education?

_____

_____

B. Discuss the questions and your answers, first with a partner, then in a group.

FOCUS ON READING

A famous person's opinion is still just an opinion, especially if the person is not an expert on the topic.

Distinguishing Fact from Opinion

One important critical skill to develop is the ability to distinguish fact from opinion. A fact is something that has been scientifically investigated and proven to be true, or something that is accepted because it has occurred in history. For example, the Earth revolves around the sun is a fact, even though most Europeans believed the opposite until the 1540s. Proof came from observation and mathematics. An opinion is something that cannot be proven or may simply be an idea that differs from person to person. You may think solar flares are the greatest threat facing Earth, but your belief does not make it a fact. Opinions are debatable; facts are not. When trying to distinguish fact from opinion, ask questions.

A. Read these comparisons of facts and opinions. Then, write an example of your own.

QUESTIONS	FACTS	OPINIONS
IS IT TRUE?	A fact is scientifically proven or agreed upon by experts: *Newspapers are printed on paper.* Example: _____ _____ _____	An opinion is a personal belief that may not be shared by others: *Newspapers are too expensive.* Example: _____ _____ _____
DOES IT EXIST?	Facts can be observed first-hand by anyone: *Loch Ness is a lake in Scotland.* Example: _____ _____ _____	Opinions cannot be observed or supported by proof: *The Loch Ness monster is an aquatic dinosaur.* Example: _____ _____ _____
HAS IT OCCURRED?	Even if something cannot be observed today, it can be established through logical thinking: *Fossils tell us dinosaurs once existed.* Example: _____ _____ _____	An opinion lacks evidence or scientific credibility: *Early humans hunted dinosaurs.* Example: _____ _____ _____

B. Decide whether these statements are fact or opinion. Discuss your answers with a partner.

1. Earth is home to billions of people. _____
2. The press has never been fair in reporting the news. _____
3. The first man to step onto the moon was Neil Armstrong. _____
4. A full moon affects a person's mood. _____
5. The moon's gravitational forces influence the tides. _____

C. Comparative and superlative adjectives can signal opinions, as can statements that feature phrases such as "I believe" or "everyone knows." Numerical data—statistics and dates—often indicate facts. Consider the words and phrases in bold and indicate which would signal a fact and which an opinion. Discuss your reasons with your partner.

STATEMENTS	FACT	OPINION
1 Exactly **37 percent** of the class are members of a gym.	☐	☐
2 The **worst** thing to do for a cold is to overeat.	☐	☐
3 The flower is sort of a **greyish purple**.	☐	☐
4 Many of the store's employees are **mean**.	☐	☐
5 Orange juice is **better** for you than apple juice.	☐	☐
6 The house has several **glass** windows.	☐	☐
7 The kangaroo is the **quickest** animal in the world.	☐	☐
8 Cheetahs run at speeds of **120 kilometres per hour**.	☐	☐

D. *Reasonable* or *valid* opinions are supported by facts. *Invalid* opinions are not supported by facts. Choose the phrase that makes each sentence a valid opinion.

1 Bananas are a healthier choice for runners than apples because bananas _____.

    a) contain high levels of potassium

    b) can be eaten more quickly

2 London is the most popular city in the world _____.

    a) because it is so beautiful and has wonderful museums and art galleries

    b) based on its ranking for the highest number of tourist visits

3 At most, people can remember five to seven things at the same time, based on _____.

    a) a few friends of different ages I asked

    b) a study by George A. Miller in a 1956 issue of *Psychology Review*

4 Most real estate agents aren't as concerned with their clients' money as with their own _____.

    a) measured by how much longer agents wait to sell their own versus clients' homes

    b) because everyone naturally looks after their own interests before the needs of others

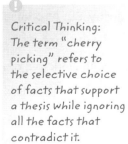

Critical Thinking: The term "cherry picking" refers to the selective choice of facts that support a thesis while ignoring all the facts that contradict it.

A. Below are words and phrases from the Academic Word List that you will find in Reading 1. Highlight the words you understand and then circle the words you use.

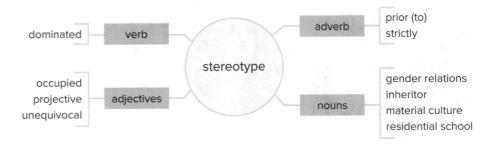

dominated — verb

stereotype

occupied
projective — adjectives
unequivocal

adverb — prior (to)
strictly

nouns — gender relations
inheritor
material culture
residential school

B. Highlight the best definition for each word or phrase.

1 gender relations
  a) how the sexes treat each other
  b) marriage options for peers

2 inheritor
  a) person who gives something
  b) person who receives something

3 material culture
  a) ideas and beliefs a group has about doing things
  b) physical objects that represent a group's way of doing things

4 projective
  a) related to the unconscious transfer of desires and emotions to another
  b) aspect of technology that moves between media types

5 unequivocal
  a) often in doubt
  b) without a doubt

C. Fill in the blanks with the correct words to complete the paragraph.

| dominated | occupied | prior | residential school | strictly |

_____ to the arrival of the Europeans, Aboriginal people relied on hunting and gathering practices. The original idea of the _____ system was to move Aboriginal people toward work in farming and industry. But Aboriginal students often found their days _____ with work that did not improve their education or their skills. The curriculum was _____ by the idea that everything Aboriginal was bad and everything European was good. Students who rebelled, by speaking their native languages, for example, were treated _____.

Seeing Red: A History of Natives in Canadian Newspapers

Beyond what we study in school or read in books, much of what we know is shaped by the news we see and hear. Editorials make it clear that they are expressing opinions, but news stories, which also often include opinion, do not. For example, a story may give an opinion on the motives of the people behind the news. If news only presents facts, you tend to form your own opinions, reflecting on how the news applies to you.

A. Oscar Wilde (1854–1900) was joking when he wrote that the one duty we owe to history is to rewrite it. But history is constantly being rewritten. Why might historians reinterpret past events?

_____

_____

_____

_____

_____

B. Read the first paragraph of Reading 1. Which statement best summarizes the writers' purpose?

☐ The writers explore the cultural richness of Canadian Aboriginals in the past and suggest that this has changed today.

☐ The writers suggest that although there were once many Aboriginals in Canada of different nations, they no longer exist today.

☐ The writers explain the diversity and cultural richness of Canadian Aboriginals and compare these to the way they are portrayed in newspapers.

> ❗ With each of the readings in this chapter, consider how the Canadian example compares to similar ones in other countries.

C. While you read, highlight the opinions that the writers put forward.

Seeing Red: A History of Natives in Canadian Newspapers

ubiquitous (adj.): found everywhere

conflate (v.): combine two or more things or ideas into one

stereotyped monolith (n.): simplified single image

non-partisan (adj.): not taking sides

1 Canada is home to more than six hundred Indigenous nations as well as roughly one-half million Aboriginals living off-reserve. Prior to the centuries-long European invasion, these groups spoke dozens of different languages, exhibited wide variety in architecture, child rearing, clothing, diet, gender relations, material culture, religion, rituals—in short, they varied in all the ways one might expect of an enormous region occupied by a wide range of cultural groups.[1] All told, in excess of 1.3 million Canadians claim some Aboriginal heritage, according to the 2001 census. This includes First Nations, Inuit and Métis.[2] Yet the country's most **ubiquitous** agent of popular education, the newspaper, has tended to **conflate** all of these peoples into one heavily **stereotyped monolith**, patterned on a colonial ideology that flourishes to this day.

2 This may come as a surprise if you think that colonialism is dead, a best-forgotten relic of days gone by in Canada. It may also surprise you if you think that the press is strictly objective and **non-partisan**. Indeed, if this is the case, you will be surprised to discover that the evidence shows something strikingly different. An examination

Develop Your Vocabulary: This article mentions "colonialism" (settling another country) and "imperialism" (extending influence through military force). Learn these and other "isms."

of press content in Canada since the sale of **Rupert's Land** in 1869 through to 2009 illustrates that, with respect to Aboriginal peoples, the colonial imagery has **thrived**, even dominated, and continues to do so in mainstream English-language newspapers.[3] Further, the press has never been non-partisan or strictly objective in Canada. A wealth of studies, and observations from daily life, readily demonstrate this.

3 Colonialism has always thrived in Canada's press. This is not a shock given Canada's **imperial birth** and its enduring colonial behaviour with respect to Aboriginals since the country's **nominal** founding at Confederation in 1867.[4] It is what David Spurr refers to when he writes that "the colonizer speaks as inheritor."[5] Paul Nesbitt-Larking notes that "the medium of print is strongly associated with the politics of imperialism and colonialism."[6] In this way, Canadian nationalism becomes imperialism because it shares the same dream.[7] Further, these colonial actions become double-edged because the mainstream positions itself as rightful owner of Aboriginal lands as well as inheritor of an English pattern of positioning itself with respect to Aboriginal peoples. Two examples exemplify the point.

4 The first is the treaty system that, to begin with, effectively stripped Aboriginals of the vast majority of their lands at the end of a gun barrel or with the implied threat of violence. This amounted to naked military conquest, though it is rarely portrayed as such in Canada. Instead, the nation insists that violence was the American way, a projective tale that serves the high and mighty purposes of elevating Canadiana over Americana at the same time as promoting the **disingenuous** and misleading idea that Indigenous peoples sought the protection of the Canadian government in their desire for treaties. Again and again in the 1870s, the press made it clear that Canada chose not to engage in all-out war because it was simply too expensive and not because it was somehow unwarranted.

…

5 The residential school system, that between 1879 and 1996 sought to disappear Aboriginal culture by vigorously educating it out of existence, serves as the second example of how the mainstream positions itself as owner of Aboriginal lands.

detractors (n.): people who criticize someone or something

genocide (n.): deliberate killing of a group, particularly an ethnic group

Detractors accurately call it a systematic attempt at cultural **genocide**. Even its few lingering supporters accept that it was morally flawed and disastrously run; and Canadian Prime Minister Stephen Harper offered a formal apology for the system on June 11, 2008.[9] As with the treaties, the historical record of residential schools is unequivocal: this was a system predicated on aggressive violence. Aboriginal children were forced to school, yanked from their families, banned from speaking their languages and often not returned for a decade or more. Sometimes years would pass and parents were not allowed even to see, let alone hug or just spend time with their children.

(648 words)

Idle No More rally, Victoria, BC, January 26, 2013

Notes

1. See Olive Dickason, *Canada's First Nations: A History of Founding Peoples From Earliest Times* (New York: Oxford University Press, 2001).

2. In some ways, the terms First Nations and Métis overlap. First Nations refers to status Natives, those who hold treaty cards. Métis refers to those of mixed European (most commonly French) and Aboriginal ancestry. A more restrictive interpretation of the term includes only those who can trace their ancestry to the Red River Settlement while a less restrictive one includes those who self-declare mixed ancestry. The overlap between Métis and First Nations occurs because many status Aboriginals also easily fit the term Métis; that is, they have some quantum of European ancestry. It is important to remember that the "status" of status has been patrolled by Canada's colonial office governing and regulating the affairs of Aboriginal peoples, the Department of Indian and Northern Affairs (INAC). In this study, we employ the terms Aboriginal, Indigenous and Native as synonyms referring to persons of any Aboriginal background. In certain contexts we use the term "Indian" to reflect the diversity of terms used over time. While considered pejorative and outdated by some scholars, it serves a number of aims, including the legal usage in the Indian Act. This is a common practice among scholars. But the other reason is that the mainstream press in Canada has tended not to distinguish among Aboriginal peoples, and typically has lumped them all together, and it is those particular images that constitute the key interest of this study. That said, we have left all direct quotes—which, as you will discover, are frequently imprecise—unaltered.

3. Mainstream values and culture derive from and are synonymous with white values and culture, sometimes referred to as settler culture. We use the terms *mainstream* and *white* interchangeably. Neither term includes all those who dwell permanently in Canada; instead, the terms refer synonymously to the dominant culture, what some would term hegemonic culture.

4. Mary Vipond, *The Mass Media in Canada* (Toronto: James Lorimer and Company, 2000), 2 and 133.

5. David Spurr, *The Rhetoric of Empire, Colonial Discourse in Journalism, Travel Writing, and Imperial Administration* (Durham: Duke University Press, 1993), 28.

6. Paul Nesbitt-Larking, *Politics, Society, and the Media, Canadian Perspectives* (Peterborough, ON: Broadview Press, 2001), 52.

7. See Benedict Anderson, *Imagined Communities: Reflections on the Origin and Spread of Nationalism* (London: Verso, 1991), 109–111 and 150.

…

9. The seven-minute apology is widely available on the Internet. See http://www.youtube.com/watch?v=qAmUe17nUdY&feature=PlayList&p=08DD57E2D5EA374C&index=0 &playnext=1 (accessed 17 April 2010).

Anderson, M.C. & Robertson, C.L. (2011). *Seeing red: A history of natives in Canadian newspapers* (pp. 3–5). Winnipeg, MB: University of Manitoba Press.

D. Indicate whether these statements are fact or opinion, according to the text. If you are not sure, read each statement in the context of its paragraph.

STATEMENTS	FACT	OPINION
PARAGRAPH 1: In excess of 1.3 million Canadians claim some Aboriginal heritage.		
PARAGRAPH 2: Colonialism is dead, a best-forgotten relic of days gone by in Canada.		
PARAGRAPH 3: Canadian nationalism becomes imperialism because it shares the same dream.		
PARAGRAPH 4: The treaty system effectively stripped Aboriginals of the vast majority of their lands at the end of a gun barrel.		
PARAGRAPH 5: Canadian Prime Minister Stephen Harper offered a formal apology for the residential system.		

E. Review the dates in the reading and write notes about each one's significance.

DATES	SIGNIFICANCE
1867	*Canadian Confederation (the joining of most of the provinces into one country)*
1869	
1870s	
1879 to 1996	
2001	
2008	

F. Indicate whether these statements are true or false, according to the text.

STATEMENTS	TRUE	FALSE
❶ The federal government never played a role in the administration of residential schools.	☐	☐
❷ Residential schools isolated students from their communities.	☐	☐
❸ Newspapers have always been non-partisan and strictly objective in Canada.	☐	☐
❹ The writers feel that the colonial powers conquered the Aboriginals, even though the term *conquest* is not used.	☐	☐
❺ Canadians Aboriginals wanted treaties to avoid the wars faced by American Aboriginals.	☐	☐
❻ The term *lingering supporters* refers to those who opposed the residential school system.	☐	☐
❼ Residential schools often did not let parents see their children for several years.	☐	☐

Active and Passive Voice

In Reading 1, you saw examples of both the active and the passive voice. Use the active voice when the subject is doing the action. Use the passive voice when the subject is being acted upon or when you are not sure who is doing the action. Form the passive voice by changing the order and roles of the subject and object in a sentence. The subject becomes the object. Change the verb to the past tense and use a form of *to be*.

A. Compare these two sentences and highlight the word that is the determining factor in each: *commission* or *children*.

ACTIVE VOICE: The commission identifies children.

PASSIVE VOICE: Children are identified by the commission.

In some sentences in the passive voice, the actor is unknown or unimportant.

PASSIVE VOICE: Children are identified.

B. Write three sentences about South African religious leader Desmond Tutu telling a story about a teenage girl. Change the form of the verb *tell*.

Desmond Tutu	girl	story	tell	teenage

❶ ACTIVE VOICE: _____

_____

❷ PASSIVE VOICE WITH ACTOR: _____

_____

❸ PASSIVE VOICE WITH NO ACTOR: _____

_____

Think about whether the "actor" in a sentence is important. Does the writer not know who the actor is or is information left out for some other reason?

C. Rewrite each sentence, either from the passive voice to the active voice or from the active voice to the passive voice.

❶ Volunteers sell lunches.

_____

❷ Dinner is cooked by her brother.

_____

❸ Students borrow many books.

_____

❹ An apology was offered by the school.

_____

❺ The thief took their bicycles.

_____

Use what you learned about the active and the passive voice when you write assignments.

A. Below are words and phrases from the Academic Word List that you will find in Reading 2. Highlight the words you understand and then circle the words you use.

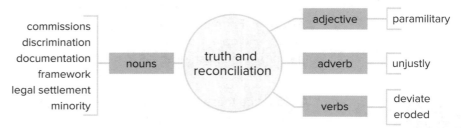

nouns
commissions
discrimination
documentation
framework
legal settlement
minority

truth and reconciliation

adjective — paramilitary

adverb — unjustly

verbs — deviate eroded

B. Highlight the word in parentheses that best completes each sentence. Key words are in bold.

1 Several government **commissions** were set up to (investigate / ignore) the abuses.

2 The purpose of the **documentation** was to (destroy / preserve) a record of the trials.

3 Human rights have often been **eroded** when governments have (given / taken) away power.

4 Building on an established **framework** requires (adapting / ignoring) what has been done before.

5 He was charged **unjustly** and sentenced to prison in a/an (legal / illegal) way.

C. Fill in the blanks with the correct words or phrase to complete the paragraph.

| deviate | discrimination | legal settlement | minority | paramilitary |

A _____ organization is typically at war with its own government.

In some cases, its members come from a single _____ group.

Frequently, this group has faced _____ and feels its only

choice is to fight back. If the government is unwilling to _____

from unfair policies, a war can continue for years. Usually, it takes an outside

authority to propose a lasting _____ that will end the fighting.

D. VOCABULARY EXTENSION: The nouns *documentation* and *discrimination* are formed from the verbs *document* and *discriminate*. Write *-ation* noun forms of the verbs. Then, write a definition for the noun form of each word.

VERBS	NOUNS	DEFINITIONS
1 cite	*citation*	*quote from a written source*
2 consider		
3 note		
4 confirm		
5 nominate		

Finding Truth and Reconciliation

Sainty Morris explained how he was punished at one of Canada's Aboriginal residential schools. Morris was taken to a dark room and forced to kneel for fifteen hours, without any food or water. Years later, he still cannot sleep in a dark room because it brings back terrible memories of school. Sharing such incidents helps survivors of the residential school system recognize how wrongly they were treated and helps ensure such things never happen again.

A. Some people do not want to be reminded of bad memories. In what circumstances would it be good to relive the past through discussing it and in what circumstances would the opposite be true? Discuss in a group.

B. Winston Churchill (1874–1965) said, "History is written by the victors." Reading 2 discusses truth (agreed-upon facts) and reconciliation (restoring a balance to relations among people). Truth and reconciliation commissions hear the stories of common people. How can sharing these stories help rewrite history?

_____

_____

_____

C. While you read, highlight one example of the passive voice in each paragraph.

Finding Truth and Reconciliation

fatal (adj.): causing death

unburden (v.): relieve someone of distress

amnesty (n.): official pardon for political offences

1 A story is told by South African religious leader Desmond Tutu (1931–) about the teenage daughter of a victim of **fatal** police brutality. She was asked, "Would you be able to forgive the people who did this to you and your family?" She answered, "We would like to forgive, but we would just like to know who to forgive" (Tutu, 2010, para. 3).

2 The teenager's answer is at the heart of the concept of truth and reconciliation. If someone close to you has been unjustly hurt, imprisoned or killed, you would naturally want to know who was responsible. If you were someone who had committed an injustice, you might wish to **unburden** yourself and share your secret. Today, truth and reconciliation commissions (TRCs) worldwide deal with similar challenges but deviate in their approaches.

3 The approach of South Africa's TRC has been to attempt to understand three hundred years of government-sponsored discrimination and violence against Blacks by the minority White population. Blacks were removed from their homes and farms. They were given lower-quality educations and medical treatment. At different times, Blacks were enslaved, barred from owning businesses, forbidden to vote, marry Whites or use the same facilities as Whites, including beaches. Blacks were often ignored by the legal system or treated harshly, and there were countless murders of Blacks at the hands of the military and the police. Like many others that followed, South Africa's TRC included opportunities for those who had offended to seek **amnesty**. But while some could plead that they were only following orders, others had to take responsibility for torture, murders and other abuses.

4 Canada's TRC is concerned with the residential school system that operated from the 1840s to 1996. The system eroded human rights and removed Aboriginal children

DNA (n.): cell's carrier of genetic information

from their homes, then subjected many to physical and mental abuse. The original idea of the residential school system was to give students skills useful in farming and industry. But, in many cases, little training was given to students. They were little more than unpaid, unskilled labourers, making shoes or using outdated equipment to grow food. Of 150,000 Aboriginals who attended these schools, at least 3000 died, many in suspicious circumstances (The Canadian Press, 2013). In Canada, thousands of Aboriginals sued the federal gov-

Frobisher Bay (Iqaluit) Federal Hostel, 1959

ernment, churches and others responsible for residential schools. In 2007, a $1.9 billion legal settlement was followed by an apology from the Prime Minister and the creation of a TRC to raise awareness of the impact on residential school children, their families and their communities.

5 Argentina's TRC focused on uncovering the truth of the detention and execution of protesters opposed to the government during the military rule of 1976–1983. During this time, the military reportedly kidnapped, tortured and killed up to 30,000 people (Crenzel, 2008). A particular concern in Argentina has been the abduction of protesters' children. Some of these children were killed, but many were secretly placed in families who were sympathetic to the military's actions. These children grew up not knowing their real parents. Argentinians in their thirties are encouraged to have their **DNA** tested if they suspect they were kidnapped as children. So far, 114 children have been identified, including a thirty-eight-year-old man whose mother had been pregnant when she was taken away; the man's grandmother had never stopped searching.

6 In these and other cases, a common thread is the involvement of governments that fail to protect and care for their citizens. With the passage of time, a deep desire to right terrible wrongs has followed the overthrow of governments. When he was Chief Justice of England, Gordon Hewart (1870–1943) expressed the idea that not only must justice be done, but it must also be seen to be done. This belief is behind the collection of witness statements and other documentation used to educate the young through revised history books and museum exhibits.

7 Around the world a voice has been given to victims, including those who can no longer speak for themselves.

(663 words)

References

Crenzel, E. (2008, June 17). Argentina's national commission on the disappearance of persons: Contributions to transitional justice. *The International Journal of Transitional Justice*, Vol. 2, 173–191.

The Canadian Press. (2013, February 18). At least 3000 died in residential schools, research shows. CBCNews. Retrieved from http://www.cbc.ca/news/canada/at-least-3-000-died-in-residential-schools-research-shows-1.1310894

Tutu, D. (2010). Desmond Tutu (South Africa). The Forgiveness Project. Retrieved from http://theforgivenessproject.com/stories/desmond-tutu-south-africa/

D. Review the examples of the passive voice you identified in task C. In each case, explain the purpose the writer might have had for using the passive voice.

PARAGRAPH 1: _____

_____

PARAGRAPH 2: _____

_____

PARAGRAPH 3: _____

_____

PARAGRAPH 4: _____

_____

PARAGRAPH 5: _____

_____

PARAGRAPH 6: _____

_____

E. Review Reading 2 and compare and contrast the work of the three truth and reconciliation commissions.

QUESTIONS	SOUTH AFRICA	CANADA	ARGENTINA
❶ Who was affected?	*Blacks who suffered under White minority rule*		
❷ What was one thing each TRC was trying to find out?			
❸ When were the victims mistreated?			
❹ How many victims were there?	*no data*		

Writing a Compare and Contrast Essay

Essays organize your thoughts in a logical order. Often, an essay is used to construct an argument, leading the reader step-by-step from an opinion through evidence toward a conclusion that may call for action. Essays are not just used in academic settings. Speeches (like Reading 3), newspaper articles, some blogs and other genres also use the essay format.

A compare and contrast essay shows similarities and differences. It has three sections: an introduction, body paragraphs and a conclusion. Because an essay is formal writing, do not use contractions and use the full forms of terms followed by their abbreviation in parentheses.

A. Read the explanations of the sections of an essay and write sentences to complete the body paragraphs.

SECTIONS	EXPLANATION	EXAMPLE ESSAY
TITLE	Engage your readers by being informative and using language that makes them curious.	*Traditional Versus Modern Justice*
INTRODUCTION	Give the reader a reason for caring about the information. Include a thesis statement that features three or more points that can be contrasted. Each point will be developed in its own paragraph.	*Traditional societies have their own methods of justice. In one example, a young man who breaks a tribal law might be sent to an isolated island to live by himself for a year. This has advantages over modern justice because it does not make others responsible for supervising the punishment, avoids surrounding the offender with other criminals, and gives the offender time to build skills and knowledge.*
PARAGRAPH 1	Develop the first—and usually strongest—point. There should be a smooth transition from the introduction to the first body paragraph. Each paragraph should provide evidence in the form of examples and explanations.	*In modern judicial systems, many people are taken away from more productive work to serve as guards and other staff at prisons. But sending a young man off to the wilderness* _____ _____
PARAGRAPH 2	Develop the second point, which is usually the second strongest.	*Statistics show that most young men who enter prison learn more criminal skills there and tend to use these skills when they re-enter society. But a young man spending a year reflecting on his own* _____ _____
PARAGRAPH 3	Develop the third—and sometimes weakest—point.	*Although many prisons now educate inmates in different skills, most are voluntary and may not be useful. A young man who has to fend for himself for a year will build character and learn* _____ _____
CONCLUSION	Summarize the points and restate the thesis statement in a new way. You may include a call to action, asking the reader or others to make a change.	*It would not be practical to send every young offender into the wilderness, but not wasting resources on supervising young offenders and isolating them from other criminals and forcing them to learn skills that build character are principles that every judicial system should consider.*

B. Following certain steps can help you write your compare and contrast essay. Number these steps in the correct order.

_____ Share your draft with a partner. Ask your partner to proofread it and to give you feedback.

_____ Use keywords from your thesis statement to search for support as well as ideas that contradict your point of view. You will need these to build your arguments.

_____ Review your draft. Read it out loud to confirm that it flows logically from point to point.

_____ While you write, check that you have clear transitions between sentences and paragraphs.

_____ Use the question or topic you have been given to write your thesis statement.

_____ When you have your notes, use a Venn diagram to determine similarities and differences.

WARM-UP ASSIGNMENT
Write an Introductory Essay Paragraph

In 1842, when he was fourteen years old, Henry Caitlin was convicted of stealing the equivalent of twenty cents. He was charged with theft and sent to work as a prisoner in Tasmania, Australia, for fourteen years. Although the punishment was according to the law, you would probably agree that he did not receive justice. *Laws* are a country's system of rules; *justice* refers to what is fair.

In the Final Assignment, you will write a compare and contrast essay. In this assignment, you will choose the essay topic and write the title and introductory paragraph.

The assignment is to find a law or a punishment that most people today would consider unjust.

A. Use the library or the Internet to find and research an unjust law. It can be an old law or a current one, but you must be able to find contrasts: either in the way the law is applied today compared to the past, or in how the law is applied in two different countries.

B. Ask your teacher for approval of your choice of topic.

C. Organize your research notes on a Venn diagram to determine the similarities and the differences.

D. Write the title of your essay.

E. Use your Venn diagram notes to write the introduction. In the introduction, give your thesis statement with the three points that will be contrasted. Review Focus on Writing, or refer to the Models Chapter (page 198) to see an example of a compare and contrast essay and to learn more about how to write one.

F. Proofread your introduction. Then, share it with a partner and ask for feedback.

Use feedback from your teacher and classmates on this Warm-Up Assignment to improve your writing.

A. Below are words from the Academic Word List that you will find in Reading 3. Highlight the words you understand and then circle the words you use.

federal — adjective — apology — adverbs — adequately / forcibly

assumption / objectives / survivors — nouns — apology — verbs — isolate / prohibited

B. Fill in the blanks with the correct words to complete the sentences.

| adequately | assumption | prohibited | survivors |

1. First Nations, Inuit and Métis languages and cultural practices were _____ in these schools.

2. It has taken extraordinary courage for the thousands of _____ who have come forward to speak publicly.

3. These objectives were based on the _____ that Aboriginal cultures and spiritual beliefs were inferior and unequal.

4. We undermined the ability of many Aboriginals to _____ parent their own children.

C. Match each word to its definition.

1. federal _____   a) put apart
2. forcibly _____   b) national
3. isolate _____   c) purposes
4. objectives _____   d) persuasively

My eLab ✎

Visit My eLab to complete Vocabulary Review exercises for this chapter.

READING ③   Statement of Apology

When Europeans first arrived in Canada, they introduced popular goods such as metal implements and guns for hunting. But diseases were also introduced. Trading for furs was a useful livelihood for most Aboriginals, but when the demand for furs fell and unfair treaties restricted where Aboriginal peoples could live, many lost their traditional way of life and were not able to adapt to a new one. Some Aboriginal leaders saw the first residential schools as an opportunity for their children to learn skills that would allow everyone to prosper. Yet, in the end, the schools did more harm than good.

A. Besides physical abuse, most Aboriginal children suffered in other ways, beginning with the rules at many of the schools. What reasons do you think those schools might have had for setting these rules? Discuss in a group.

- Students must never speak their own language.
- Students must not mix with the opposite sex, even brothers and sisters, or receive presents or letters from family.
- Students must work for the school, even in unsafe environments.

B. Although Reading 3 was delivered as a speech, it takes the form of an essay and has been widely shared. After a one-sentence paragraph, the introduction continues with background to the issue of residential schools and then introduces the thesis statement with three points.

> Today, we recognize that this policy of assimilation was wrong [1], has caused great harm [2], and has no place in our country [3].

While you read, number the paragraphs that are used to develop each of the three points.

Statement of Apology

obligations (n.): moral or legal duties

assimilate (v.): become part of something bigger

inferior (adj.): lower in rank or status

legacy (n.): something left to the next generation

The treatment of children in Indian residential schools is a sad chapter in our history.

For more than a century, Indian residential schools separated over 150,000 Aboriginal children from their families and communities. In the 1870s, the federal government, 5 partly in order to meet its **obligations** to educate Aboriginal children, began to play a role in the development and administration of these schools. Two primary objectives of the residential school system were to remove and isolate children from the influence of their homes, families, traditions and cultures, and to **assimilate** them into the dominant culture. These objectives were based on the assumption that Aboriginal cultures 10 and spiritual beliefs were **inferior** and unequal. Indeed, some sought, as it was infamously said, "to kill the Indian in the child." Today, we recognize that this policy of assimilation was wrong, has caused great harm, and has no place in our country.

One hundred and thirty-two federally supported schools were located in every province and territory, except Newfoundland, New Brunswick and Prince Edward Island. 15 Most schools were operated as "joint ventures" with Anglican, Catholic, Presbyterian and United Churches. The Government of Canada built an educational system in which very young children were often forcibly removed from their homes, often taken far from their communities. Many were inadequately fed, clothed and housed. All were deprived of the care and nurturing of their parents, grandparents and communities. 20 First Nations, Inuit and Métis languages and cultural practices were prohibited in these schools. Tragically, some of these children died while attending residential schools and others never returned home.

The Government now recognizes that the consequences of the Indian residential school policy were profoundly negative and that this policy has had a lasting and 25 damaging impact on Aboriginal culture, heritage and language. While some former students have spoken positively about their experiences at residential schools, these stories are far overshadowed by tragic accounts of the emotional, physical and sexual abuse and neglect of helpless children, and their separation from powerless families and communities.

30 The **legacy** of Indian residential schools has contributed to social problems that continue to exist in many communities today.

resilience (n.): ability to recover

impediment (n.): obstacle to doing something

Chamber (n.): reference to where the Canadian government meets to make laws

void (n.): emptiness

undermined (v.): weakened someone or something

It has taken extraordinary courage for the thousands of survivors who have come forward to speak publicly about the abuse they suffered. It is a testament to their **resilience** as individuals and to the strengths of their cultures. Regrettably, many
35 former students are not with us today and died never having received a full apology from the Government of Canada.

The government recognizes that the absence of an apology has been an **impediment** to healing and reconciliation. Therefore, on behalf of the Government of Canada and all Canadians, I stand before you, in this **Chamber** so vital, so central to our existence
40 as a country, to apologize to Aboriginal peoples for the role the Government of Canada played in the Indian residential school system.

Prime Minister Stephen Harper and National Chief of Assembly of First Nations Phil Fontaine, June 11, 2008

To the approximately 80,000 living former students, and all family members and communities, the Government of Canada now recognizes that it
45 was wrong to forcibly remove children from their homes, and we apologize for having done this. We now recognize that it was wrong to separate children from rich and vibrant cultures and traditions, that it created a void in many lives and communi-
50 ties, and we apologize for having done this. We now recognize that, in separating children from their families, we **undermined** the ability of many to adequately parent their own children and sowed the seeds for generations to follow, and we apolo-
55 gize for having done this. We now recognize that far too often, these institutions gave rise to abuse or neglect and were inadequately controlled, and we apologize for failing to protect you. Not only did you suffer these abuses as children, but as you
60 became parents, you were powerless to protect your own children from suffering the same experience, and for this we are sorry.

The burden of this experience has been on your shoulders for far too long. The burden of this experience is properly ours as a Government, and as a country. There is
65 no place in Canada for the attitudes that inspired the Indian residential school system to ever prevail again. You have been working on recovering from this experience for a long time and in a very real sense, we are now joining you on this journey. The Government of Canada sincerely apologizes and asks the forgiveness of the Aboriginal peoples of this country for failing them so profoundly.

70 Nous le regrettons. We are sorry. Nimitataynan. Niminchinowesamin. Mamiattugut.

(751 words)

Harper, S. (2008, June 11). Prime Minister Harper offers full apology on behalf of Canadians for the Indian residential school system. Retrieved from http://www.pm.gc.ca/eng/news/2008/06/11/prime-minister-harper-offers-full-apology-behalf-canadians-indian-residential#sthash.e1TgHbH7.dpuf

C. Choose the phrase that best completes each sentence.

1. Residential schools were in place for over _____.
   a) a decade
   b) fifty years
   c) a century

2. The Government of Canada became involved in residential schools _____.
   a) as part of its obligations to Aboriginal children
   b) in part to earn additional income from schools
   c) as a way of controlling the entire population

3. The Government of Canada once believed Aboriginal cultures and spiritual beliefs were _____.
   a) based on Christian ideals
   b) inferior and unequal
   c) superior to Christian ideals

4. Residential schools were run in cooperation with _____.
   a) church groups
   b) Aboriginal leaders
   c) local officials

5. While attending residential schools, some children tragically _____.
   a) dropped out
   b) died
   c) returned home

6. Although some former students have spoken positively about their experiences, _____.
   a) most experiences were profoundly negative
   b) they likely attended schools located in cities
   c) it is possible that they were completely mistaken

7. A major result of the residential school system was _____.
   a) the completion of grade 12 certificates and university entrance
   b) meetings among former students with their teachers
   c) social problems among former students and their families

8. One fault of the government was that the residential schools _____.
   a) were not their responsibility
   b) were inadequately controlled
   c) were independently funded

D. At the end of Prime Minister Stephen Harper's speech, there are apologies in Canada's official languages: French and English, as well as three Aboriginal languages. What do you think is the significance of the repetition of certain phrases in the two speeches? Discuss in a group.

E. An apology is a symbolic gesture to show regret, but this apology to Canada's Aboriginal people was also marked with payments to victims and the establishment of a truth and reconciliation commission. Why do you think an apology from the government might be important to former residential school students?

_____

_____

F. How does the concluding paragraph summarize the speech's ideas?

_____

_____

Academic
Survival Skill

Preparing for an Exam

After months of lectures and tutorials, you will probably face exams. It can be a stressful time, with last minute cramming, practising new skills and trying to understand and remember hundreds of details. But understanding, remembering and applying what you learn should begin the first day of class, not just when you need to pass an exam.

A. Here are some tips on how to prepare for an exam. Discuss these with a partner. Talk about what you already do and what you might do in future.

HOW TO PREPARE FOR AN EXAM	
FIND SPACE TO STUDY	Find a study space free of distractions, including from technology (e.g., your phone) and friends. Make sure you have the right tools and resources: books, notes, etc.
FIND TIME TO STUDY	Study after each class. Turn your notes into points to remember and questions to research.
PREDICT	Predict questions you might be asked based on the type of exam. Multiple-choice tests focus on many small details while essay questions deal with understanding broad themes and evidence to support them. Write practice questions and answer them.
SHIFT INFORMATION	Shift information in your brain. Rewrite your notes in graphic organizers and summary paragraphs. Discuss with a study partner. Read your questions and answers out loud. Create flash cards to review while waiting in lines and on public transportation.
KNOW THE DETAILS OF YOUR EXAM	Imagine yourself at the exam and think through all the steps that will get you there. Confirm the time, place and type of exam (ask your teacher if you are unsure).
EXERCISE, EAT AND SLEEP	Be physically and mentally fit. Get enough good food, water, exercise and rest.
DURING THE EXAM	Don't panic. Scan the exam to understand the questions. Check the marks' weighting to see which sections are worth more than others and budget your time accordingly.
AFTER THE EXAM	Evaluate your study plan. If you didn't make the right decisions, revise your plan for the next time.

B. Think of an unsatisfactory exam experience you had in the past. Write what you could have done differently, and why. When you finish, discuss in a group.

_____

_____

_____

FINAL ASSIGNMENT
Write a Compare and Contrast Essay

Use what you learned in this chapter to write a compare and contrast essay.

A. Start with the title and introductory paragraph you wrote for the Warm-Up Assignment. Consider feedback you received and make appropriate corrections.

B. Do additional research to develop your body paragraphs. Look for evidence to support the ideas in your thesis. Keep complete bibliographic notes on your sources.

SOURCE 1: _____

_____

_____

SOURCE 2: _____

_____

_____

SOURCE 3: _____

_____

_____

C. Organize your research notes on a Venn diagram. Then, use your notes to write your body paragraphs. Choose the point-by-point method or the block method to make comparisons. Try to use both the active and the passive voice (see Focus on Grammar, page 173). Use compare and contrast words and transition words to ensure unity and coherence (see Chapter 6, Focus on Writing, page 125).

D. Write your conclusion. Your conclusion should relate to and/or restate your thesis. Review Focus on Writing (page 178), or refer to the Models Chapter (page 198) to see an example of a compare and contrast essay and to learn more about how to write one.

E. Proofread your essay. Then, share with a partner and ask for feedback.

F. Make corrections and write a final copy.

How confident are you?

Think about what you learned in this chapter. Use the table to decide what you should review.

I LEARNED ...	I AM CONFIDENT	I NEED TO REVIEW
vocabulary related to human rights;	☐	☐
to distinguish fact from opinion;	☐	☐
the correct use of the active and passive voice;	☐	☐
about the compare and contrast essay format;	☐	☐
tips on preparing for an exam;	☐	☐
how to write a compare and contrast essay.	☐	☐

VOCABULARY
Challenge

Think about the vocabulary and ideas in this chapter. Use these words to write two sentences about rights and obligations.

dominated	isolate	minority	prohibited	strictly	unjustly

_____

_____

_____

_____

_____

My eLab ✎
Visit My eLab to build on what you learned.

MODELS CHAPTER

This chapter provides models for the writing assignments found in *LEAP Intermediate: Reading and Writing*. All are based on the city. Using the city as a common topic lets you see how similar information can be organized for different writing assignments.

Before each model,
you will find

- instructions that highlight the key characteristics of the writing assignment;

- if applicable, the plan that the writer used to prepare for the writing assignment.

MODEL 1 **How to Write a Descriptive Paragraph**

The paragraph is the basis of many kinds of writing, including news articles and essays. A paragraph is a group of connected sentences on the same topic. It includes a topic sentence, supporting sentences and a concluding sentence.

Instructions

- Write a topic sentence to suggest the reason you are writing, such as answering a question or solving a problem. The topic sentence explains your main idea but doesn't give detailed information.

- Add supporting sentences that expand on the idea or ideas of your topic sentence. These usually include facts, examples and explanations. There may be three or more supporting sentences in a paragraph. Sometimes more than one sentence is used to explain a single detail.

- Close with a concluding sentence that brings your ideas together. This sentence may restate the topic sentence in a different way or summarize the supporting sentences. Sometimes the concluding sentence is a transition to a new topic in the next paragraph.

- Choose a mind map as a graphic organizer when you are brainstorming ideas for a descriptive paragraph. If you are describing something over time, use a timeline. For the example topic (a description of Venice from the outside in), you could brainstorm on a copy of a map of Venice.

Example of a Descriptive Paragraph

Describe the city of Venice.

WRITER'S PLAN	
CHOOSE A WAY TO DESCRIBE IT	• work from the outside in, from the sea surrounding the city to the public squares at its centre
TOPIC SENTENCE	• introduce the city and stress that it differs from other cities • note it is worth exploring
SUPPORTING SENTENCE	• 118 islands separated by canals and connected by bridges • no cars so you walk or take boats
SUPPORTING SENTENCE	• daily markets offer fresh meats, fish, poultry and fruits and vegetables for 270,000 locals
CONCLUDING SENTENCE	• public squares = heart of Venetian neighbourhoods • tourists (22 million) visit, but squares for Venetians

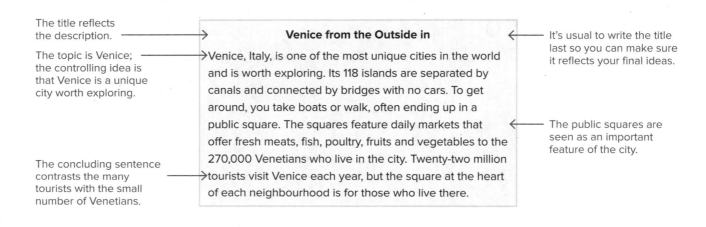

The title reflects the description. →

The topic is Venice; the controlling idea is that Venice is a unique city worth exploring. →

The concluding sentence contrasts the many tourists with the small number of Venetians. →

Venice from the Outside in

Venice, Italy, is one of the most unique cities in the world and is worth exploring. Its 118 islands are separated by canals and connected by bridges with no cars. To get around, you take boats or walk, often ending up in a public square. The squares feature daily markets that offer fresh meats, fish, poultry, fruits and vegetables to the 270,000 Venetians who live in the city. Twenty-two million tourists visit Venice each year, but the square at the heart of each neighbourhood is for those who live there.

← It's usual to write the title last so you can make sure it reflects your final ideas.

← The public squares are seen as an important feature of the city.

MODEL 2.1 **How to Write a Likert Survey**

A Likert survey collects first-hand information (primary data) about opinions, attitudes and frequencies.

Instructions

• Decide what information you want to gather. Write the question you want to answer or the hypothesis that explains what you expect to find.

• Select the respondents. Choose people who have common connections to the survey statements, such as those of a similar age, gender, membership or occupation.

• Use statements (not questions) to collect responses. Make sure each statement is a single idea.

• If you have several statements that are on the same topic (e.g., costs), create a statement stem (see example) to avoid repetition.

• Test the survey with a smaller group to get feedback and ensure the statements and format are clear.

• As a graphic organizer, consider using a mind map to help you brainstorm.

Example of a Likert Survey

What do college students think about the cost of living in Montreal?

Survey: College Students' Perceptions of the Cost of Living in Montreal

For each statement, circle the answer that is true for you.

COST OF LIVING IN MONTREAL FOR ...	VERY INEXPENSIVE	INEXPENSIVE	UNDECIDED	EXPENSIVE	VERY EXPENSIVE
clothing	1	2	3	4	5
household supplies	1	2	3	4	5
personal care	1	2	3	4	5
recreation and entertainment	1	2	3	4	5
transportation	1	2	3	4	5
utilities	1	2	3	4	5

Findings of Cost of Living in Montreal Survey (20 Respondents)

COST OF LIVING IN MONTREAL FOR ...	VERY INEXPENSIVE	INEXPENSIVE	UNDECIDED	EXPENSIVE	VERY EXPENSIVE
clothing		3 (15%)	1 (5%)		16 (80%)
household supplies		4 (20%)	3 (15%)	11 (55%)	2 (10%)
personal care	5 (25%)	14 (70%)		1 (5%)	
recreation and entertainment	2 (10%)	18 (90%)			
transportation		20 (100%)			
utilities				8 (40%)	12 (60%)

MODEL 2.2 How to Write a Report

A report is a summary of data that has been collected and organized. Usually, a report interprets the data to explain what it means.

Instructions

- Begin with a topic sentence that lets readers know what your report is about.
- Include the reason you are writing the report: what information you are sharing and why it is important.
- Include the questions from your survey and the results. Put the results together and present them with numbers, percentages and expressions that are easy to understand.
- Explain the findings (results).
- Use a version of the survey as a graphic organizer when you write notes for a report.

Example of a Report

Write a one-paragraph report explaining what college students think about the cost of living in Montreal.

WRITER'S PLAN	
TOPIC SENTENCE	• 20 college students • perceptions of the cost of living in Montreal
BACKGROUND	• Likert scale used for data collection • statements based on cost of clothing, household supplies, personal care, recreation and entertainment, transportation and utilities
DISCUSSION	• include findings; use the term *mostly* rather than percentages • readers can consult the findings table for exact figures
CONCLUSION	• weather might play a role in utilities statistics

The title is as factual as possible. →

The topic sentence introduces what the survey is about as well as when it was conducted. →

The term *mostly* is used; percentages could be used instead, but a one-paragraph report only gives a general idea. →

A Report on College Students' Perceptions of the Cost of Living in Montreal

This report is based on data collected in January, 2015, from twenty college students, about their perceptions of the cost of living in Montreal. The students responded to Likert scale statements on clothing, household supplies, personal care, recreation and entertainment, transportation and utilities. Personal care, recreation and entertainment and transportation were mostly considered inexpensive or very inexpensive. On the other hand, clothing, household supplies and utilities were mostly considered expensive or very expensive. Some aspects of the survey, such as the perception of high costs for clothing and utilities, may reflect the fact that the students live in Montreal during the winter and the survey data was collected then. See findings table, for a detailed breakdown.

← The second sentence identifies how the data was collected.

← The phrase "on the other hand" indicates contrast.

← The final sentence explains part of the data. A full interpretation could be in a separate paragraph.

MODEL 3 How to Write a Compare and Contrast Paragraph

A compare and contrast paragraph shows similarities and differences. When you compare two or more items, you list similarities. When you contrast items, the focus is on differences.

Instructions

• Decide what you are explaining using points of comparison or contrast.

• Use one of the two methods of organization: the *point-by-point method* or the *block method*. The point-by-point method compares or contrasts each fact before moving on to the next. The block method talks about all the points of one of the things being compared or contrasted first and then repeats with the second thing being compared or contrasted.

- Comparison words include *similarly, likewise* and *in the same way.*
- Contrast words include *although, however* and *but; yet* and *on the other hand* highlight contrasts.
- Use a topic sentence, supporting sentences and a conclusion. Note: the block method often requires two paragraphs.
- Use a Venn diagram as a graphic organizer for your compare and contrast paragraph notes.

Example of a Compare and Contrast Paragraph

Compare and contrast religious buildings in Cologne, Germany, and Kyoto, Japan.

WRITER'S PLAN	
INTRODUCTION	• religious buildings worldwide (comparison) • different materials: stone and wood (contrast) • different materials available in different places (contrast)
POINT-BY-POINT METHOD	• how long it takes to build a cathedral (Cologne Cathedral, 600 years) contrasted with a temple (Kiyomizu-dera, 2 years) • contrast roles of the craftsperson: stonemasons out of work after a job is done and don't pass down their skills; carpenters need to pass on their skills for repair and replacement work • conclusion: fire not a big threat to cathedrals, therefore stonemasons' skills unnecessary; fire a threat to temples, therefore carpenters' skills necessary
BLOCK METHOD	PARAGRAPH 1, CATHEDRAL: • time required to build a stone cathedral, up to 600 years • example Cologne Cathedral, Cologne, Germany • conclusion: stone masons' skills were not passed down after completion because they were not needed PARAGRAPH 2, TEMPLE: • time required to build a large wooden temple, 2 years • example Kiyomizu-dera, Kyoto, Japan • conclusion: carpenters' skills are passed down because repair and replacement is constant with wooden structures

POINT-BY-POINT METHOD

The title summarizes the three points. ——→

The topic sentence identifies the common factor (religious buildings) and a difference: stone versus wood.

Cathedrals, Temples and Skills

→People have always built religious buildings from stone or wood. Building a stone cathedral was often a multi-generational undertaking, lasting as long as six hundred years, as in the case of the Cologne Cathedral. On the other hand, Kyoto's Kiyomizu-dera wooden temple was completed in just two years. Stonemasons who finished a cathedral would find few opportunities to use their skills. In contrast, wooden temples need constant upkeep as weathered, burnt or insect-eaten portions are replaced. Stone walls may have preserved cathedrals from fire, but fire may have preserved the skills of Japanese carpenters.

← Related points are set together for easy comparison.

The point-by-point format makes it easier to create a concluding sentence, in this case, contrasting the role of materials in preserving skills.

BLOCK METHOD

The title summarizes the three points.

The topic sentence identifies the common factor (religious buildings) and a difference: stone versus wood.

Cathedrals, Temples and Skills

People have always constructed religious buildings from stone or wood. Building a stone cathedral could take as long as six hundred years, as in the case of Cologne Cathedral. Stone walls generally preserved cathedrals from fires, erosion and attacks so, after the completion of a cathedral, stonemasons were no longer needed and their skills were often not passed down to the next generation.

Only two years were required to build one of Kyoto's largest wooden temples, Kiyomizu-dera. Unlike sturdy stone cathedrals, wooden temples need constant upkeep to replace weathered, burnt or insect-eaten portions. This requires generations of skilled carpenters. For this reason, Japanese carpenters have always passed down their skills.

This first paragraph focuses on aspects of a stone cathedral.

This second paragraph focuses on aspects of a wooden temple.

MODEL 4.1 | How to Write a Short Definition

When you introduce a new term or concept in an assignment, you can include an informal definition or a formal definition.

Example of a Short Definition

Define a city.

Use one or more of these strategies to write a definition.

STRATEGY	EXAMPLE	EXPLANATION
synonym	A city is a **big town**.	Synonyms are usually informal definitions.
examples	A city, **like London or New York** ...	Examples should be clear enough that they are not confused.
words and phrases that signal a definition	A city can be **defined as** a large town.	Expressions include "that is to say" or "can be defined as" and "in other words."
a second sentence	A city is a big town. **A city can be several towns that have merged.**	The second sentence should repeat the key word to signal that it is a definition.
what it is not	A city **is not like** a town, which is unlikely to have all the professional workers that the general public requires.	When defining something by what it is not, choose something close in meaning, but not easily confused.
part of speech	A city (**noun**) is ...	This and the next two items are used in more formal definitions.
the class	A city (noun) is a **place** where a large number of people live and work.	A class defines the group the term belongs to.
an expression that separates the term from its class	A city (noun) is a place **where a large number of people live and work** with a population in excess of fifty thousand people under a local political administrative unit.	Separating a term from others is called *disambiguation*.

How to Write a Definition Paragraph

A definition paragraph is an extended explanation of a term. It often combines several of the strategies in Model 4.1. Use a definition paragraph as a part of an essay where a common understanding of a key term is essential before further explanation can take place.

Instructions

- Write a topic sentence that gives a simple definition.
- Use supporting sentences to give additional information.
- Do not write a concluding sentence; it is seldom necessary in a definition paragraph unless the point of supplying the definition is to transition to another paragraph.
- Use a mind map as a graphic organizer when you are brainstorming ideas for a definition paragraph.

Example of a Definition Paragraph

What is a city?

WRITER'S PLAN	
TOPIC SENTENCE WITH A SIMPLE DEFINITION	• a city is a place • a large number of people live and work there
EXAMPLE WITH DETAILS	• Hong Kong began as a small village • grew into a major port because of its deep harbour
EXAMPLE WITH DETAILS	• surrounding farms have slowly been converted to land for homes and businesses
WHAT IT IS NOT	• no urban sprawl like Los Angeles • mountains and the ocean divide urban dwellers from those who live in rural villages

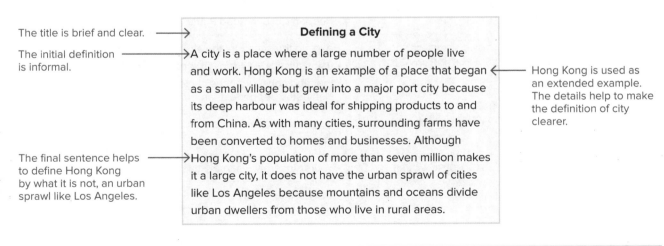

The title is brief and clear. →

The initial definition is informal. →

Defining a City

A city is a place where a large number of people live and work. Hong Kong is an example of a place that began ← as a small village but grew into a major port city because its deep harbour was ideal for shipping products to and from China. As with many cities, surrounding farms have been converted to homes and businesses. Although Hong Kong's population of more than seven million makes it a large city, it does not have the urban sprawl of cities like Los Angeles because mountains and oceans divide urban dwellers from those who live in rural areas.

Hong Kong is used as an extended example. The details help to make the definition of city clearer.

The final sentence helps to define Hong Kong by what it is not, an urban sprawl like Los Angeles.

How to Write a Formal E-mail

Unlike informal messages to friends and family, formal e-mails are written to share important information in academic, business and other contexts.

Instructions

- Confirm the correct e-mail address of the person you are writing to.
- Make sure your own e-mail address is serious and clearly identifies you; avoid playful addresses.
- Explain your topic in the subject line; recipients may not read the e-mail if they think the subject is unimportant.
- Use a paragraph format for the body of the message. Include a topic sentence that explains your reason for writing (e.g., a question, request or message of thanks).
- Add supporting sentences with brief facts, examples and explanations.
- Write a concluding sentence. If your e-mail is a request, include a clear statement of what you would like to happen as a result of the message. The term for this is *a call to action*.
- End with a closing—a farewell word or phrase followed by your name. Formal e-mails most often close with *Yours sincerely*.
- Signatures are not required on e-mails. If appropriate, include your name and title or role.
- Explain any attachment. In letters, the term *encl.* (enclosure) is used but e-mails more commonly use the word *attached*.
- Use a mind map as a graphic organizer when you write notes for an e-mail.

Example of a Formal E-mail

Write a formal request to modify a building site.

WRITER'S PLAN	
TO	• the mayor (the person most likely to be able to help with the problem)
SUBJECT LINE	• Reopen Caliban Road Paths
TOPIC SENTENCE WITH SUPPORTING IDEAS	• explain the situation: the site is currently used as a path • use statistics: 642 trips (514 pedestrian; 128 cyclist) • mention consequences of closing the path: an additional 11 minutes per pedestrian trip
CONCLUDING SENTENCE	• emphasize the mayor's concern and role in the issue • make a specific request
CLOSING/SIGNATURE	• Yours sincerely + name + title
ATTACHMENT	• copy of the survey

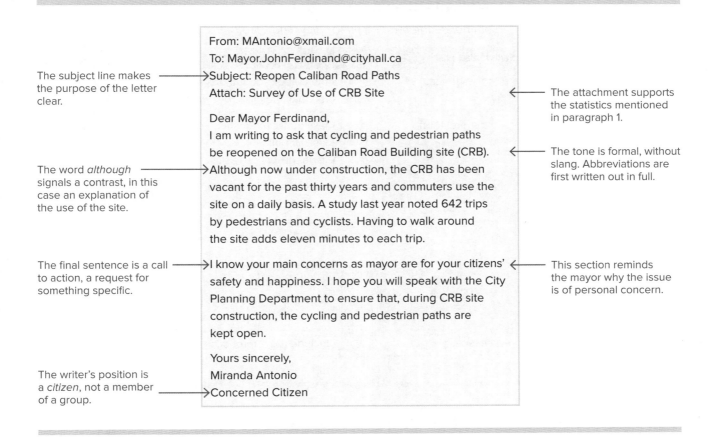

The subject line makes the purpose of the letter clear.

The word *although* signals a contrast, in this case an explanation of the use of the site.

The final sentence is a call to action, a request for something specific.

The writer's position is a *citizen*, not a member of a group.

From: MAntonio@xmail.com
To: Mayor.JohnFerdinand@cityhall.ca
Subject: Reopen Caliban Road Paths
Attach: Survey of Use of CRB Site

Dear Mayor Ferdinand,
I am writing to ask that cycling and pedestrian paths be reopened on the Caliban Road Building site (CRB). Although now under construction, the CRB has been vacant for the past thirty years and commuters use the site on a daily basis. A study last year noted 642 trips by pedestrians and cyclists. Having to walk around the site adds eleven minutes to each trip.

I know your main concerns as mayor are for your citizens' safety and happiness. I hope you will speak with the City Planning Department to ensure that, during CRB site construction, the cycling and pedestrian paths are kept open.

Yours sincerely,
Miranda Antonio
Concerned Citizen

The attachment supports the statistics mentioned in paragraph 1.

The tone is formal, without slang. Abbreviations are first written out in full.

This section reminds the mayor why the issue is of personal concern.

MODEL 6 How to Write a Summary

A summary gathers the key points of a longer article, book or lecture. Summaries are used in paragraphs or essays or for study. Attribute the source material with the names of the authors, the date and publication details. This helps you find the source material later and reference it in an essay or presentation.

Instructions

- Skim the source text to get a general understanding. Then read in detail, asking yourself *who, what, when, where, why* and *how* questions. Highlight key points.

- Write a topic sentence that explains what the summary is about. Include the author's or authors' name(s) as well as the title and the source of the text.

- For each paragraph, write one or two sentences that summarize the main idea. Filter the information by asking yourself what is worth knowing. Ignore unimportant details.

- Write notes in your own words. However, don't add personal opinions; keep your summary factual.

- Review your summary to ensure you have unity and coherence.

- Use a mind map as a graphic organizer when you write notes for a summary paragraph.

Example of a Summary

Summarize the reading titled "Bicycling: Health Risk or Benefit?" from page 53.

WRITER'S PLAN	
TOPIC SENTENCE	• the author's or authors' name(s) and the date • the main points about ways of promoting cycling
SUPPORTING POINTS	• less traffic congestion • less air pollution • fewer greenhouse gases
DRAWBACKS (POINTS AGAINST)	Canadians cycle less than some Europeans due to: • fewer bicycle lanes because of car users' opposition • cyclist safety concerns • limited helmet use concerns
CONCLUSION	Drawbacks can be overcome/managed by: • establishment of bike routes • reduction in car speeds • promotion of helmets
REFERENCE	• include the reference in APA format

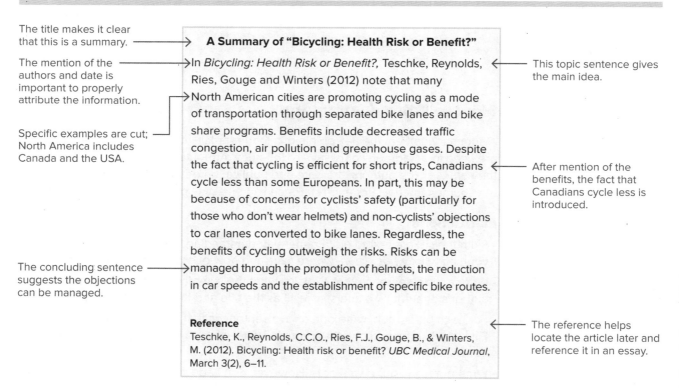

The title makes it clear that this is a summary. →

The mention of the authors and date is important to properly attribute the information.

Specific examples are cut; North America includes Canada and the USA.

The concluding sentence suggests the objections can be managed.

A Summary of "Bicycling: Health Risk or Benefit?"

In *Bicycling: Health Risk or Benefit?*, Teschke, Reynolds, Ries, Gouge and Winters (2012) note that many North American cities are promoting cycling as a mode of transportation through separated bike lanes and bike share programs. Benefits include decreased traffic congestion, air pollution and greenhouse gases. Despite the fact that cycling is efficient for short trips, Canadians cycle less than some Europeans. In part, this may be because of concerns for cyclists' safety (particularly for those who don't wear helmets) and non-cyclists' objections to car lanes converted to bike lanes. Regardless, the benefits of cycling outweigh the risks. Risks can be managed through the promotion of helmets, the reduction in car speeds and the establishment of specific bike routes.

Reference
Teschke, K., Reynolds, C.C.O., Ries, F.J., Gouge, B., & Winters, M. (2012). Bicycling: Health risk or benefit? *UBC Medical Journal*, March 3(2), 6–11.

This topic sentence gives the main idea.

After mention of the benefits, the fact that Canadians cycle less is introduced.

The reference helps locate the article later and reference it in an essay.

How to Write a Process Paragraph

A process paragraph explains how something is done or how something happens (e.g., how to find a bus station or how buses make commuting more efficient).

Instructions

- Review the question to understand what process—or part of a process—is being asked about.
- Choose a topic that you understand well and include it in your title.
- Consider your audience. Decide how much background information you will need to give.
- Write a topic sentence to explain what will be covered and why.
- Explain technical terms at the beginning of the paragraph or as part of the step where they appear.
- Write the steps in the correct order. Use transition words to signal the order of steps, e.g., *first, begin by, before, next, then, as soon as, finally* and *last*.
- Use a flow chart as a graphic organizer when you write notes for a process paragraph.

Example of a Process Paragraph

How do cities grow in response to transportation needs?

WRITER'S PLAN	
TOPIC SENTENCE	• write generally about how cities form
SUPPORTING SENTENCES	• outline the process with an example of one city on the banks of a river • note how the arrival of each group creates new needs and develops the city
CONCLUDING SENTENCE	Note: process paragraphs don't need a concluding sentence but you can add a benefit or extra point. • explain that even if the original reason for the city disappears, the city continues to grow

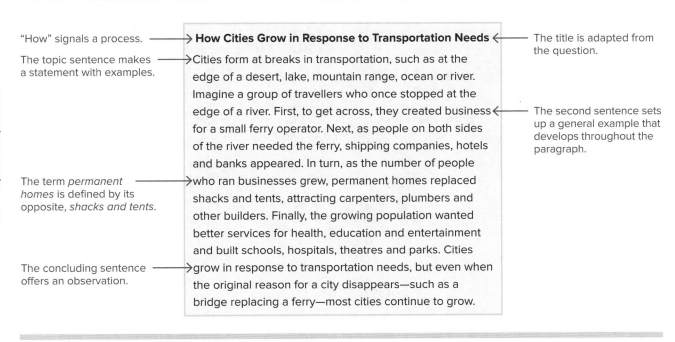

"How" signals a process. ——→ **How Cities Grow in Response to Transportation Needs** ←—— The title is adapted from the question.

The topic sentence makes a statement with examples. ——→ Cities form at breaks in transportation, such as at the edge of a desert, lake, mountain range, ocean or river. Imagine a group of travellers who once stopped at the edge of a river. First, to get across, they created business ←—— The second sentence sets up a general example that develops throughout the paragraph. for a small ferry operator. Next, as people on both sides of the river needed the ferry, shipping companies, hotels and banks appeared. In turn, as the number of people

The term *permanent homes* is defined by its opposite, *shacks and tents*. ——→ who ran businesses grew, permanent homes replaced shacks and tents, attracting carpenters, plumbers and other builders. Finally, the growing population wanted better services for health, education and entertainment and built schools, hospitals, theatres and parks. Cities

The concluding sentence offers an observation. ——→ grow in response to transportation needs, but even when the original reason for a city disappears—such as a bridge replacing a ferry—most cities continue to grow.

How to Write a Compare and Contrast Essay

An essay is organized in three sections: an introduction, body paragraphs and a conclusion. There are usually three or more body paragraphs. A compare and contrast essay shows the similarities and differences between two items or ideas. Use the point-by-point method or the block method to organize the similarities and differences (see Model 3, page 190).

Instructions

- Choose the point-by-point method or the block method to make comparisons.
- The introduction states the topic of the essay and the items that are being compared and contrasted. Introduce ideas in a way that attracts the reader's interest. Write a thesis statement with three points. Each point is developed in its own paragraph.
- Use the body paragraphs to explain each point being compared and contrasted. Offer evidence in the form of examples and explanations.
- Avoid contractions; keep your essays formal by using the full forms of abbreviated terms followed by the initial letters in parentheses.
- Add a conclusion that summarizes the points and restates the thesis statement in a new way. Some essays include a suggestion for something to happen, such as the reader to take an action.
- Choose a graphic organizer such as a Venn diagram to write your compare and contrast essay.

Example of a Compare and Contrast Essay

Compare and contrast Beijing and Rome.

WRITER'S PLAN	
CHOOSE A WAY TO ORGANIZE	• choose the point-by-point method this time, not the block approach
TOPIC SENTENCE AND THESIS STATEMENT	• explain that a city's history is important • three points: preserving architecture, expanding transportation networks and limiting growth
SUPPORTING PARAGRAPH	• similarities: villages on trade routes • differences: preserving their architecture
SUPPORTING PARAGRAPH	• similarities: expanding transportation networks • differences: focus on subway systems
SUPPORTING PARAGRAPH	• similarities: limiting growth • differences: natural barriers
CONCLUSION	• population size forces difficult decisions

Beijing and Rome: Balancing History and Population

The first sentence gives general background.

Physical reminders of the history of ancient cities usually include their buildings and monuments, but these are often threatened. Beijing and Rome are two ancient cities with different approaches to preserving their architecture, expanding their transportation networks and limiting their growth.

The title sparks interest.

The topic sentence focuses on three points, each of which is developed in its own paragraph.

The second paragraph starts with similarities that lead into a description of the city walls and how these are different in each city.

Beijing and Rome were both villages on trade routes that became politically important cities. As each village grew, it required defensive walls. In Rome, the walls built in 271–275 AD are generally well-preserved. In Beijing, city walls built in the 1400s up until 1543 were largely torn down in 1965. The walls in both cities protected ancient palaces that, in Rome, have fallen into disrepair. However, Beijing's Forbidden City complex, completed in 1420, remains the centre of the city and is now a museum. While Rome has been labelled an open-air museum because of the extensiveness of its architecture from different ages, many of Beijing's old buildings have been demolished to make way for new developments.

The idea of the walls serves as a transition into a description of palaces. Palaces serve as a transition into the idea of museums.

The previous paragraph ends on developments, and this third paragraph expands on the idea of the needs of growing cities before highlighting the importance of transportation.

Growing cities need to expand their transportation systems. In Beijing, private car ownership was limited until the 1990s, and most people cycled or walked. To serve its citizens, Beijing built a subway network of 465 kilometres and is proposing another 708 kilometres. In contrast, Rome has only 40.4 kilometres of subways and plans for expansion have been abandoned. Unlike Beijing, Rome carefully preserves its past and subway lines are often halted—sometimes for years—when archaeological treasures are uncovered.

Both cities have subways (a similarity) but the scale of the subway network is far different (a contrast).

Contrasts can be inferred. Beijing's continued subway construction suggests it has different priorities than Rome.

Transportation links this fourth paragraph to the third.

With expanding transportation systems, cities quickly grow. Beijing sprawls without breaks of green space and absorbs neighbouring towns. Similarly, the suburbs of Rome are also spreading, but are contained by mountains to the east and the sea to the west. Another difference is vertical growth. A 2000 year-old law forbids buildings in Rome higher than 21 metres. Beijing is a different story, where the tallest skyscraper is 405 metres.

The inference is that although Rome is spreading, the natural barriers stop it spreading too much.

Vertical growth is contrasted by the numbers 21 and 405, without need for further explanation.

The use of "however" in the conclusion points to a difference that is more important than some or all of the previous differences; more people means more growth.

However, comparisons between the two cities cannot ignore their most dramatic difference: population. While Rome has a population of 2.8 million, Beijing has a population of 19.6 million. City planners balance the needs of a growing population against the challenge of preserving layers of history, and sometimes have to make difficult decisions.

The conclusion avoids suggesting one city is better than the other. Despite their differences, Beijing and Rome are both popular places to visit and live and work in.

PHOTO CREDITS